MW01243227

A BATTLEFIELD ENCOUNTER

By

ROSEMARY FROST KIDD

A division of Squire Publishers, Inc.
4500 College Blvd.
Leawood, KS 66211
1/888/888-7696

Printed in the United States

ISBN: 1-58597-080-8

Library of Congress Control Number: 2001 130435

A division of Squire Publishers, Inc.
4500 College Blvd.
Leawood, KS 66211
1/888/888-7696

Dedicated to

John Gentry Frost

*whose own experiences before,
during, and at the end of World War II
inspired this story.*

PART ONE

Munich, Germany — 1932-33

CHAPTER ONE

Glockenspiel — Munich

CHAPTER ONE

Munich, Germany, 1932

Two twenty-year-old American youths stood entranced on the street of Munich listening to a man addressing an immense gathering in the streets of the city. In spite of the size of the crowd, it was extremely quiet, as if each and everyone listening wanted to hear every word the man said. Only when the speaker paused was there a bit of frenzy among the throng. Everyone, including the two young Americans, began jockeying for position — each wanting to get a step or two closer to the charismatic figure speaking to them.

"Who is that man?" one American asked the other.

"I don't know, but he has this whole city in his hand."

"I wonder if he knows the power he has? He's appealing to all the people still suffering from the World War."

The two young men had come over to Europe to attend the University of Munich, each specializing in a different study. They had met on the ship, had toured other parts of Europe before arriving in Munich in time for their school year to begin. One of the students was named Jordan Fisk, Jr., the other was Samuel Bradshaw.

"What an introduction to Munich," Samuel said.

"I want to find out who he is," Jordan said. "He might be worth knowing."

"By the size of this crowd, our school year will be over before you can get close to him," Sam joked.

"I expect we'll find out a lot more about him while we're here. He can't gather crowds like that without being known all over Germany."

That was the first awareness the American boys had of the man called Adolph Hitler. After they had enrolled in their separate schools of study and were proceeding along with their studies, they learned much more about that man from their classmates as well as from other daily contacts, but Adolph Hitler was of no particular interest to either of them for some time.

Six college age students sat in a booth at a beer hall drinking beer and smoking cigarettes. All of them were not of German nationality. One of them was an American boy, one a French girl, and another an Italian boy. The other three were German, two boys and one girl. They were all studying music at the University of Munich.

The small beer hall, packed with many young people, had become filled with haze from the smoke of many cigarettes. The German girl, Grenythe Karlstein, began waving her hands back and forth in front of her face and said, "I can't breathe in here any more!" Though she spoke in German, the three foreign students had no trouble understanding her message. One of the requirements in their music education was the ability to know five European languages; two of the foreigners found that assignment no problem at all, that is, the French girl and the Italian boy, who from their early years had been learning the neighboring languages. The American boy had studied the German language three years in college and could converse in it to some extent. He had little or no training in any other foreign languages and had to listen closely to comprehend the French or Italian words that crept into the general conversation.

The other five students paid little attention to Grenythe's complaining, and in various languages continued the discussion of their music assignment. They laughed as discrepancies occurred when they each tried to mimic the others' words. Jay Fisk, the American student, took the cigarette out of his mouth, stubbed it out in the ash try in front of him and remarked, "I'll put mine out. I can wait until I get outside."

One of her other countrymen scolded, "Grenythe, old girl, you've been getting this smoke every evening for the last month, why are you complaining now?"

"And you look like an old woman waving a dish rag!" another said.

Grenythe had already gotten up from the table and pushed her way past some of the others to get away. She said, "I want to get out of here!"

Jay, the American boy, graciously got up to let her by and remarked in an off-hand manner, "Perhaps I'll go out, too, but not for long. I don't want to miss any part of the conversation. It is the only way that I am going to learn all these languages."

The two of them walked out the door together and headed toward the park on Koniginstrasse. They had walked less than half a block when Grenythe said, "It –"

Her companion interrupted, "Then it won't bother you if I light a cigarette now?"

"No. I just wanted to get away from Georg. He kept whispering about getting our group involved in the Nazi party political movement before the election comes up in November. I don't want to get involved in politics right now."

"Well, you know Hitler likes cats and opera, and I know you do, too," Jay teased.

"I still don't want to join that party!" Grenythe answered.

"I heard Hitler when I first arrived here in Munich. He is one powerful speaker!"

"You must like him?"

"I wouldn't say that — I'm apolitical!"

"Then why have you grown that Hitler mustache?'

"Oh, just to be in the crowd with all the other guys in school."

"I think that is silly, but I won't argue about that, but I don't want to talk about the Nazi party."

"I won't argue about that, but I don't want to talk about the Nazi party."

Their conversation lagged a bit and Jay said, "Let's not be gone too long — I'll try to keep the conversation concentrated on music — okay?" Jay had spoken in German until the very last word which he said in English.

"Okay?" his companion quizzically repeated.

"Grenythe, you've heard me say that word hundreds of times — it means all right," Jay informed her.

After Jay finished his cigarette, the two walked back to the beer hall. They joined their companions who were still sitting in the same booth where they had left them.

Since many customers had already left the pub, the cacophony of the crowd was gone, and the conversation of their friends could be heard by most everyone in the room.

"Helene, don't be an idiot!" Franz Luebeck was almost shouting. "Even if he did write in *Mein Kampf* that movement to the south and west would be stopped, and that Germany would move to the east and eventually move into Russia, you'd better believe that France will be in his path, too."

Tony Riccionne, the Italian boy, and Georg Blaich, another German, sat quietly by and listened, while Helene kept saying, "Shush, shush, not so loud!"

When Grenythe Karlstein and Jordan Fisk, Jr. (Jay) again sat down in the booth, the arguments stopped for a moment, as Jay said, "Let's forget politics now and talk about something more pleasant. How many of you are going to go with me tomorrow night and see the opera *Reingold*?"

"You can get standing room for a mark." Grenythe remarked.

"And for five pfennings you can get a little copy of the libretto, but don't forget that 'standing room' is in the side aisles," Georg added.

"Tony, you haven't said a word. Are you going to the opera with us, or aren't you?" Helene queried.

"Oh, opera is all right, but I enjoyed our political discussions here more," Tony replied. "That Hitler is quite a man. He's the best speaker I've heard in a long time."

Grenythe looked at Jay, for she remembered that he had also remarked about Hitler's oratory, then she asked, "What's it to you, Tony?"

"It should mean a lot more to you, Grenythe. He will

make your nation a lot stronger and he will make this, your own town, the center of the new government. Munich people should be very happy with him."

Grenythe had meant to stop the discussion about politics with her remark to Tony, but instead, the whole topic heated up again. For nearly an hour, the six students of four international heritages argued about the political power that was rising around them.

The end of the war in 1918 left the German soldiers with nothing to do, no war to fight, no other occupation. Much of the rest of the German populace found itself penniless, bankrupt from the cost of the war. Battle devastation had not only shattered the livelihood of many families, it had left scarcely any finances in the country with which to rebuild.

The common misery of both the military and unemployment of the ordinary citizen brought about a combined rebellion against the Versailles Treaty that had prohibited the use or the production of arms. This situation created a perfect atmosphere for the uprising of several different political parties opposing the Weimer Republic, which was the ruling government of Germany after the war. The Communist party met with a bloody repression from former military men and others with patriotic idealism. One organization was usually called The Freikorp, though it assumed other names in different parts of the country. Captain Ernst Rohm, a former officer of the German army, led his soldiers in a fight against the government, saying that the Weimer German Republic was a farce. Another rising party, the National Socialists, was gaining strength along the same lines, with a leader known for his eloquence in public speaking, Adolph Hitler.

Hitler was propelled to the front of the Socialist party by other leaders who wanted to use his persuasive speech to further their cause. Little did they realize that Hitler had a plan of his own — to use that ability to further his individual power. He had been imprisoned for his earlier treacherous fight against the government, but while in prison he wrote a book called *Mein Kampf,* proclaiming (as well as later in his oratory) that it was the Jews and the Bolsheviks who had caused the defeat of the German army in the war, and that these same enemies were also responsible for the present unemployment and hardship of the working class people. He was gaining momentum day by day, yet in August 1932, though he was defeated in his bid for Chancellor of the German Government, he kept pushing for further acceptance of his views.

The growing unpopularity of the present government was not lost on Paul von Hindenberg who had been president of the Weimer Republic since 1925. He was considered by most Germans to be the top man of the time, the best soldier, the best leader. He was a military man and kept himself above the different party squabbles. The Weimer Republic during Hindenberg's first years had been a prosperous dictatorship, but when the depression came, he was unable to meet the challenge.

Hitler's stronghold was the Bavarian area of which Munich was the center. Though his backers were many, there were some who looked askance at his leadership. This was the situation about which these six University students talked and argued. The three foreign students,

American Jordan Fisk, French Helene Dolmet and the Italian Tony Riccionne, were all close friends with the three German students. The three foreigners listened to their hosts' opinions, not always agreeing with them, or with each other, on the political trend that was developing in Bavarian Germany.

When a pause came in the discussion, Grenythe stood up and said, "Come, we better get some studying done tonight. Tomorrow night, if we are going to the opera, we won't get home before eleven o'clock and we won't have time to study much then." Helene got up to leave, joining Grenythe. When the two girls started walking away, the boys one by one followed them out the door.

It was a solemn and disturbed Jordan Fisk who briskly walked the remaining few blocks to the residence that he had called home for the last six weeks. Jay had always enjoyed nature and the outdoors. Ordinarily he would have been enchanted with the feel of the crisp air of a lovely autumn evening, and he would have noticed with satisfaction how much closer to the earth a full harvest moon seemed on a clear, cool October night. It was not only the argument about the worthiness of that upcoming man called Hitler that disturbed him, it was the fact that he knew he was at a direct disadvantage, on any subject, in a discussion with his fellow students. Though he spoke the German language he had learned in school fairly well, he heard how much better the French girl and the Italian boy were able to fit into the informal conversation with their German friends. Sometimes he felt he was no better than a mute.

He knew he had to make some change if he wanted to improve his daily use of the German language, and to know more about what was going on around him. He expected to study here for just one year, and he knew he could not get the most out of his studies (or think intelligently about the political turmoil) if he could not speak and understand the street usage as well as the text book version of the native language.

The problem was Sam! Jay wished Sam had gone along with him to the beer hall tonight, then perhaps he would have understood why he, Jay, needed to make a change. Samuel Bradshaw and Jordan Fisk had met on *The Albert Ballin*, the German ship on which the two young students had sailed from New York to Hamburg in late August. They learned that they were both on their way to Munich, Germany, to obtain their junior year's college credit, each for further study in his own particular line, sponsored by their respective universities. Samuel was studying engineering; Jordan was specializing in music. As their friendship developed on the ship, they decided that they would find a place where they could room together.

Jay admitted that the six weeks with Sam in a pension boarding house had been fine. Being together far away home had kept the two twenty-year-old boys from getting too homesick living in a foreign country with no other familiar friends. But Jay realized that the six weeks in the pension with other Americans had not improved his speaking of the German language. He felt he had to tell Sam, tell him tonight, that he was going to look elsewhere for a place to stay, perhaps with a German family where he would have to speak German all the time. He hoped that Sam would understand and not think him unappreciative of their friendship. Before Jordan arrived at the pension, he did not know whether he would be glad if Sam were home, or if he would feel relieved if he were not, thereby postponing the painful task of breaking the news of his very recent decision.

Sam was sitting at the little table he used for a desk, hunched over and absorbed in his studies, when Jay stepped into the room. "Sam," he remarked, "I have something I want to talk to you about."

"Umm," Sam mumbled, sounding like an old furnace letting off steam, never looking up from his work

"Listen, Sam! It's important!" Jay's voice became louder.

"Okay, let me finish this first." Sam still did not lift his head from his books.

Jay removed his jacket and was in the process of hanging it up. Before he had time to turn around, Sam said, "Now, tell me what's so important that you couldn't wait to get your coat off before you interrupted my study."

"Sam, now don't get me wrong, but I think I need to move out of this pension. I am not picking up enough German here. There are too many Americans in this building and I find I am speaking more English than German. I did not know until tonight how far behind I was."

Sam sat looking at Jay for a moment then said, "What about me? Who am I going to get to split the rent with me here? And what are you going to do?"

"I don't know yet. There are a lot of Americans around." Jay lit a cigarette and stood silently a moment before he continued, "I'll help you find someone to move in here, Sam. I thought I would go looking for a room in some German home where I had to speak German all the time, then I might be able to carry on a decent conversation with all my classmates."

"Are they all German, Jay?"

"No. That's the problem. They come from other European countries and they all speak much better German than I do — I thought I was pretty good in my classes back home. Sam, maybe you might like to go into a private home, too."

"I don't know about that. When are you leaving?"

"I'll be here all this next week? Why don't we get together with all our friends who are going on the ski trip to Austria. Someone in that group night want to move in here with you. Maybe someone will know where I can find an inexpensive place in some German home."

"That'll give us a week to make our plans, I guess. Right now, I have some more studying to do."

"Me, too." And Jay turned to the small corner designated as his own study space.

The colorful brisk and exhilarating days of early autumn had given way to the doleful, gray days of late November. Though the calendar marked the days to be in the autumn season, the weather seemed more like winter to Jay Fisk as he walked from the University to the home of a widow where he had procured a room and breakfast. The home was in the northern section of the city known as Schwabing, a convenient location for access to the University. A widow and her teen-age son owned and lived in the house.

As Jay surmised, he had to speak German with the landlady since she spoke no English. The widow's son was named Paul. Paul was delighted to have an American student move into his home — it would help him learn to speak better English. Jay Fisk did not know whether speaking too much English with the boy would impair his own desire to speak better German. At least he had a daily lesson in translating the foreign words he heard into his own language and vice versa.

When he had first moved in, he made a point in starting a conversation with Frau Weis by asking her about her husband. She refused to talk with him. At first Jay thought she did not understand the textbook German he was speaking, but it soon became clear that she did not want to talk about her husband. She was not a talkative person anyway, and the subject of her widowhood was verboten. One day in a German/English conversation Jay had with the boy, Paul, he asked in a roundabout way about his father. The boy, much like his mother, seemed reticent to talk about it, but before he clammed up entirely, he mumbled, "He disappeared."

It was one mid-week day in late November when Jay walked in the door of the Weis house, feeling an aloneness that was just as gray as the weather. For the first time in the weeks since he had lived in the Weis home, he missed his American friend Sam, and was sorry he would not be opening the door to greet him. Expecting to see no one, he was surprised to find Frau Weis waiting for him. She even had an infrequent smile on her face.

In very broken English she said to him, "Happy Birthday!" as she handed him several letters and cards.

"How did you know?" Jay blurted out in English.

She immediately said it in German, "Froehlicher Geburtstag." Then she told him that Paul had taught her how to say "Happy Birthday" in English. She and Paul had learned about his birthday from Samuel Bradshaw who had come over that morning to leave an invitation for Jay to join him for dinner that night. When Frau Hannah Weis heard about what Sam had planned, she offered her own invitation — she invited Sam to join her and Paul for a birthday dinner for Jay right here at their home. A smile replaced the glum countenance on Jay's face, and tears came to his eyes, when Mrs. Weis told him that Samuel had accepted her invitation and would be here at six o'clock to have dinner with them.

Jay could not suppress his joy on this news, nor did he try. He had been feeling so blue — it was his birthday, and he thought he would spend it all alone in his room with no one caring — no one knowing!

Now with a big smile on his face, he planted a quick kiss on Mrs. Weis's forehead and dashed up the stairs to get ready for dinner, eager as a six-year-old on Christmas morning, waiting to open the cards and letters he had received from home.

When Jay had found the Weis place where he could get room and breakfast, he did not know or care that the Weis family was Jewish. But as the days passed he kept hearing subtle remarks from some of his schoolmates. Though Jay enjoyed the company of his classmates as a rule, he could not but notice the vague yet growing change in their attitude toward the Jewish situation. One day while he and a few of his classmates were eating lunch at a small restaurant near the campus, one of the students remarked, "I bet those Jews are getting awfully tired of eating chicken all the time."

"Why do you say that," Jay Fisk asked.

"Don't you know those crazy people won't eat pork."

"Oh, but they can have beef, can't they?" Jay pressed the subject.

"Yes, but beef is very expensive," Grenythe Karlstein, one of Jay's closest friends, explained. "You know, very few of us can afford to eat beef. You in the United States have acres and acres of land where you can raise cattle. We don't have that kind of land here, so we eat mostly pork or chicken that can be produced in much less space." Grenythe explained.

"That's not all," Tony Riccionne laughed, "the grocers won't sell beef to Jews nowadays."

"That's what I meant about Jews getting tired of eating chicken. They can't buy beef and their religion won't let them eat pork, so what else can they eat?" Helene said.

"They can eat lamb or mutton, I guess," Jay said as he remembered the excellent lamb dish that his landlady had prepared for his birthday dinner.

"That is expensive, too, and scarce. I hear that some of the grocers won't sell lamb or mutton to the Jews, either."

When Jay heard that, he thought of the difficulty Hannah Weis must have gone through to prepare such a wonderful meal for him on his birthday. He made a promise to himself that he would make it a point to buy special meat for her when he could.

In the evenings, Jordan Fisk usually went to a kaffebar, or beer hall, for a bite to eat and was often accompanied by one or more of his closest friends, Helene, Grenythe, Tony, Franz or Georg. They also attended the operas together after they had eaten. They would buy a "stehhplatz" (standing place) ticket and after the third bell, when every one is supposed to be seated, if there happened to be unoccupied seats they could sit down. Sometimes there would be just one, sometimes more. Jay never pushed to occupy a seat when there were not enough to go around. He said that if he sat down for a four-hour opera, he would probably go to sleep if he did not understand all of the German language. The operas, whether French, Italian or German, were all rendered in German. Another reason Jay did not push for a vacant seat was that he noticed Jewish students were shoved aside, even for the better standing room.

"It was so funny!" one of the female students laughed so hard she could hardly get the words out of her mouth, "Did he tickle her on purpose?"

"Why doesn't Hindenberg do something about him?"

"I think the mountain climbing would be a great extension!"

"Listen, everybody, we want to tell you about it!" a couple shouted together.

The group had not all been together for several weeks and in their exuberance in seeing each other they were all talking at the same time, and not about the same subject, sounding like a bunch of chattering magpies.

Jordan Fisk with five of his classmates, Helene Dolmet, Grenythe Karlstein, Tony Riccionne, Georg Blaich and Franz Lubeck, had met with several of their mutual friends to discuss their plans for the Christmas vacation that would be coming up in the next few weeks. Jordan (Jay) had brought along his friend Sam Bradshaw, and most of the others had brought along one or two of their friends whom they thought might be interested in joining them in their arrangements. It was late in the evening, later than they usually stayed out on a school night, but some of the students had gone to the opera and could not meet any sooner and others could not come in the hours before the opera.

It was Jay Fisk and Grenythe Karlstein who had been laughing and called out that they wanted to tell the rest of the group something funny. When they got the attention of the others, Franz Lubeck asked, "Is it about the ski trip?"

"No," Jay and Grenythe both laughed, "it's about the opera."

"Let's get our ski trip plans settled first, then you can make us laugh later." Franz stated, "And what were you talking about, Helene?"

"I was arguing about Hindenberg and Hitler with Tony and their friends."

"That, too, can wait until later. What we need to do right now is decide what we are going to do about our ski trip. Georg, why don't you tell them what has come up?"

There were fifteen youths, boys and girls, between the ages of nineteen and twenty-one or twenty-two in a small beer hall. They were crowded together around a table designated to accommodate twelve people. Georg started to speak. "You better stand up, Georg," one of the group suggested.

Georg got up and spoke, "You know what we first planned — to leave the day after Christmas and go to Austria where there is more snow and the skiing is better. Well, here's what came up while we were talking about the trip with friends. Some of them say that they wanted to go, but they were not very good at skiing; then one of the guys said that he was a good teacher and that he would give them instructions. Then another boy said he, too, was better than just a good skier. He suggested that we should divide the groups into two sections — the beginners in one group, the experienced ones in another. The two would-be instructors said they would do that for a very small fee. What do you think about that plan?"

"That's not all, Georg, "Franz prompted. "Tell them about the climbing."

"Oh, yes. They said that it would be fun to spend the first day or two climbing some mountain, the Zugspitze, if possible."

"How can we do that? There will be too much snow," someone interrupted.

"How can we do that if we have no mountain climbing equipment?" another asked.

"That was discussed when they brought it up and they said we would not take hard climbs, just fun climbs that anyone can do by following the climbing trails that have been marked. We would not try the Zugspitze if there has been a lot of snow, but take one of the lesser mountains where we would have little trouble. Gallen said we could all start the climb and if it was too much for anyone, he could turn back at any time. I am not a good climber, but I like to do it. We should decide if we want Galen and Ed to go with us and sort of manage the group."

"Do we have to decide tonight?" Sam Bradshaw asked.

"Why don't we think about it while I tell you about the opera?" Jay Fisk suggested.

"Yes, you ought to hear this," Grenythe agreed.

"Well, I know it will be about a good opera because tonight's opera was *Tristan and Isolde* and that's by Wagner. He's the greatest, and he's Hitler's favorite, too," Tony Riccionne broke in.

"It was at the end when Isolde has died," Jay begins, "that scene, by the way, is over one-half hour long and so much sadness can become a bit tiring. Well, tonight during the performance when he is mourning over her body after Isolde has died, he bent too low and accidently tickled her. She, although 'dead,' suddenly jumped! All the audience saw it, and the death scene became hilarious — not in keeping with the theme at all." Jay was laughing again, as were the rest of the students who had seen the opera.

"Now you know what we were laughing about when we came in and what we wanted to tell you before you got into any serious business," Grenythe said.

"That's what we were asking — do you think he tickled her on purpose or was it purely accidental?" Helene asked.

"If he did it on purpose, he could be fired from the cast — couldn't he?" Grenythe questioned her own statement.

"I don't know," answered another of the music students loudly to be heard over the group still laughing about the incident. "Why don't we ask our teacher tomorrow?"

"Why don't we ask what Gus and Helene were arguing about?" Franz Lubeck said as he pointed to a young man across the table.

"She thinks Hindenberg should get rid of Adolph Hitler. I think Hitler is best thing that Germany has had since the war. He has more charisma than any man I've ever known." Gustav Streicher turned toward Jay Fisk and Sam Bradshaw. "Hitler even put your Kaltenborn in his place."

Jay, who had remained aloof to most of the arguments he heard around him daily, could not let this statement pass. "Gustav, I am not interested in your politics, but I think you should be advised that Kaltenborn merely asked Hitler why he was so antagonistic to the Jews and it was *Hitler* who could not give Kaltenborn a straight answer. Hitler just said Germany had a right to deal with anti-German elements, then Kaltenborn asked him why he thought the German Jews were anti-German. All Hitler did was just make a long speech with no answer at all."

"Gus is right, though," Tony Riccionne joined the argument. "Hitler is great. He and Mussolini will stand together, and Italy and Germany will control France and all these countries that are coming under the influence of the Communist Party."

"Now, wait a minute!" Helene almost shouted, "What do you mean that Germany will control France?"

"Had you forgotten that Alsace/Lorraine belonged to Germany and that the French took it after the war?" Gus reminded the group. "You don't think Hitler is going to let that stand, do you?"

"Germany lost the war!" Helene argued. "They lost that territory!"

"They won't lose the next time."

The voices were getting more belligerent as opinions were clashing around the table. Only Sam Bradshaw and Jay Fisk kept quiet. Finally Jay, in his quiet manner, yet loud enough for all to hear, spoke, "Franz, why don't we get back to our ski plans?"

"You are right. Have all of you had time to think about what we want to do? First, will we accept the instructors on our trip as Georg outlined, and second, will we stop on the way to Austria for a day or two of mountain climbing?"

Because additional snow had fallen on the Zugspitze, the group knew that trails would be closed and any attempt at mountain climbing would be too dangerous for inexperienced mountain climbers. They agreed that they would go on to their selected skiing area and if there was a peak nearby that offered a one day's climb on a trail that was open for hikers, they would do that the first day, then spend the rest of their holiday skiing. That way they would not have to move from one place to another. Other plans were discussed briefly, and the group agreed that the instructors would be included in their coming trip.

The Christmas season was approaching — it was actually a few days before the official first day of winter, but already greetings along the streets in Munich were "Merry Christmas" instead of the customary "Gruss Gott."

From the weather reports, the snow in the nearby Bavarian Alps was enough to prevent climbing the Zugspitze, but the new snow in the higher mountains near Innsbruck, Austria, would provide great skiing slopes. The two instructor students at the University were organizing and dividing the beginners from the more experienced skiers.

Jay felt that he fit into the experienced group, because he had climbed a few mountains and skied in Colorado, though he knew he was a long way from being accomplished at either sport. Sam felt he, too, could fit into the advanced group. Both boys were exuberant about the plans. Being away from home for Christmas for the first time in their lives, this trip buoyed their spirits. The trip was scheduled to leave the morning after Christmas.

Jay expected to have a good time. What he did not anticipate, however, was that two seemingly insignificant happenings would affect his thinking for the rest of his life.

CHAPTER TWO

CHAPTER TWO

JAY FISK WAS DELIGHTED that two particular girls were going on the ski trip. He liked being with Grenythe Karlstein because she enjoyed the same music that he did. He had also noticed that she was kindhearted and tolerant of other people. He found Helene Dolmet different from Grenythe, but he liked her just as much. It was a pleasure to be around Helene because she had a great sense of humor, and she was so full of fun when she helped him with his French. Jay appreciated the fact that both of these girls seemed to like him, too, for they made arrangements to be with him often.

Jay was aware that the political atmosphere seemed to be escalating in intensity among most of the university students, Grenythe and Helene included. The same attitude prevailed in the general population as well as among the children on the streets, around their homes or in the schools. Everywhere people were getting involved in the aura. The despair that had hovered over the nation for years was giving way to a buoyancy and a trust in the promises of a charismatic man who was reaching out to them with promises for a brighter future.

Jay remembered hearing this man, Adolph Hitler, early after his arrival in Munich. He sensed the power that this man held over those who listened to him, and now a few months later it was evident to Jay that the promises Hitler was making had not convinced all the citizens of Germany. With every promise there was a message of hate and ridicule against the Jews and other political parties, such as the Communists, the Prussians and often the Protestant Churches in the Prussian area. Since Jay considered himself apolitical, he listened but paid little attention to the arguments that were developing among his friends and acquaintances. Helene and Grenythe both expressed the thought that Hitler was nothing more than a loud-mouth who wanted to get attention by reviling the Jews, the Communists and some protestant churches. The girls both remarked that he could not really mean all the abominable atrocities of which he accused any of them. Jay had heard Franz Lubeck tell Grenythe Karlstein that she would be wise to keep her criticism of Hitler to herself, or she might disappear like some other people he knew about. Grenythe had not replied to Franz but had just walked away from him.

Franz's remark made Jay think about Mr. Weis, the husband of his landlady. The only information Jay had about that incident came from the man's son, Paul, who had said but two words — "He disappeared."

One day late in the afternoon, shortly before Christmas, Sam Bradshaw was walking beside Jay as they sauntered down Ludwigstrasse away from the University. They were going to a meeting with the others that had been assigned to the more "experienced" of skiers that were planning the upcoming excursion to Austria. Their group was under the tutelage of a student named Galen Schirach.

Jay remarked, "You've met six of my closest friends in my music classes. The other day Helene Dolmet said that since she was such a bad skier, she hoped Galen would not kick her out of the advanced group."

"She's so much fun to be with, that I think Galen will want to keep her in our group anyway," Sam said.

"Helene and Grenythe are bringing two other girls along. They say that they are good skiers."

"Do you know them, Jay?"

"I've met them, and there is one named Lizbet and another Katherine or something — I forget her last name — I could not help but notice her. She reminded me of my sister, Roxanne, because she has red hair and blue eyes. Her whole attitude and personality reminded me of Roxy."

"Oh! Oh! You sound like you like her a lot."

"Don't get me wrong. I don't know her. I don't know whether I would like her or not. I couldn't help but look at her though, because she reminded me of Roxanne. She did not really look like Roxy — it was just her red hair."

"What about the other girl? What was her name?"

"Katerina, or something like that. That would be Katherine at home."

"What did she look like?"

"Sam, she was just a pretty girl. I just got to meet them for a short time and did not have time to *study* them." Jay laughed. "We'll get to be with them a lot on this ski trip. You can make up your own mind which one you like the best then."

"I don't want to cut you out, Jay, if there is one you like," Sam bragged.

"Better be careful, Sam," Jay teased, as he slapped Sam across the back. "I like them all."

As the boys walked briskly along the street to the Kaffeehaus where the meeting was to be held, they paid little attention to the drab terrain around them. Only a few weeks before, the beauty of the bright autumn colors had gone, leaving the trees shorn, yet creating a delicate vision of their own. The tiny unclad branches formed a lacy pattern against the gray skies, reaching up into the winter atmosphere as if welcoming the flakes of the first white snow that had fallen gently down. The blanket of new snow had given the whole territory the aura of freshness and exhilaration. Then came the melting and the slush!

The white blanket of snow had turned into a dull brown cover that could have left a dismal atmosphere in the area — but it had not been reflected in the folk on the street. The enhancement of the first snow was carried over into the spirit of the people as they walked, as they spoke and as they greeted each other. A new salute was being heard everywhere — "Heil Hitler."

This was how Jay and Sam were hailed by several as they entered the kaffeehaus, even by three of the girls in the group — all except Grenythe Karlstein. Jay not only noticed that she did not sing out "Heil Hitler," he noticed a slight shake of her head. Two of the boys greeted them in another different fashion — they said, "Guten morgen."

When everyone arrived, Galen Schirach took charge of the meeting, which turned out to be short and agreeable. Galen said that he had hoped to get a larger group, but many students did not have enough extra money to make the trip. The plan was that they would leave early the morning after Christmas Day, which proved very convenient since Christmas Day came on a Sunday. They agreed that they would stay in pensiones, the least expensive places they could find. When the meeting was over, it was Galen who dismissed them and bid them goodbye with a salute — and "Heil Hitler!"

In the early morning hours, the train trip to Tirol, Austria, was a delight for Jordan Fisk, Jr. and Samuel Bradshaw. Neither of them had ridden an electric train before, and the scenery over the mountain passes provided them with an unexpected thrill. They felt the feeling of power under them, as the train climbed slowly up the steep passes. The two American boys left the car in which they were riding with their friends and moved up through the cars as far as they could go toward the front of the train. There, as the sun rose over the peaks, they could see displayed before them the magnificent scenery, mile after breathtaking mile.

The spectacular beauty of the surroundings did not lend itself to the pensiones where the two groups settled for the first night. They had agreed at their earlier meetings that they would find inexpensive lodgings. They quickly found a place where they could get a bed for one-half mark, which amounted to about twelve and one-half cents American money. That was even better than they had expected. After paying in advance they moved into their quarters, only to find that these cheap rates had sheets on the beds that were not too clean, and there were lice and bed bugs in abundance. They looked around for rats and would not have been surprised if they had seen one appear to wish them welcome. They had already paid for one night, so these twenty students, not having much money, resolved to stay this one night but to find a better place for the rest of their stay.

The two instructors, Galen Schirach and Edvard Bloch, called the two groups together and told them there was only one mountain feasible for climbing. It was a small mountain on the windblown side of the range, and if they decided to go, they should get started immediately. On that mountainside the snow, instead of accumulating, had been blown free on most of the trail, so they could still make the climb and get back before dark if they started at once. Galen's *experienced* group of ten listened as Galen expressed the desire to hurry.

"I heard a man say we were crazy to try to do any mountain climbing in the winter," Jacob Stein observed.

"I expected you to back out," Galen sarcastically answered.

"I did not say I was backing out — I might not have any better sense than you," laughed Jacob. Several of the others laughed along with Jacob, but the remark did not amuse Galen.

"Well, how many of you want to climb?" Galen looked over the entire group of eighteen students and the other instructor.

"Galen," Edvard Block stated, "we, not professing to be as sturdy as some of you, have been convinced by the comments around town that we are nuts trying to climb any of the peaks at this time of year." He shook his head as he said it.

Galen turned to the nine members of his group. "Well?" he said.

Helene said she did not want to go. "I am afraid, Galen."

"Honey," Galen put his arm across her shoulders. "I'll take care of you. If you get too tired, you can turn back." Turning to the others, he asked, "How many of you are willing to start the climb? We have to get started at once if we are going!"

Katarina Polz spoke up, "Come on — let's get started!" And she started for the door.

Jay Fisk was grinning as he poked his friend Sam in the ribs, "Remember when I told you that girl reminded me of my sister, Roxanne. That's just the way Roxy would have reacted. Act now, think later."

"What do you think?" Sam whispered.

"I'm the more cautious type. I think it a risk to try such a feat when everyone around us is saying it is too dangerous."

"Then you are not going?" Sam asked.

"Oh, I'm going!" Jay answered.

Sam and Jay joined the others of the group as they were moving out the door, bundled up for a climb on a windswept mountain. They asked those staying behind to change the bug-infested, dirty sheet accommodations for a better place. Then they said, "See you later!" as they waved goodbye.

The four girls started out with the five boys and Galen. Galen, smiling at Helene, told her to stay with him, that they would be walking at a rapid pace and he didn't want to lose her. He also told the girls that if they were not able to stay with the group they could quit at any time — that the trail was well marked and they would have no trouble finding the way back to the village.

The ten grabbed their water bottles and what other little necessities they had in their rucksacks, and they were on their way. To save time, they hired a cab to get them to the foot of the mountain. It was already after nine o'clock in the morning, and they had to allow six hours to climb to the top of the mountain and three hours for the return. It would be six o'clock in the evening before they would return, and the sun was expected to set about four forty-five.

On the way to the mountain, one of the girls asked Galen, "Are you sure we can find our way back in the dark?"

"We can if we watch where we are going and don't dilly-dally along the way. If we can make the climb in less than six hours, it will be to our advantage," he replied.

Sam Bradshaw had paid little heed to the arrangements that were being made around him — he just followed the others. His whole attention was on Lizbet. When he had first seen her at the meeting in Munich days ago, he had looked forward to this trip — not for the trip itself, but a chance to be with Lizbet. He had learned her last name was Greenberg. He wondered it that was a Jewish name, but it made no difference to him. He was in love! From the moment the touring students had gotten together this morning of departure, Sam had sought out Lizbet.

Jay was aware of Sam's infatuation and, smiling to

himself, kept his distance so that Sam could operate his love game without feeling any interference. The trail was wide at the beginning, and it was natural that the ten would pair off as they climbed. Galen had already expressed his desire to have the French girl, Helene Dolmet, walk with him, and Sam had stuck by Lizbet's side. The other two girls, Grenythe and Katarina, walked together. Jay would have liked to have had a better opportunity to talk with Katarina, because he wanted to tell her that she reminded him of his sister, Roxanne, but he also liked Grenythe. He could see that his two German friends, Georg Blaich and Franz Lubeck, also liked the two girls and that they stayed right at their heels as they hiked along the trail.

The Italian boy, Tony Riccionne, was a natural-born comic. In the first two hours of the climb, with his wry humor he kept making some remark that kept the rest of the group in a happy mood. The only person he did not amuse was the instructor, Galen Schirach. Jay wondered if it was because Tony was always attracting the attention of the students, when Galen, the instructor, wanted to be the big cheese, or was it because Tony was of another nationality. They hadn't climbed for more than an hour before Tony, as well as the rest of the climbers, became too short of breath to talk or to laugh — yet they continued on up the trail.

The first two hours of hiking were not as easy as they expected, even though it had not yet become steep. The difficulty came because of some ice and snow had clung to the trail in spite of the constantly blowing winds. Galen was generous in letting them stop frequently to catch their breath. Though he did curtail the length of the interludes, he made it a point to let them know that time was of the essence.

As the altitude increased and the climb steeper, their breath became shorter and more labored, the stops more frequent. The trail was also narrower, and they had to walk in single file.

Helene kept falling back behind the rapid pace of Galen — he would step back, get her by the hand and almost pull her onward and upward. Franz and Georg each got behind one of the other girls, "We're in a position to push if necessary," they laughed, but Katarina and Grenythe were making it a point to keep up with the ones ahead of them, saying that they would more likely be the ones doing the pushing. Jay and Joseph were also having no trouble keeping up with the others.

Sam, who had taken Lizbet by the hand in the early hours of the climb, did not want to let go. I think he deliberately slowed them down so that they could talk a bit with one another, and before anybody noticed, they could not be seen around the last bend of the trail.

After three hours of climbing, with stops now occurring frequently, the group now of just eight stopped and sat on the bare rocks with a cold, intense wind blowing across the peaks. The very thing that had kept the snow from accumulating in the earlier storms was now making their climb miserable — a strong, bone-chilling wind. Jay found shelter under one big rock and told the girls to come join him. He reached in his pocket for a cigarette and found that he was out of them. He asked the girls if any of them could lend him one. The girls had none. Jay got up from his sheltered spot to ask the boys if they had any cigarettes. No one had a cigarette to spare. Jay, for the first time on the climb, seemed disturbed and nervous. "I've got to have a cigarette!" he exclaimed.

"You smoke too much, already," Grenythe told him.

"We got ready in such a hurry back at the pensiones that I didn't pack any cigarettes," Jay complained. "I need one!"

"That's your problem," Galen said, then called to the group to get on their feet — it was time to be moving. He told them that they had made good time, and if they kept going they would reach the top in less than the six hours they had planned. If they did, they could get back very soon after dark.

"I can't go any farther!" Helene exclaimed without moving from the sheltered spot behind the big rock.

"Yes, you can," Galen said, as he pulled her up from her position. The tone of his voice was not as cajoling as it had been in the earlier hours. "We must go on. We can't spend the night up here in this cold."

"We can go back," Helene insisted.

"I am going on," Galen announced to the rest of the group. "You can come with me, or you can head back. It's your choice."

Grenythe and Katarina were already heading up the mountain. That was all it took for the rest of them to join in the upward progress. Jay felt he would have no trouble climbing the rest of the way, but for a moment he thought he would rather get back as soon as possible, if for no other reason than to get a cigarette.

In less than an hour, exhausted and short of breath,

the eight climbers saw minimal flakes of snow and sleet. Each step became harder with occasional slipping and sliding, slowing their progress. Their chances of reaching the summit in the time planned was not only questionable, it now looked practicably impossible. They knew the little tea house that stood on the summit to welcome the climbers in the summer season was closed. If they reached the top, they had no place where they could escape the bitter cold. The chance of a heavy snow would make their descent hazardous — it could even trap them on the cold, windswept peak. There was little conversation among the climbers as they considered their predicament.

When they finally reached the top, Tony wrote "Snow" on a note and passed it around to get all their names; then putting the date on it, he slipped it inside a little plastic container that one of the climbers provided and stuck it under a rock. He half jokingly said, "That's for Sam and Lizbet if they ever catch up with us." His companions did not think the note was a joke, and most of them turned to begin their descent.

Someone muttered, "Sam and Liz were smart to go back!"

"But we didn't, did we?" Tony answered, still in a joking tone of voice.

"Why did you really want to leave that note, Tony?" Helene asked.

"Oh, no reason particularly!" he answered lightly.

"Tony, you thought there was a chance that we might not get back, didn't you!" Grenythe stated, not in a questioning tone.

"We should never have started on this ludicrous junket!" Franz Lubeck said.

"You didn't have to come, you know!" Galen countered.

"Let's stop the quarreling and try to get safely back," Jacob said as he took his first step down the mountainside. The rest of the group followed.

Galen reluctantly turned with the rest of the students and said, "I'll bring up the rear to see that everyone returns safely." Again, he placed Helene directly in front of him as they followed the other six, who were finding more and more slippery patches on the downward trail.

It was Tony who started the derisive remarks as they continued their hurried descent, meaning to put a bit of humor into their mountain-climbing feat. He turned from his position toward the head of the line and yelled back, "Gallen, this whole idea was a little *off key*, wasn't it?"

"Yeah, it was *flat!*" Grenythe laughed.

Jay Fisk grinned as he yelled, "And the band leader was *fortissimo.*"

The six music students were all donating their critique in musical terms. Tony turned all the way around. Facing back up the slope toward the others, he yelled, "And sometimes the band leader was too *sharp!*" As Tony made that remark, his foot slid out from under him as he took a step backwards on an ice covered rock. In a split second he fell backward off the narrow path down the side of the cliff.

The chuckling among the students was suddenly replaced by screams of terror as they saw their good friend disappear among the trees and underbrush down the steep side of the mountain! For a few seconds they stood silent and petrified in the cold. Soon they were saying, "Let's get some help — what are we going to do —?"

It was Galen who yelled, "Listen, you clowns, we can't just stand here and freeze to death, or wait for help to come. Two of you guys come with me and we will make our way down the mountain to find Tony. One of you boys will accompany the girls back to town, and get help to us as soon as possible!"

All four boys, Franz, Jay, Jacob and Georg, volunteered to help Galen find Tony. Katarina and Grenythe both said they would like to help find him, too.

"You girls aren't strong enough to carry Tony if we find him in very bad shape," Galen advised. "You girls and Jay go get help!"

Grenythe said, "I expect it would be better for Jay to help you, Galen, because he may not be able to speak the dialect well enough with the rescue people."

"She's right, you know," Jay agreed, and told the girls they should get started back immediately.

"All right, then. Franz, you and Jay come with me, and Georg, you take the girls back," Galen announced.

"What about me?" Jacob Stein, who had been completely ignored, asked.

"Oh." Galen shrugged his shoulders and said indifferently, "You might as well go back with the girls."

Georg and the girls were already making their way carefully, but as hurriedly as possible down the slick path when Jacob joined them. Galen, Jay and Franz were just as careful as they climbed down the steep slope in the direction that Tony had fallen.

It was not hard for the three young men to follow the track of Tony's downward plunge. The density of the trees had kept the incessant wind currents from blowing away the previous snows. It was also the trees that had kept his companions from spotting him from the trail, for he had not fallen far. Soon the three rescuers came upon Tony's still body sandwiched between a tree and a large rock. He was lying with his head down against the rock and his feet up the slope.

The boys hurried to him and found him still warm and, to their relief, still breathing. "Two of us will make a pack for him to sit on, the other will hold his arms around the packers' necks, and we'll get him out of here and back upon the trail," Galen instructed,

We can take turns, of course, forming the pack," Franz suggested. "Jay and I will make the first pack, and Galen, you can get him sitting on our arms and hold him."

"Galen, why don't we head slightly uphill, but otherwise parallel with the trail. We'll make forward progress without such a difficult climb instead of going straight back up that steep slope," Jay suggested.

"Good idea!" Galen answered laconically.

"My head hurts!" the muttering of words below them startled the three youths who were discussing rescue plans.

"Did you hear that?" Franz asked excitedly. He leaned over the boy lying in the snow. "Tony, Tony, are you all right?"

"Do I look all right?" came the disgusted answer from the prone figure trying to reverse his position and get his head above his feet.

"Lie still, Tony," Galen said. "You mustn't move too fast. You probably struck your head on that rock when you fell."

"How long have I been here?" Tony asked as he made an effort to stand up.

"You four-flusher," Franz joked. "You've pretended to be hurt, lying here for hours, and had us sending for the troops to rescue you."

"Really? Has it been hours?" Tony inquired.

Galen was smiling, "Can't you see how dark it is?" The clouds and compact forest made the light of the day seem much dimmer than it was.

"I'm sorry. I did not know about anything until just a few minutes ago. I know I have a bump on my head and it hurts." Tony was very apologetic.

"They are just getting even with you, Tony. It is their time to tease. I do think we better get moving. We were making preparations for carrying you out of the forest," Jay said.

"Jay's right — we must get going. Do you think you can walk? Do you hurt anywhere besides your head?" Galen asked.

Tony looked at his watch for the first time. "Why, it hasn't been but thirty minutes since I fell."

The other three were laughing as they helped Tony get to his feet. Galen pulled Tony's arm around his neck and told Franz or Jay to support him on the other side. "We have to get back to town before it gets dark, and it is beginning to snow a little harder now. I know you cannot feel too good after that fall, so we will help you along as much as we can."

The four boys walked so fast that they met the rescue party just starting up the mountain trail. Soon they were rejoicing with the rest of their group over Tony's miraculous escape from serious injury. They were also greeted with the good news that more acceptable accommodations had been procured for the rest of the week at a gasthaus for one mark per night (only 25 cents in American money), still an inexpensive cost in this depression time.

While students of both the groups were mingling and exchanging pleasantries, Grenythe, in a chiding manner, called over to Jay who was standing nearby, "Now, friend, you can get your precious cigarettes."

"Uh, uh," was the only reply Jay made, as he shook his head.

Surprised at Jay's response, Grenythe walked over to him and enquired, "Did I take that to mean 'no'?"

"That's right — I'm not going to smoke anymore."

"Well, well, what brought that on?" Grenythe tauntingly remarked.

"You wouldn't understand," Jay was in a pensive mood, shaking his head slightly and looking off into the distance.

Grenythe made no reply but stood quietly by Jay's side for a few moments, "I might — if you let me," she said, as she turned to move away.

Jay took one step after her, then stopped. Grenythe was aware of his action. She turned back to him and said, "Do you want a cigarette or not?" Jay said nothing, and Grenythe continued, "Do you want to tell me about it?"

Jay took Grenythe by the arm and pulled her away from the rest of the students who were milling around on the sidewalk in front of the pension.

"Grenythe, remember a short time ago after Tony had fallen and Galen asked for volunteers to help him search for Tony? For just one second I thought I wanted to get back to my room and get a cigarette, let the others look for Tony. That was the moment when I could not believe that I, even for a second, had such a thought! I decided right then and there that I could not let a cigarette ever again have such a hold on me, that I would think it more important than saving a life. That's why, Grenythe, I will not add to that addiction, not ever, ever again."

The days that followed were delightful, that is, weatherwise, for the two Munich groups of students who were in Austria for holiday skiing. The new snow that had fallen had not been heavy enough to make skiing difficult, but enough to cover spots where much skiing had made them too slick.

Jay Fisk's group of the more experienced skiers were appreciative of the good instruction given them by their leader, Galen Schirach. Jay and his American friend, Sam Bradshaw, accepted the fact that they weren't the best skiers in the group, probably the least experienced. Jacob Stein, one of the boys in their group, they considered to be better than they were; yet they were puzzled that their instructor criticized him continuously most of that first day. Possibly, Jay first thought, Galen did it as an example to point out to the rest of them an error that they all had made.

The next day, Jacob Stein was again ridiculed even more by the instructor. Jay and Sam, talking to each other, could not understand why Galen was picking on Jacob. When the third day came and the same thing happened, Jay said, "Sam, the poor fellow is not the best at skiing, but he's just as good as we are. I wonder what he's done that has brought on the wrath of the teacher."

On the fourth day, Galen Schirach threw Jacob out of the first group. "You are not good enough to be in this group. Go back to the inferior skiers." After he was gone, the instructor openly said, "Thank God, that Jew is no longer with us!"

That night Jay and Sam talked with Grenythe Karstein, Franz Lubeck and a few of the others that they knew well and mentioned the dismissal of Jacob from their group. There was a little bit of humming and hawing among the students, but few made any comment, either for or against, the action taken by their instructor. When they were ready to say goodnight to each other, Grenythe whispered to Jay, "I think I need to talk with you in private."

"Let's take a walk," Jay said. The two of them told the others that they were going to walk around the town a little bit before going to bed. A few smirks on the faces of other students showed that they thought Jay and Grenythe were getting away alone for romantic reasons.

When they were out of hearing distance, Grenythe said, "Jay, I don't think you know how much the hostility is building up against the Jews in Germany. That's why Galen got rid of Jacob."

"What about Edvard? He has Jacob in his group now. How will he treat him?"

"I don't know. But everybody isn't as prejudiced as Galen. I don't know about Edvard Block. I haven't heard him say anything yet."

"Well, Grenythe, it's none of my business. I don't pay attention to these political matters — they don't mean anything to me. I just want to learn more about great music."

"You *better* pay attention, Jay. You are living in a Jewish home. Be careful!"

When the holidays were over, Jordan Fisk, Jr. went back to Munich, less the carefree youth he had been when he started. For the first time he realized that cigarettes were like many other drugs — addictive, and he wanted no more to do with them.

He also knew there was something wrong in Germany when the deep prejudice against the Jewish people was gaining momentum. He could not help but notice the attitude of Galen Schirach on their ski trip — so solicitous and worried about the welfare of Tony Riccionne when he fell, yet so contemptuous of and insulting to Jacob Stein for no obvious reason, except his being Jewish.

CHAPTER THREE

Linderhof

CHAPTER THREE

WHEN THE TWENTY STUDENTS returned to Munich after their ski trip, it was again time to take up their studies. They saw little of their holiday companions except those in the same classes at the University.

Jay Fisk was in daily contact with his five closest friends who were also studying music. One day Grenythe said, in an amused voice, "Jay, you better tell your friend Sam to take it easy."

"What about him?" Jay was puzzled.

"I guess you haven't talked with him or seen him since we got back."

"No, I haven't! What's he done?"

"I see Lizbet now and then, and she told me that Sam is on her doorstep every day."

"I know he liked her a lot," Jay laughed, "but I don't think we should worry about it. He'll be going home after the school year."

"Jay, he's trying to get her to go to the United States next year. He wants her to finish her education there," Grenythe said.

"What does she say about it?" Jay asked, in a more serious mood.

"That's the problem, Jay. She says wants to go, but I

don't think she's sure — she keeps saying that she doesn't have the money."

"I don't know any way that I can help, can you?" Jay shrugged his shoulders.

"Of course not!"

"Grenythe, we'll get together and talk with them about it — it might be fun. In the meantime, I want to enjoy the operas."

Though Jay especially concentrated on opera, he found concerts, cathedrals and architecture worth his attention. Neither he nor most of his classmates (all in their early twenties) paid little attention to a man named Hitler, a man not yet too well known, and in no way considered dangerous. In the autumn school months of 1932, students had other interests and thought little about politics — they thought of Hitler as a man who loved opera. They had heard that he liked Wagner operas especially. So some of the students, too, took special interest in them.

Jay found all the opera performances in Munich wonderful. He was so impressed that one evening in a letter to his sister, Roxanne, he wrote about them:

> *I liked the Wagner operas the best of all. They start at six o'clock in the evening and last until eleven o'clock. (There is a thirty-minute break, when the patrons go to the lobby to eat). The stage settings are very realistic. In Rheingold, the Rhine maidens appeared to be really swimming under water.*
>
> *My favorite of all operas is Tannhauser. When Wolfram comes out and sits near the front of the*

stage and sings, "O du holder Abend-stern" (O, you lovely evening star) in the sky at the rear there gradually appears the bright star — well, that's a moment to treasure.

I loved it! I was so taken with Wagner, I rode my bicycle to Bayreuth, visited his house, reveled in the atmosphere. The fact that he was anti-Semitic didn't register with me.

At the end of Parzival when that holy grail ascends a shaft of light, the audience was so stunned, impressed, immersed in the scene, that when the curtain went down, there was no applause — no one felt like breaking the inspirational atmosphere. I looked around and could see the humility on all faces.

No appearances in front of the curtain — nothing — we just got up quietly and left.

Well, Rox, I can't think of anything more to say.

Jay was sitting at his desk, musing about that great opera, when he unconsciously reached into his pocket for a cigarette — then remembered he no longer smoked. He contemplated whether to write any more, or to sign off and continue another time. While he sat there, he heard a slight tapping on the back door of the house. There were three taps, a pause, then three more taps. Jay's room was on the second floor at the back of the house. His curiosity aroused, he got up and went to the window. If he pulled back the curtain, more light would shine down on the back fence, and whatever or whoever was down there would know he was watching them

— spying! So he watched as best he could through the curtains. He saw Mrs. Weis answer the door, and he heard her whisper to the caller, "Be quiet, I don't want to wake Paul."

Jay wondered what was going on in such a secretive manner. Perhaps his landlady had an admirer, or maybe, just maybe, it could be her husband who was making a home call after being gone for a long time!

Soon after he heard the back door downstairs close, Jay went back to his desk, but before he did curiosity prompted him to pull the curtains aside, so that if another chance presented itself he could get a better view from his window. After what he had seen and heard, Jay couldn't concentrate any further on letter writing, nor could he give full attention to his books, even though he tried to focus on tomorrow's assignments. In a short time he heard the sound of the back door opening again. Jumping up, he got to the window in time to see a furtive figure hurrying across the limited back yard and jump over the fence and disappear.

What bearing did that small incident have on what was going on in Germany's political situation? Jay did not want to upset his landlady by letting her know what he had heard and seen. He wondered if it had anything to do with the Hitler uprising, or with the condemnation of the Jews because Mrs. Weis was Jewish. The American boy wanted no involvement whatever with what was taking place in this foreign country, but he was aware that some great changes were in the making by this man called Hitler. It was in the newspapers, on the radio, in the movies and in torch processions. Just a few days after he and his friends had returned from their Christmas vacation, it was known that a supposedly secret meeting had taken place on January 4, 1933, to plan the future of Germany. It was between the banker, Baron Kurt von Schroeder of Cologne, Papen, who wanted to be the next Chancellor, and that upcoming man called Hitler. Hindenberg, the beloved old General, was at the mercy of the intrigues around him. When Hitler pointed out that he would *not be* a part of the Papen-Hitler government that was proposed, Hindenberg accepted the alternative — it would be the Hitler-Papen government. It was no surprise when on January 30 in Berlin, Hitler was sworn in as the new Chancellor. After dark, a torchlight parade marched through the Brandenburg Gate in Berlin, as Hitler watched it from the upper window of the Chancellery. The Third Reich was on its way!

Most of the people in Munich, including the University students, had participated in or watched the parades in Hitler's campaign for Chancellor. Hitler was greeted with great fanfare, and his Nazional Sozialist political party became the Nazi party, using just the first four letters of the original party name. Though the party was named Socialist, it wasn't in any way socialist — it was fascist. The socialist name was used for propaganda.

While Hitler was fast becoming a dictator, the students were going about their business of getting an education and paying little heed to political events. Sam Bradshaw was sitting on the steps of the Weis home one cold winter afternoon when Jay returned from his classes.

"What are you doing here out in the cold?" Jay asked.

"I need to talk with you," Sam replied.

"Then come on up to my room and get warm. How long have you been sitting out here?"

"Just got here." As soon as they got to Jay's room, they removed their coats and Jay told Sam to make himself comfortable; then he left the door open and went downstairs to see if Mrs. Weis might make them some hot tea. Soon he came running back up the steps, saying the hot tea would be coming shortly.

"Now what was so important to talk about?" Jay grinned as he added, "Lizbet?"

"Yes! How did you know?" Sam asked.

"Oh, I hear by the grapevine that you've been seeing her a lot."

"Jay, I want to marry her, but I don't have any money. I don't know what to do."

"Well, Sam, I don't know what to do either. You are only twenty-one years old. Perhaps you better wait a year or two."

"In a year or two?" Sam scoffed, "I'm supposed to leave Germany at the end of this year, and I don't have enough money to stay any longer — and she'll still be over here. That's not all, Jay — she says there are many people in Germany who don't like Hitler, and they think he is heading Germany into another war. Lizbet would like to get out of Germany now. I think she likes me as much as I like her. I want to get her out of here, and I don't know how."

"What makes her think there's going to be another war?" Jay questioned. He had heard no rumor along that line.

"Don't tell anybody what Lizbet said about a war.

She said if anyone heard that she had said that, it might get her in trouble and she could be arrested. They would want to know where she had heard such talk, and that would get her friends in trouble, too."

"Wow! It looks like you are in a predicament all right, Sam." Jay gave a little laugh that he and Sam both knew was not in amusement. He then continued, "Why don't we just go about our studies and forget Germany's politics? They don't mean anything to us."

"They do to me, Jay, because Germany's politics affect Lizbet."

"You are in love, aren't you, Sam? I don't think there is anything you and I can do about it. We are just two poor American students with just enough money to last us until we go back to the United States next fall. If Lizbet wants to get away, it's up to her to arrange it."

Mrs. Weis came in the open door about that time with a tray of hot tea, cups and saucers. She had included a few biscuits with the tea. She smiled at Sam and told him she was glad to see him again. She looked directly at Sam for a few seconds and said, "Come see me again." The few seconds that the two of them stared into each other's eyes was not lost on Jay. It made Jay think of the incident some nights ago when the stranger had come calling at the back door. Maybe Mrs. Weis did have something going on. He wondered if he should tell Sam about that night caller, but decided he had better put it off for the time being.

When Hannah Weis had left, Jay looked at Sam and said, "Maybe there is something that can be done to get Lizbet out of Germany, but I don't know what it is. I'll keep my ears open and let you know if any information comes my way. Is Lizbet Jewish?"

"No, I don't think so, because she says her church thinks all this propaganda against the Jews is wrong."

"I agree, Sam, but I can't do anything about it. And so far Hitler can't do much, either. Even with his popularity, he doesn't have the power to displace the top leaders. And like I said, it's none of our affair."

Jay's statement that Hitler did not have the power was not just a school boy's opinion. To improve his knowledge of the German language, he read articles in magazines, books and the newspapers. He learned that there were good and powerful men who were doing all they could to keep Hitler from getting that power. One of those good men was Erwin Von Witzleben, a field marshal who was horrified by the cruelty and baseness of the Nazis; Dr. Carl Goerdeler, a civilian resistance leader; and Ludwig Beck, a Colonel-General, the one-time German Chief of Staff who became the military leader of the resistance against Hitler. There was Wilhelm Canards, head of the German Counter-Intelligence who abhorred National Socialism (Nazis), and there was Peter Count Yorck Von Wartenburg who fought Hitler and Nazism because of his own unshakable devotion to Christian moral principles.

Then Hitler became Chancellor! His party did *not* have the power or the strength to change the constitution to his liking, and he knew he could *not do it legally.* Falsifying elections and the trickery of dissolving the Reichstag *before* the election and the Communist party *after* the election, he maintained the illusion that he had done it legally.

One day in the spring of 1933, the Nazis closed a big department store named Tietz in downtown Munich. It was a store owned by a Jew! There was a storm-trooper with a gun in front of every door, and a big sign posted in front saying "This store is closed because the Jews in foreign lands are spreading false information about the New Germany." The store remained closed for only *one* day. Even the Nazis were not anti-business, not by any means! When the protests arose about the store's closing, even from the majority of Hitler's followers, it was allowed to reopen. The students, foreign and native, thought the whole thing funny and held no grudge against Hitler for the one-day closing.

Jay and his usual student friends, sixfold, were gathered at their customary kaffeehaus finishing their drinks after seeing the opera.

"Did you like it?" Helene Dolmet asked the rest of them.

"Well, 'Der Vogelhandler' is my favorite opera on the light side," Tony Riccionne said. "I think that old 'bird dealer' did a great job."

"Since it was partly in the Bavarian dialect, even though I couldn't read along with it, I was able to understand it pretty well. And it had everyone's favorite conductor, Knappertsbusch," Jay added.

"Ooh, ooh! He is young, vigorous and I think he is wonderful, too," Grenythe expressed her praise.

"Since it's a modern current opera with no written text, if you cannot understand the dialect, you might not be able to enjoy it," Franz said. "You haven't said anything about it, Georg. Did you like it?"

"With the singing and acting, I think anyone would enjoy it, even if there is no script to go with it, and it was by no means entirely in dialect."

"Does anyone have a list of the rest of the season's operas?" Helene asked.

"You know we'll see more of Wagner. Because Hitler likes them, we'll probably see more Wagner than anything else — Lohengrin, Die Meistersinger, The Flying Dutchman —" Grenythe said.

"Are they on the list?" Georg asked.

"I don't have my list with me, but I remember those three. And I think Mozart's Magic Flute is another one.

"What about Verdi's Masked Ball? I hear Hitler likes that one," Franz said.

"Are you saying we aren't going to see any operas that Hitler doesn't like?" Tony asked.

"I don't think it makes any difference. I hear that Hitler likes all operas."

"Well, good for him!"

"I've something else to ask about," Jay said. "Spring break is coming up soon, and I want to take that time to see more of the rest of Europe. I can take the trip on my bicycle. Any of you want to go with me? Italy, more of Germany, a bit of France — and Austria." Jay looked around the group, "Anyone?"

Several hands went up, the boys and both the girls.

"Maybe all six of us can go," stated Helene, "and perhaps go through Alsace, and we can all stop at my home."

"And my friends, Lizbet and Katarina, might like to go," Grenythe said.

"If Lizbet goes, then Sam will go, too," Jay laughed.

The gathering broke up, with the understanding that they would all get together to plan a bicycle trip during the spring break.

A few nights after the music students had decided to bicycle over Europe for two or three weeks, Jay Fisk was walking with his friend, Sam Bradshaw. They came upon a book burning in a downtown Munich square. Jay was six feet tall and could see over the heads of the crowd. Sam, who was two inches shorter, had to pry his way among the spectators to see the exhibition. They watched the fire for awhile and asked a few questions of those around. Jay had always said he was apolitical and Germany's politics were none of his business. The book burnings made him aware that something was drastically wrong in this country.

"You know that's pretty dumb, burning all those books," he said to Sam. They found out that **all** books by Jewish authors were being banned and these burnings were books by Jewish authors.

"I wonder if they will burn all books written by Jews?" Sam asked.

Jay had read one book by Stefan Zweig which he liked very much. Later on, when he tried to buy another of Zweig's books, he was unable to find any. One store owner told him that he had put all books by Jewish authors on a back shelf out of sight. Other store owners had destroyed them.

The book burnings in Munich and elsewhere in Bavaria changed Jay's attitude. From the moment he and Sam watched the spectacle in Munich, he refused to give the Nazi salute of "Heil Hitler" and continued to say "Gruss Gott' instead. Another thing Jay did — he shaved off this Hitler mustache!

The spring break came in March at the University of Munich. Of Jay's six music student friends, Tony Riccionne and Georg Blaich chose not to go on the proposed cycle tour. Sam Bradshaw and Lizbet Greenberg joined the group. Jay Fisk asked his good friend, Grenythe Karstein, why Katarina was not going with them.

"Katarina said she spent all her money on the Christmas trip. Jay, I don't know if you have noticed, but many of us here in Germany are strapped for money. I can go on this trip because we are bicycling. Most of us have enough money to get by, have a few little extras and pay for our education — that is all. I think Helene has more money than most of us, and possibly Tony," Grenythe explained.

"Then I wonder why Tony isn't going?" Jay asked.

"You'll have to ask him."

"That'll have to wait until we get back, I guess," Jay answered. "We won't be back in class until after the break."

The group, six University students in a gay mood, made their way out of Munich headed northwest into Germany. They had not ridden far before they paired off, two by two. Sam Bradshaw made sure that he would ride along beside Lizbet Greenberg. The other two girls, Helene Dolmet and Grenythe Karlstein, rode together, as did Jay Fisk and Franz Lubeck. Many times they had to go single file, but whenever space was available they enjoyed visiting with each other as they rode along side by side. Once in awhile the girls slowed the procession, saying they were going too fast, but Sam and Jay, the two American boys, agreed with the girls, saying they did not want to go faster than they could absorb the scenery as they went.

The students found the flat land between Munich and the Black Forest excellent farmland, and they made good time, pedaling faster there than they could in the hill country. Also they liked to stop and talk with the farmers they encountered along the way. They ran into one farm occupational practice that they were not expecting. The farmers fertilized with manure from the farm animals that had been diluted with urine. The mixture was placed in a long barrel-like wagon and driven out to the fields. There a plug was removed, and as the wagon was pulled along by horses, the highly odorous solution sprayed out over the ground. The farm hands who were doing this work, over the course of the day, could not help but get their clothes contaminated, and when the students came near them, the farm hands were, to put it mildly, very smelly!

"If Tony had been with us, he would have had some comic remark to make about these farmers," Helene said.

"You better be glad Tony is not with us, " Franz joked, "or he would have found a way to maneuver one of you girls into the spray."

"Which reminds, me — why isn't Tony with us?" Grenythe asked.

"Oh, he wanted to go to some political meeting with

Galen," Helene told them

Jay and Sam both spoke at once, "He wanted to go to that meeting instead of take this trip?"

"You knew about the meeting?" Grenythe asked.

Jay spoke first, "We both got notices of that meeting. It announced that the Nazi party wanted to inform all foreign students about the great reforms the Nazis had for the German government."

"We chose not to go," Sam added. Then he turned to Franz and asked, "Did you know about it?"

"Of course, but I was more interested in this trip," Franz replied.

"What about Georg?" Sam and Jay both asked.

"He wanted to hear what was said at the meeting," Franz told them. "He's going to tell me about it when we return."

The political subject was not mentioned again for some time. Helene took command of their routing, advising the best way to Strasbourg, France, and her home in a small suburb nearby. They reached the Alsace region of France early on the fourth day and again stopped to talk with some farmers. Jay could not resist asking them what they thought about the Hitler situation in Germany. These farmers, though they spoke German fluently, considered themselves French, and said they were satisfied that Hitler would keep his word and would not invade French territory.

It was only fifteen years after World War I when the students were making this trip. Though these scenes were commonplace to the European students, Jay Fisk and Sam Bradshaw were amazed at seeing the old battlefields through the Rhineland, especially in the provinces of Lorraine and Alsace. There were stalks of blasted trees with new growths coming up and battle trenches still unfilled along the way.

The weather had been good with a mild west wind as they biked through the Scharzwald and into France. The students thought that since they had gotten here earlier than expected, they would still have time in the three-week spring break to bike on down the Rhine River shoreline into Switzerland. Then, if time permitted, they could see a bit of northern Italy before crossing the narrow neck of Austria back into Germany. Jay compared his bicycle with those of the others. He had a coaster-brake model without a high gear and knew he could not travel as fast as his friends with more modern vehicles. Helene had one of the best models available — she said that was the only reason that she could keep up with the rest of them.

On the fourth day of their journey as they approached Strasbourg, Helene, leading the procession, pulled over and stopped at the side of the road and announced that she and Lizbet had some important business to take care of, and would *not* go into central Strasbourg with the others. Sam objected and argued that he wanted to go wherever Lizbet went.

"Sam, come here!" Helene, her right hand on the handlebars of her bicycle, lifted her left hand and motioned for Sam to approach her. The rest of the group were talking among themselves, as they watched Sam, with a reluctant look on his face, move slowly up to Helene. When he reached her side, she pulled his head down and whispered something in his ear. When he raised up, he looked first at Lizbet and then back to Helene, nodding his head as he walked back to his bike.

When he got back to his place in the line, Jay Fisk, who was right behind him, asked, "What was that all about?"

"I can't tell you." Sam, no longer objecting to the arrangement, had a pleased expression on his face.

"Helene, if you and Lizbet leave us, do you plan to join us later?" Franz asked.

"Of course!" Helene answered. "Since I have lived most of my life in this area, I do not want to spend any time sightseeing in Strasbourg, but it would be interesting for you two Americans to look around, and Franz, you and Grenythe have not been here before — I think you would enjoy it, too."

"How long before you meet us, and where?" Franz insisted.

"Noon tomorrow, we'll meet in front of the Cathedral."

"Which cathedral? — I see there are several important churches in Strasbourg," Franz interrupted.

"Franz! Only *one* is a cathedral — The Cathedral of Our Lady of Strasbourg — Strasbourg's pink angel. You can start a walking tour there — in fact, that's where you can start any of your walking tours. From there you can see St. Thomas' church and the most important museums. I like The Kammerzell House, and the Chateau des Rohan — these were once homes, but are now museums, and there's the museum Ouevre Notre Dame. The different bridges across the rivers are interesting—especially the covered bridge with its towers, and there's the

Crow's bridge." Helene paused a moment, then laughed before she continued, "And don't miss the Market Place of the Suckling Pigs Place."

"I think we need you to guide us, Helene," Jay said.

"You can buy a little walking tour guide as soon as you get into town. Find your pension for overnight now, and by noon tomorrow you should have covered all the important sightseeing spots." Helene turned to Lizbet, "Come on, friend, this is where we leave our good companions."

The three young men were sprawled upon the steps in front of the Cathedral, while their female companion sat primly by as all four of them discussed what they had seen in the city of Strasbourg in the last two days.

"I couldn't get over the difference in the information from guides inside the museums and churches," Sam Bradshaw observed.

"Which differences?" Grenythe asked.

"You remember when I asked the guide here at the cathedral yesterday if there was a synagogue in the city ..." Sam began.

"Yes, and I wondered why you asked," Grenythe interrupted.

"Oh, I just wondered! Then I asked if it was because there were no Jews in the city. Remember that she answered that there were Jews, lots of them, but they did not have a permit to build a synagogue."

"Sam, I thought you were going to get us thrown out of the cathedral when you kept quizzing her," Franz laughed.

"Well, don't you think it was funny when I asked her about protestant churches, and she said they didn't have any *American* protestant churches — that no place in France except Paris had American Protestant churches. She said she had heard that there was one in Nice. I wanted to know what she meant by American Protestant churches."

"That's when ***I*** thought she would throw us out," Jay said. "And remember that's when I told her we Americans were curious people and didn't want to upset her, to just forget all the questions."

"I thought it was important that we heard Strasbourg sheltered more than 15,000 Huguenots in 1575," Franz said. "You know most of those Huguenots fled into Germany where they were not persecuted."

"That's when Sam asked his most delightful question!" Grenythe started laughing, and Franz and Jay joined in her amusement.

Sam's face turned red and he muttered, "So what if I didn't know what a Huguenot was!"

"It was a good question, Sam, "Jay consoled. "That's the way you learn. I bet you'll never forget that the Huguenots were French Protestants persecuted by the government when all religions were banned except Roman Catholics."

"What happened to the Protestant Christians then is what is happening to the Jews in Germany now, isn't it?" Sam mused.

The conversation was cut short when a car drove up into the square and a young woman jumped out and ran up to them. The four young people on the steps jumped up to greet her.

"Hello, hello!" Helene exclaimed, "Did you enjoy your sightseeing?"

"We saw everything you mentioned and much more, Helene," Jay assured her. "Now I know why we hurried through Germany, first Augsburg, and then you rushed me through Ulm when I wanted more time to see the Butcher's Tower, and the Crooked House — and I wanted to stay and watch the Cathedral's radiant glow as the setting sun cast its golden rays upon it. You knew Strasbourg had more to offer, didn't you?"

"Where's Lizbet?" Sam queried.

Helene did not answer Sam, but said, "What I have to offer you now is lunch at my house. My mother has invited us all for a noon meal, as soon as we can get there. Here are the directions to my house. I don't think you can go fast enough to follow my car." Helene gave Grenythe a piece of paper with drawings of lines and street names through the south end of Strasbourg to the Dolmet's home address. "I wish I could take you there in my car, but I can't carry your bikes. We can leave this afternoon on our way down the Rhine — after lunch, of course!."

"Where's Lizbet?" Sam insisted.

"Oh, Sam, quit being so possessive of her. She's at my house — you'll see her when we get there." Helene stood a moment, looked at her car and then back at Sam. "Sam, do you think you can get your bike in the boot of my car? If you can, you can go back with me and we'll be there in fifteen minutes." Before she was finished speaking, Sam was lifting his bike into the small trunk of her car.

"Do you have a rope that I could use to fasten it?" Sam asked.

"No, but you can take off your belt — that will hold it."

Sam laughed and jokingly said, "How'll I keep my pants up?"

Helene turned to the others and called out, "Anyone have a safety pin that Sam can use to hold up his pants?" The three other students, joining in the teasing, were all offering Sam pins of all sorts and suggesting the best place to stick them.

Once the bike was securely fasten in the car, Helene gave the others further instructions on finding her home, telling them it would take about forty minutes or less for them to get there. Then she and Sam drove off.

When Jay Fisk, Franz Lubeck and Grenythe Karlstein arrived at the Dolmet home, they were graciously welcomed, not only by Helene, but by Mrs. Dolmet and Helene's younger sister, Marie. Soon after the reception they were ushered into the dining room, with assigned places at the table. Sam Bradshaw and Lizbet Greenberg were nowhere to be seen, nor were there any places set for them. Almost immediately, Jay asked, "Where are Sam and Lizbet?"

"They have already eaten. They'll join us shortly," Helene told him, then hurriedly changed the subject to their own afternoon plans — how far they could expect to travel before dark — how soon they would reach Switzerland on the following day.

Before their meal was completed, Sam and Lizbet

came walking into the dining room, holding hands and smiling happy greetings to those at the table. Their joyful mood seemed to portray the fact that wherever they had been and whatever they had done was a complete success, but it did not ward off the questions from their three friends.

"Where've you been?"

"What's going on between you two?"

"Why're you so secretive about it?"

Sam turned red in the face when the questions kept popping up. Lizbet was a little more composed as she answered, "We just like being together — that's all."

"There is nothing more than that to say," Sam joined in Lizbet's explanation.

No more questions were asked as all the young people thanked their hostess profusely about their wonderful meal and the cordial invitation she had extended to them. It was two hours after midday before they were on their bicycles and headed south along the Rhine River en route to Switzerland.

As they stopped periodically to rest along their route, Sam talked quietly to Helene. "They keep asking questions. Why can't we just tell them what we are doing? I know Jay would keep it secret — he's my good friend."

"Sam, Lizbet is afraid. She doesn't know how Franz and Grenythe stand on the political issues, or if what they are thinking now might not be the same as they will think in the future. And she doesn't know Jay that well."

"Then how are we going to keep answering all their questions?"

"I'll think of something — just don't say anything

more than we have already said. Just say it's a secret and laugh — laugh! You hear?"

When they stopped for that night at a small hostel for students, the questions began again among the six. Grenythe told Helene and Lizbet that they were treating her like an outsider and she felt hurt.

In the boys' room, both Jay and Franz were pestering Sam to let them know what he was doing. Sam got up and left the warm bed, not knowing how he could put up with any more probing. When he got outside the boys' sleeping room, he met Grenythe, alone, leaning against the wall.

"Grenythe, what are you doing here?" Sam asked.

"What are you doing here, yourself?" Grenythe said, and Sam saw tears in her eyes. "Why are the other girls excluding me? Are they trying to say they wish I were not along?"

Sam put his arm around Grenythe's shoulder and pulled her to the door of the girls' sleeping hall, "Go in there and tell Helene and Lizbet that I want to see them — right now!"

The three girls came out of the hall into the corridor, and Sam said, "I think we better tell Grenythe and the others what's going on. It isn't fair for you two to keep Grenythe in the dark. And Jay is my best friend. But I don't want to leave Franz out, either. Helene, you said you would …"

"Yes, I did. All right, get Jay and Franz out here and I'll give you a rundown on what's happening."

When she said that, Lizbet turned deathly pale. She moved to Helene's side and whispered, "How can you …"

"Shhh ...!"

When the boys joined the girls, they all gathered close, and Helene, keeping her voice down so as not to disturb any sleepers in the adjacent rooms, "I suppose we will have to tell you what is going on — if you haven't already guessed — but it will have to be kept a secret. Do you hear?" The three students not involved promised to abide by that decision. "Well, Sam and Lizbet want to get married. That is the only way Lizbet thinks she can get into the United States. Sam wants to finish his college education when he gets back, and he thinks his father will not furnish the money if Sam comes home with a wife. Now you see their problem — getting married, yet keeping it a secret at the other end of the line. Now you know the whole story. If you have any suggestions, let them know."

"Well, why didn't you tell us?" Jay asked. "I don't know of any way, right off, that I can help, but at least I can think about it."

Lizbet and Helene both put their arms around Grenythe, and the three girls went together back into the dormitory. Jay and Franz were both slapping Sam on the back and congratulating him, agreeing that he did have a problem, yet not knowing how they could help.

The following day nothing more was said about Sam's and Lizbet's situation, but plans for the days ahead were discussed instead. If their expectations were met, they would get to Switzerland within the morning hours. The four hours they had traveled out of Strasbourg the previous afternoon had put them a few miles south of Colmar. They thought they could cover the seventy-five kilometers to Basel by early afternoon, then they would decide the direction to travel from there — whether across the northern part of Switzerland to see Zurich, Lucern and St. Gallen, or should time and weather would permit, go on further south to Bern and Thun viewing the higher Alps.

It was springtime, and though the weather had been comfortable for their journey so far, it was not yet balmy, and they knew it would be much colder in the mountains. As soon as the travelers got into the higher altitudes, they would know if they were prepared for winter temperatures. Already the foothills of the mountains had slowed their progress. In the early planning of their trip, they had estimated that they could travel *leisurely* about twenty to twenty-five kilometers an hour for about six hours per day. Jordan Fisk and Samuel Bradshaw had already converted those figures into miles — about twelve to fifteen miles per hour, for six hours. That would have them covering about seventy-five miles per day. That had proved true in their ride across Germany into Strasbourg. They hoped that it would do so through the rest of their journey.

The six students made frequent stops to rest and catch their breath, but the stops were short. They rode single file some of time, though the original pairings were frequent. The two boys, Frans Lubeck and Jay Fisk, led the procession for the first session; then Grenythe Karlstein and Helene Dolmet would take the lead. After the girls, Sam Bradshaw and Lizbet Greenberg took their turn. The pace was set by the leaders (or leader, when the line-up was single file).

The first few hours went smoothly, though the terrain was getting hillier mile by mile and progress was slower than they had hoped. Even though they were following the Rhine River shoreline as near as possible, they still had the Vosges Mountains skirting the river all along the way. They arrived in Basel (Basle) later than expected, but it made no difference in their destination for that day. Basel had so much to offer to these eager sightseers, that they had planned to stay here for the night anyway. The two American students, Jay and Sam, had already made a list of the things they wished to see, such as the Cathedral, built in the eleventh century over another old church that was already four hundred years old; the Art Museum with paintings from all the great painters of the world, and the zoo, which many say is one of the best in the world. And surrounding the charming square of the cathedral, there are still standing some of the old medieval houses, all worth seeing.

Finding a resting place for the night at a rate the students thought acceptable was not easy, but they didn't waste too much time looking. They took a pension in walking distance of the Cathedral. They wanted to start their sightseeing as soon as possible, visiting the outdoor places before it got dark, leaving the museums to the last. Following this plan, they became the last ones to leave the art museum before it closed for the night.

The next morning all six were up early, ready to start the journey on their chosen itinerary — to Bern and Thun. As they were eating breakfast, Jay and Sam heard English spoken by two young travelers who were sitting at a table next to them.

"Are you American?" Sam asked them.

Before they could answer, Jay whispered, "I think from their accent that they are English." The two sitting at the table heard Jay's whisper and smiling said, "Yes, we are English."

In the conversation that followed between the six youths from Munich and the English couple, the students stated that they planned to travel south across Switzerland to visit Zermat and see the Matterhorn before returning to Munich. The English couple told them that they had better reconsider any plans to go south — a heavy snowstorm had developed down there and they might find some of the highways impassible.

"Where have you all traveled?" Jay asked.

"We have been traveling in Italy and across Switzerland and are on our way to Paris," the young woman answered.

"That's the reason we wanted to head south, so we could see northern Italy before returning," Jay told them.

"You wouldn't have enough time in Italy to make it worth the trip. There is a big depression there, and the poverty you see everywhere is appalling. Little thieving children would brashly try to reach into our pockets, so we had to keep our own hands in them to hold onto our possessions. The police just smiled and seemingly sympathized with the children. If you had two or three weeks to see Naples, Rome, Venice and Milan, then a trip to Italy is worthwhile — not for a day or two."

The six students from Munich looked around at each other and back to the strangers they had just met. Almost in one voice the Munich travelers thanked them for the advice and assured them they would review their plans. After finishing their breakfast, sipping their last drop of black (very black) coffee, they left the restaurant.

"Well, I guess we'll skip Italy. That will give us more time in Switzerland," Helene stated.

"I don't think we can see all we want to in Switzerland, either," Grenythe announced, "not since we can't go into the mountains because of the blizzard."

"Since we are going to Lucern and Zurich, why don't we go to that little country Liechtenstein after we leave St. Gallen?" Lizbet suggested.

"I'm for doing that!" Sam spoke eagerly.

"Why?" Franz asked, more as a comment, than really wanting to know.

"If Lizbet says it's worth seeing, then I take her word for —" Sam answered.

Jay interrupted, "Lizbet, what is there to see in Liechtenstein?"

"I don't know," Lizbet laughed, "but it's on the way, and I haven't been there. Surely there must be something worth seeing. Doesn't any one of you know?"

"Yes!" Franz spoke almost simultaneously with Grenythe.

"Yes!" Grenythe repeated.

"Then one of you tell us about it," Jay said.

Franz bowed his head toward Grenythe, but she told him to go ahead with what he knew. Franz laughed before he started speaking, "Do any of you need false teeth or glasses? Now this is just what I remember — Vaduz, the capitol, had a factory for making false teeth and producing optical instruments. If none of you need help there, you can visit the art gallery which contains many of the Prince's collection. The Prince lives in a seven-hundred-year-old castle with his family. The castle is on the top of a hill above the Rhine River and overlooks most of the country. It's that small. Oh, the country is also known for its stamp collection."

"That's all?" Sam asked.

"That's all I know about it. My parents took me there years ago when we were on a holiday."

"Okay, then let's go!" Sam enthusiastically exclaimed.

After filling their water bottles, the group were soon on their way, Grenythe and Helene were the first ones to lead the procession. They planned to spend that day traveling to Lucern. After overnight and sightseeing the following morning, they would travel on to Zurich for the next overnight stop.

It was close to one hundred kilometers and they judged it would take them six hours if they did not encounter too many steep inclines. At the first stop they happily estimated that they were making better time than expected. The skies were clouding up, but the temperature, though cooler than they had encountered so far in their journey, was not uncomfortable. They changed line-up positions, with Jay and Franz now taking the lead, followed by Sam and Lizbet, Helene and Grenythe bringing up the rear.

The time gained in the first few hours of their biking were fully appreciated when they ran into a cold rain as they approached Lucern. They had to make an extra stop to unpack and get out their rain gear. Progress was slower on the wet road and they tired quickly, so rest stops became more frequent. They were happy to arrive in Lucern and find a warm, comfortable pension on the River Ruess, not too far from the old fourteenth-century covered bridge. They saw the familiar Lion Monument commemorating the Swiss guards who attempted to save the life of Marie Antoinette.

The following morning the weather had not improved, and their proposed bike climb to Mt. Pilatus was discarded in favor of taking the cable car. After descending the peak, they headed north to Zurich, hoping to find warmer and clearer surroundings there.

Whether it was the uninviting damp climate, the big city atmosphere, or perhaps the fatigue of nine days of constant travel, the six students were not in a pleasant mood when they arrived in Zurich, Switzerland's largest city.

"I think we have missed the best part of Switzerland," Jay complained. "I think we should have followed our original plan and proceeded on to Zermat."

"What makes you think we could have gotten there through a lot of snow?" Helene argued.

"I think we should have tried," Franz agreed with Jay.

"What would we have done when we got trapped on a mountain pass in a snowstorm?" Grenythe added to the argument.

"We have two weeks and I think we are pushing too hard," Lizbet interrupted the quarrelsome tones of the others with a sweet and eager voice. "Why don't we just stay over a night or two in one place and enjoy the scenery?"

Sam put his arm around Lizbet and said, "Now you see why I like this girl. She makes life a joy."

"Okay, Joyful, what do you suggest?" Franz asked.

"Let's find a comfortable place to spend the night in Zurich; then why don't each of us go our own way for the rest of the day, seeing the museums and city sights as we wish — then tomorrow morning decide where and when we want to go," Sam proposed. His plan was accepted, and a pension not too far from the center of town was obtained. Then the group paired off, making no plans to see each other the rest of the day.

The two girls, Helene and Grenythe, said something about visiting one of the famous department stores and doing some shopping. "I don't have much money to buy anything, but I like to look," Grenythe said.

"I want to look at the watches," Helene said. "I had planned to do that in Lucern, but we were too busy sightseeing. Sam was right, we are traveling too fast and not taking time to smell the roses."

"The roses aren't in bloom yet," Grenythe laughed.

"Okay, okay, then try the lilacs!" Helene, in her usual joking and jovial spirit, replied as the two made their way down the street.

Jay and Franz planned to start their day seeing the sights; then they both wanted to shop for watches. They spent more time in the Rietberg Museum than they expected, and it was late when they entered one of the shops on Bahnhofstrasse. The watches were not the first thing they saw! Leaning over one of the display counters were Helene and Grenythe.

"Hello, girls!" the boys exclaimed loudly, as they came

up suddenly behind them.

The girls jumped and turned, "Well, hello!" they replied.

"I guess Liz and Sam aren't interested in watches," Jay remarked as he looked around the store, "or they'd be here, too."

"He's so in love he couldn't see anything but a cuckoo clock!" Franz chuckled.

"I wonder where they are." Grenythe pondered.

"We'll find out when we meet for breakfast in the morning, or perhaps when they turn in for the night." Helene tugged at Grenythe's arm, "I think we'll be on our way — see you later," she said, as the two girls turned and left the store.

That evening When the six met for dinner, the questions thrown out to Lizbet and Sam were, "Where've you been? What did you see?" and the only nonchalant answer was, "Oh, things, just things."

"This is murder!" Lizbet stopped and got off her bicycle. "I can't go any farther!" She was fifth in the line of single file bikers, as they struggled up a very steep incline.

Jay Fisk, who was just in front of her, also came to a stop and said he couldn't peddle any more either. "I know what you mean! I am going to push my bike up this mountain; it is easier than trying to ride it up."

"You wanted to see more mountains, Jay," Sam chided, "Well, here we are, right in them!"

The riders ahead stopped, all of them puffing for breath. The thin air of the altitude, along with the cold and dampness, made their progress slow. The students had left Zurich late that morning in good spirits, rested from their earlier continuous travel. They expected to arrive in St. Gallen today if travel was not too difficult. If they found they could not make it in one day, then they would stop along the way at a convenient spot — after all, they had plenty of time before they had to be back to Munich in time for school.

Short of the summit of one very steep mountain, the six pulled off the road to talk and rest. They noticed very few cars going in either direction. While they stood idling there on the side of the road, one car came over the top of the mountain and down past them. Franz exclaimed, "Did you see what I saw?"

"What?" they all asked in one voice.

"There was snow on that car!"

"Then we had better get going — we don't want to get caught up here in a snowstorm," Grenythe advised. All six bikers started immediately toward the top — pushing their bikes up the steep incline. Walking and pushing the bikes was easier than trying to peddle up the steep slopes, riding their bicycles. When they got to the top, they stopped once more to look ahead, expecting to see snow.

"Good! No snow yet," Helene said.

"But mountains as far as you can see, Jay!" Lizbet called out.

The stop was short. They all agreed that they mustn't take too much time loitering. Once more on their bikes they almost flew down that incline and had a good start up the next one before they once again were slowed down.

For a little over an hour, the six youths progressed up and down over one high summit after another. Before long they reached sections on the road which were speckled with snow — where some spots were slushy, others slick. They stopped after they reached the summit of one of the mountains. In the valley below, they could see more snow than they had yet observed, even though little bits of sleet and snow that had been stinging their faces for some time.

"We can't go on in this," someone remarked, but was immediately interrupted. "We can't stay here, either!" came a quick answer.

"We aren't too far from St. Gallen. Perhaps we can get there before dark," Franz suggested.

"Let's see how far we can go. If we find a good place to stop, we'll take it," Jay offered. The others agreed with that plan, and soon they were on their bicycles and headed down the hill, with Franz leading the way, followed closely by Jay.

It was Jay Fisk who brought the single line to a halt. He almost screamed at everyone to stop. He himself tried to stop, but he couldn't stop his bicycle's slide on the ice. He jumped off, grabbed his bike as he watched Franz, ahead of him, tumble down the hill, off the road and into the ditch.

The startled cries of alarm from the five companions was broken in seconds by Jay Fisk who called out, "Sam, you get his bicycle out and I'll take care of Franz! You girls stay back!" Jay's quick commands were unthinkingly shouted out in English. He had always made a conscious effort to speak in German. He did not even realize he had spoken in English as he followed Sam into the ditch where he was pulling the bicycle up and away from Franz.

Also down in the ditch, leaning over Franz, Jay asked, "Are you hurt?" Franz had lain quietly as if stunned for only a minute or two, then he was trying to get up almost before Jay could get to him. Franz struggled a bit as he got to his feet. "I'm all right, just roughed up a bit," he replied in German.

Jay realized that he had reverted back to his own language when he spoke spontaneously in the emergency. He laughed as he helped Franz gain his equilibrium. They walked slowly down the incline as they made their way back onto the road. Sam was following with Franz's bicycle. "Franz, I'm glad you can walk, I don't think your bike is in the best of shape," Sam called out.

Grenythe had hurried down the road to where Jay, Franz and Sam were standing. She noted the bruises, abrasions and scratches on Franz's face and hands. "I think we better get those wounds cleaned out before you go on," she said. "Sit down, Franz." She reached into her rucksack for her kit, ready to perform the necessary first aid.

Sam and Jay had gone back to get their bikes, and with the two girls they joined the nursing process that was taking place at the side of the road. In the conference that took place while they were there, few cars went by in either direction. One car going their way stopped, and the passengers asked if they could help.

"How far is it from here to St. Gallen?" Lizbet asked.

"About ten kilometers," the motorists responded.

All five friends suggested that Franz accept a ride into town, but he refused. Very graciously he thanked the people in the car for the offer, and insisted to his companions that he could make the rest of the trip with them.

When the car had moved on, Jay looked at his watch. It was four o'clock in the afternoon, the time they should have been in St. Gallen if traveling had been normal. The cold and slick road had slowed them down, and Jay figured the ten kilometers meant six miles yet to go. If they could ride their bikes, they still might get to St. Gallen before dark. In this inclement weather, the intermittent sleet they had experienced in the last hour before Franz's accident had now changed to a wet snow and it was sticking to the ground.

The six travelers soon found that most of the time they had to walk, pushing their bikes up and down the slopes. Franz's bike did not push too well, and it was impossible to ride since damage from the plunge into the ditch had caused the front wheel to be out of line. After struggling along for a while, Franz came to a stop and called to the rest, "I think we better find a place as soon as possible where we can hole up for the night." The others, knowing he was smarting from the accident, were quick to agree with him. They, too, were getting cold and wet from the melting snow, and they all realized the light of the day was fast disappearing. Jay thought that they had sporadically walked or ridden about three or four miles. Surely they couldn't be too far from the town.

As they came to the top of the next hill they could

see lights in the valley below. Expressing their glee, they all let out their yelps like happy pups, as they moved eagerly down the mountainside.

CHAPTER FOUR

St. Gallen

CHAPTER FOUR

THE GROUND was already covered with snow, and the wind had picked up. Six shivering bicyclists, for the first time, saw bright lights ahead. The sign read "RESTAURANT AND BAR." The building was standing alone by the highway, with no others around it or even close. The six youths rushed through the door, like hungry animals trying to see which one could be first at the food trough. Their noisy entrance suddenly became very quiet, as they noticed that the place was empty! The room was warm, tables were set as if guests were expected, but no one was behind the counter, and the lights overhead were very dim. They stood around for a minute or two and Franz called loudly, "Where is everybody?"

In a moment a middle-aged woman came through a door at the back of the room, wiping her hands on a soiled apron. "Hello," she said.

The young people greeted her, then several speaking at once, said, "We are looking for a place to stay." Before the woman could answer, Grenythe asked, "How far away is St. Gallen?"

"It's about three kilometers to the center of town. How long are you planning to stay?" The woman stood before them, wondering who they were, dubious of their intentions. They all looked bedraggled and scruffy. She noticed that one of the boys had small bandages on his forehead and scattered over one side of his face. She wondered is he had been in a fight. As she looked over the six of them, she paid special attention to the three girls. The taller girl had wet, stringy blond hair — the other two were shorter. One had brown eyes and dark brown hair that was mostly covered with a scarf. The other one had chestnut-colored hair, and a golden glint made the color of her eyes almost match the color of her hair. The woman was staring at the golden brown eyes of that girl, when Helene stepped forward, and in her sweet and pleading manner, asked the woman if she had a warm drink, tea, coffee, hot chocolate — anything that would warm them up; they were cold and tired. Then others of the six, a few at a time, told the woman that they were students from the Munich University on a bicycle holiday, that they had run into bad weather, and one of them had an accident. They needed to find a place to stay and get warm.

After they had explained their identity and needs, the woman smiled. She offered her hand and said, "My name is Kate. My husband, Karl, and I own this place. We were in the kitchen doing the cooking for our evening business when you came in." She turned from the visitors toward the back of the room and called for Karl to come out front. Soon he came through the same door where Kate had entered, and she told him of the young people's problem.

Karl greeted them and said, "If you patronize our restaurant, you can sleep three nights in the loft above this dining area, free of charge.

"Oh, we can't do that!" Lizbet exclaimed, "We are going to Liechtenstein tomorrow."

Kate and Karl looked at each other, then both shook their heads, and Kate amusingly said, "Dear, you haven't heard about the weather, have you? This is the worst spring snowstorm we have had in years. We said three nights, because we don't think you can go anywhere before that time."

Jay, thinking about the offer, asked, "Won't the loft be too cold for us?"

"The heat from the restaurant makes it always warmer than you would expect," Kate told them.

"But we carry only light blankets with us. We don't have any heavy blankets or clothing," another of the students said.

"There are some horse blankets in the barn that you could use," Kate said.

"Kate, there are only three blankets, and there are six of them," Karl added.

"Do you have two lofts, one for the girls and one for the boys?" Helene asked, half jokingly, then more seriously, "We need separate sleeping arrangements."

"Sorry, just one loft, and we don't have any other space where we can put you," Kate told her.

The six youths talked among themselves, then turned to the proprietors and asked if they could have something to eat right now, then they would let her know if they would accept the generous offer of the loft.

Soon Kate and Karl brought sandwiches, hot tea and hot chocolate to the table where the students had seated themselves. They had shed their wraps, after warming up from the chill they had absorbed during the last hour of walking and cycling in the snow.

"How are we going to get along with our light blankets in that loft?" Helene queried.

"There are the horse blankets!" Franz laughed.

"Who gets them?" Helene shot back.

Sam said, "That's no problem at all! Lizbet and I will cuddle up under the same one."

"Has *she* said so?" Helene looked over to Lizbet. But Lizbet didn't say anything. Sam continued, "You two guys, Jay, you and Franz can use one, and Grenythe and Helene can use the other one."

"Sam," Jay asked, "do you have any idea on the size of a horse blanket?" Sam shook his head and Jay continued, "They are hardly long enough to cover my feet if I stretch out," Jay continued.

"Well, we can sleep spoon fashion." Sam insisted.

"Stop it, Sam!" Grenythe scolded him. "You know you guys will have to sleep at one end of the loft and we three at the other."

The offer of free sleeping space was no longer argued when the six vacationers counted what money they still had, and what they still needed to get home. Time was running out, and they had to get back to Munich in time for school this coming Monday. It was now Thursday evening. They decided to accept the offer — at least for one night.

"That offer was for three nights — not one," Franz recalled. Since any exercise for him after the accident was slightly hampered, Franz thought three nights in one place sounded good.

The plan was again discussed, and Helene asked, "What are we going to do for three days — just sleep in the loft?"

"We can hike into St. Gallen and see what the town has to offer. St. Gallen is listed as a resort town, so there must be something there to do," Grenythe said. "And maybe there is a bicycle shop where Franz can get his bike repaired."

When they had finished eating, Kate had returned. They told her they were going to accept the invitation for the three nights in the loft. Kate told them that she would show them the way at once, since the evening patrons would be coming in soon, and she and Karl would be very busy for long hours after that.

Kate took them to the barn where they picked up the horse blankets. The boys asked if they could take some of the hay from the barn to the restaurant loft, to use as a mattress. They promised that they would return it before they left. Kate was reticent at first, but when they argued that the hay would add warmth as well as comfort for their beds, she consented.

After preparing the loft for their sleeping, the six young people took their bicycles into the barn to shelter them from the elements. By the time they had accomplished this, patrons of the bar and restaurant were arriving. As the crowd expanded, the racket of the gaiety also increased. In the loft right above this din, the six travelers could not get to sleep, so they joined the revelers — dancing, drinking and visiting. They even joined these customers in their favorite drink at the bar. It was a mixture of vodka and cherry brandy, strong but tasty. The students did not stay in the restaurant until closing time. When some of the customers were drinking too much and falling around, the six left for the loft. They were tired enough that they fell asleep in their makeshift sleeping accommodations, in spite of all the racket.

They appreciated the hay! Though it had been harvested months ago, it still had the faint fragrance and freshness of new-mown hay. What they had not counted on was the smell of the horse blankets. The boys took two of the blankets to their side of the loft, and the girls took one and added it to the lap-robe that Kate had lent them. They slept in their clothes, hoping that would help keep them warm enough through the cold night.

The travelers did not grasp the trouble that might come from their sleeping arrangement until the second day. The first morning they were tired and did not get up until nearly noon. After they had their lunch, they set out for a visit to the town of St. Gallen.

All six were expressing their delight for the forced stay in the area when they saw the frozen waterfalls and the snow-covered ice of the fountains in the parks of St. Gallen.

Looking at this winter wonderland, Lizbet said, "Jay, I think this should suit your fancy."

"Yes, it is beautiful, isn't it?"

The second morning they were up and moving by nine o'clock, but they quickly learned that their hosts did not customarily go to bed until three o'clock in the morning and therefore seldom got out of bed before noon — every day! The six loft guests found that they had to go into town to get breakfast. It was over breakfast that they figured they would have to take a train to get back home by Sunday. They traipsed through the new fallen snow to the railway station to find out the cost for transporting themselves and their bicycles to Munich.

After hearing the cost, the six youths stood around the station, each separately counting their money and calculating how much they would have left available for meals for the next two days, after they purchased the tickets.

To get them back in time, the train they needed to take would be leaving on Sunday morning at eleven-sixteen and would arrive in Munich at three-twelve that afternoon. The only problem was that they had to change trains in St. Margrethen with only twenty-two minutes to get their bicycles out of the baggage car and onto the other train to Munich. The station master told them not to worry — that if they missed the earlier train, they could get on another just three hours later. They bought the tickets, hoping they could make the first connection at St. Margrethen.

Still counting their money after buying the tickets, they joked about how poor they were. "You'll have to forego that vodka and cherry brandy, Sam!" Helene teased.

"And you should spend your lunch money on perfume, Helene. You smell like a horse, a sweaty horse," Sam retorted.

Jay Fisk, grinning from ear to ear, began sniffing around each of the others and remarked, "We all smell like sweaty horses." The others were laughing and sniffing at each other. They had slept in their clothes and covered themselves with the horse blankets provided by their hosts. It was inevitable that they would pick up the odor from the blankets.

"Do you think they will let us on the train smelling like this?" Lizbet asked, and the discussion began on what they could do about their unpresentable hygienic condition. They still had two days to go. They could keep one complete change of clean clothes in their rucksacks, and early on Sunday morning they would use the toilet facilities at the restaurant to wash themselves as best they could, put on their remaining clean clothes, pack their own (now smelly) blankets and clothes and be ready to board the train in their only inoffensive dress. Today and the next day they would get along wearing whatever they had that was the least contaminated with the hint of horse and save their clean paraphernalia for the ride home.

The young travelers spent their time exploring the beautiful scenic trails in the St. Gallen area, seeing the waterfalls, the streams, the mountains and the museums in the town itself. They felt that it was relaxing and pleasant to do their sightseeing each day, knowing they had a place to stay for the night and good meals available.

The train moved swiftly through Switzerland, around Lake Konstanz, Austria, and into Germany's Bavarian Alps. In one car of the train, Jay Fisk, sitting next to the window with Franz Lubeck beside him, watched the rapidly passing landscape. In the valleys between the majestic peaks, Jay noted tiny villages, each with the spiral of a church reaching up into the heavens. Now and then he noted a castle perched high upon a hill, looking down over valley and stream like an overlord scrutinizing what lay below. Jay merged as one with the unblemished peace around him and realized how fortunate he was to be able to enjoy this experience. He thought about the young man sitting next to him. He had first become acquainted with Franz in their music classes at the University, but being with him on the ski trip in December and on this school break, Franz had become a closer friend, a friend he would like to keep forever. He and Franz could sit in silence much of the time and still communicate, happy just being with each other.

The general atmosphere of Munich appeared changed during the absence of the vacationing students. The ardent marches, the processions, the "Heil Hitlers" that were taking place when they left seemed tempered with a quality of uneasiness upon their return. On March 23 Hitler had enacted a new law entitled "Law for the Relief of the Distress of the People and the Reich." This act gave the government the power to act contrary to Article 2 on the Constitution — in other words, it meant that Hitler could deviate from the Constitution in any way, at any time, as he wished.

In February, Hitler had appointed Josef Goebbels to head the Ministry of Enlightenment and Propaganda. Goebbels was club-footed and mean-spirited. He was the ideal person to carry out the diabolical plans of Hitler. When the March edict was passed, it was Goebbels who carried out the new list of books to be burned, and carried out further persecution of the Jews. Even old Hindenberg, who seldom knew what was going on around him, rose up in protest about the Jews being thrown out of their jobs, being refused service in many establishments, etc.

Many Germans, churchmen, theologians and teachers opposed Hitler's attitude as an absolute tyrant. They called him an uneducated barbarian. Hitler's jibe was "Yes, we are barbarians. We want to be barbarians. It is an honorable title."

As the weeks passed, Hitler began to suspect treason among his own followers. He had but one reaction — death to the dissenter. What was once free and joyful to the German people vanished on Hitler's orders, and in their place came harsh, senseless orders and just as equally senseless punishments. Hitler allowed only one interest, one devotion — ardor for Hitler.

In the familiar small beer hall, the six college students met, as they often did, after seeing a pleasing opera together. Jay Fisk, the only American foreign student, did not feel at all alien to the group, because Helene Domet was French and Tony Riccionne was Italian. By now, Franz Lubeck had become his best friend, and Grenythe Karlstein was the girl friend he saw most often. And Georg Blaich was also a good friend whom Jay found especially pleasant to talk with because he was talented in so many musical categories. It was nearing the end of their school year, and Georg, like a broken record, began his praise of Adolph Hitler, saying how great he was for the German people.

Grenythe could not let this adulation go unanswered, "Yes, that was great when he burned down the Reichstag in Berlin!"

"The Communists set the fire to the Wallot Palace," Georg argued. (Paul Wallot was the designer of the Reichstag, so the building was sometimes called the Wallot Palace).

"You are a fool to believe that! Everyone knows that Goering had orders to set fire to it with instructions to blame the Communists. You forget that months ago Hitler called the Wallot Palace, a symbol of decadence, that it ..."

Franz Lubeck interrupted Grenythe, "Grenythe, I want to talk more about the opera. Jay, you and Helene or Tony are not interested in these arguments about our politics, are you?" Underneath the table Franz put his hand over Grenythe's leg and pressed hard. Jay Fisk, sitting on the other side of Grenythe, noticed.

Jordan Fisk, Jr. (Jay), always considering himself to be apolitical, had paid little attention to the rise of Adolph Hitler in Germany. He considered it none of his business — he would be going home at the end of one year's music study in Germany, and he felt the change of power in Germany from the time he had arrived to the end of his stay would in no way affect his life in the United States. But he couldn't help but be saddened by the useless deaths of Hitler's protesters, the victimization of the Jews, the burning of more and more good books, even American books.

He heard Franz whispering to Grenythe, telling her,

as he had many times before, that she must not keep objecting to Hitler or she could face disaster. Franz never would discuss Hitler with Jay, but Jay felt Franz couldn't possibly agree with Hitler's policy, but he said nothing for the same reason he was advising Grenythe to keep quiet The whispering advice made Jay remember one day when he and Franz were leaving one of their classes, Franz had said, "Jay, remember when I told you that you had better move — well, you'd better!" Jay asked him why and Franz replied, "Things are going to get worse."

After the meeting of the music students came to an end, Jay bid goodbye to his special friend Franz; then he and Grenythe departed together. He had already made plans to walk with Grenythe to her residence to discuss some of the things about the opera, and also some other studies in the classes they had together. The opera they had attended was in a little theater near the University, not in one of the bigger theaters in the center of town.

Grenythe did not live as near the University as Jay did, so after he left Grenythe, Jay's walk home was longer than he would otherwise have made. But it was a pleasant late spring evening and Jay was reminiscing about another walk he had made in the autumn, also one after the opera meetings with his classmates. He remembered how reticent he was about arriving at his pension and telling his roommate, Sam Bradshaw, that he wanted to move. The move had been helpful in perfecting his use of the German language, but he and Sam had still remained good friends. With Sam on his mind, he suddenly thought it had been some time since he had seen him — not since they went on spring break!

Jay knew, of course, that Sam was all tied up with Lizbet, and didn't seem to have time for anyone else. The more he thought about it, the more he thought there was more to their relationship than just getting married. He remembered on that trip last March, the first night out of Strasbourg, when Helene had brought them all together to tell about Sam and Lizbet. He remembered how white and scared Lizbet had looked when Helene said she was going to tell everyone their secret, and how the color came back to her face quickly as Helene told about the marriage deal. Then Jay remembered the startled look on Sam's face, how his eyes had bugged out, when Helene said Sam was afraid his father would not finance the rest of his education if he got married. "There is more going on with those two than Helene's story implied," Jay mused, "but what?" He must see Sam to say goodbye before the school term was over, for Sam was leaving for America just as soon as he was out of school.

As he neared his residence, Jay was swayed from his musing when he glanced up. The old time-worn phrase "Speaking of the devil!" rushed through his mind, for there were Sam and Lizbet coming down the steps from Jay's rooming house, barely visible in the dim street light.

"Oh, so there you are! We were giving up on getting to see you," exclaimed Sam, in a voice much louder than necessary, especially at this late hour in the evening when neighbors could be sleeping.

"I am glad to see you — anything particular you wished to see me about?" Jay asked, speaking softly, hoping to tone down Sam's loud voice.

Sam, still speaking loudly, "I need more information

on the tour itinerary we are taking after school is out." Sam had moved down to the bottom step close to Jay.

"But I thought ..." Jay started.

He was interrupted by Sam's low whisper in his ear, "Just listen," and then in a much louder voice, "Yes, you thought I wasn't going to go with you, but I'm about to change my mind. That's why we came by to talk with you."

"Well, shall we sit down here on the steps and I'll tell you the tentative plans."

"Jay, let's go up to your room, if you don't mind. I want to jot down a few notes, and it is dark out here." Unobserved, even by Lizbet or anyone else who might have been in the vicinity, Sam had taken a firm grip on Jay's arm, slightly pressuring him up the steps.

"Wish I could go with you two," Lizbet added, in a voice like Sam's — too loud for the time of night.

"You guys better keep your voices down. Most people around here are asleep by now," Jay warned.

"Okay, okay!" they both uttered in lowered voices, as the three headed quietly into the house.

Jay's room was comfortable and satisfactory for just his own use — a place to rest and sleep and a place to study. Inside the room besides the bed, he had a clothes closet, a desk with a chair and one larger chair that he used to sit when he just wanted to read and did not need his desk.

As soon as the three entered, it was obvious that only two chairs were available. Jay motioned for Lizbet to take the lounge chair and Sam the other. Jay sat on the bed. "Now, tell me what's going on!" he asked his two guests.

"You don't know at all what's going on inside Germany, Jay," Lizbet said. Hitler's coming into power with his diatribe against Jews is NOT, Jay, not just talk. My father is a Christian, but my mother is part Jewish — that makes me part Jewish. My father is afraid for me and my mother. He has made a connection with friends in France, who are also friends of Helene's parents. They are Jews who will take in Jews from Germany who are trying to get away from Hitler. The French say that the Jews will be safe in their country. Hitler has said that he will not be attacking the west."

"What do I have to do with it?" Jay asked. "I have no interest in Germany's politics. How am I involved?"

"Not you personally, Jay," Sam said. "But Lizbet's father is trying to save the Jewish boys. Hitler is planning to take *all* boys fifteen years old or over at the end of this school year and induct them into the army. He plans to put the Jewish boys up at the front of the line in time of battle. He thinks this is the easiest way of obliterating the young Jewish males, as well as protect the Aryan boys."

"What does he plan to do with the girls?" Jay questioned.

"That's what my father is worried about," Lizbet answered. "He doesn't know whether Hitler will pass on me and my mother or not, since we are not one hundred percent Jewish, but we don't know."

"Then what is it you are working on?" Jay got up from his bed and walked over to a pitcher of water he had on his desk. He held up an almost empty pitcher and asked, "Shall I get some water for us?"

"Please do," Sam said.

Jay took the pitcher and left the room and quietly made his way down the stairs to the kitchen. He would need to bring back two extra glasses as well as the pitcher of water, because he had just one glass in his room. The door to the kitchen was open, and he was shocked to see Mrs. Weis, fully dressed, bent over the table with her head on her arms and sobbing. He had been so careful in approaching the kitchen so as not to wake either Hannah Weis or her son Paul. When he saw her here crying, he said in a voice slightly above a murmur, "Mrs. Weis, Mrs. Weis!"

She looked up at him and smiled through her tears, "Please forgive me for being such a coward."

"Mrs. Weis, I don't know why you are crying, but I'm sure you have a good reason."

Hannah Weis, still sobbing but trying to control herself, said, "My Paul's gone — I'll miss him so much!"

"Gone? Gone where? Oh! Tell me about it."

"Then you don't know," Hannah Weis looked up into Jay's eyes. "I should be crying for happiness — thanks to you and your friends."

"I don't know what your are talking about, Mrs. Weis," Jay frowned. He was still holding the pitcher in his hand and unconsciously waved it upward.

"Do you need some water, Jay? I'll get you some." Mrs. Weis was up from the table and took the pitcher from his hand.

"I'll need two more glasses, too," Jay stated.

"Of course — for Lizbet and Sam. Let them tell you all about Paul." Mrs. Weis handed the pitcher full of water and two glasses to Jay and ushered him out of the kitchen.

Back in his room, as Jay poured three glasses of water, he told Sam and Lizbet about his happening upon Mrs. Weis and her suggestion that he get the details about Paul from them.

"Well, you already heard me tell you our fears of Hitler ..." Lizbet began, but she was interrupted by Sam.

"I'm sure you've guessed by now that our meeting you out front was a set-up. Jay, we knew you would go to the opera, but not how long you would be before you came home. We came over here about the time the opera would be near its end and waited for you. We just watched and waited and when we saw you way up the block we made our exit, acting as if we couldn't wait any longer to see you. We tried to make it quite a scene to attract any attention if anyone was spying on us, and we kept it up long enough for Hannah Weis to get Paul out the back and over the fence with his uncle who will get him into France. Now you know why we kept up the charade in front for so long."

"Yes, but what has my planned tour for this summer got to do with it?" Jay asked.

"More than you know," Sam told him. "If we are ever questioned on why we are coming to the Weis house, we have to tell them it is to see you — just you. Your summer itinerary seems like the reasonable excuse to see you. You see?"

"Yes," Jay nodded. "Is that all?"

"No! No!" both Sam and Lizbet said at once.

Sam continued, "Jay, you need to give us a complete

run-down on your itinerary, so if we are questioned, we will know exactly where and when you are going."

"But your interrogators will find out you are not taking the trip with me," Jay protested.

"We have that all figured out," Lizbet laughed. "I will find that I don't have enough money to make the trip and Sam refuses to go without me."

By now Jay had become interested in the machinations and remarked, "And *you* plan to marry Sam to get out of Germany that way."

"That's another problem," Sam shook his head. "She says she doesn't want to get married right away. I'm the one that's saying that's the solution."

Lizbet then told how she and her mother were going to France when school was out to visit relatives there. Her father thinks no one has yet discovered their Jewish relationship, so if they go soon enough, no question will be asked.

"So now, Jay," Sam insisted, "tell us as much as you can about your summer tour — where you are going, how long you will travel, oh, and who's going with you."

Jay gave a brief outline of the itinerary he and his friends expected to cover in about two months. He would be traveling with another American student, Wilbur Jones. Since Wilbur had more money than most of the foreign students, he had a car, so they would be touring by auto. Wilbur was taking his girl friend, Nell Crawford, also an American student. Jay had arranged for Franz Lubeck to also be included in the plans. Nell Crawford told the three boys that she wanted another girl to also go along. Franz and Jay persuaded Grenythe Karstein to join the group. That would make five of them traveling together in Wilbur's car.

A few weeks later the school year ended, and Jay said goodbye to many of his friends, to Sam Bradshaw who left for his home in the United States, and to Lizbet Greenberg who left with her mother for France as a place of safety from any persecution they thought Hitler was planning against Jewish people

Jay and his friends had chosen Italy as their first destination on their summer tour. As Jay saw these places for the first time, he thought how much better he could have described the itinerary for Sam. He reflected that Sam *might* have appreciated seeing Leonardo da Vinci's "The Last Supper" in Milan, but *might not* be interested in the famous La Scala opera house. And he would probably like Ponte Vecchio (the old bridge) in Florence more than the art. He would have loved *Harry's Bar* in Venice.

In Rome, Sam would remember the story of Italian poverty as told by the English couple they had met in Basle, about the hungry children filching anything they could get off strangers.

When the five summer travelers were in Rome, the boys wanted to see Via Appia and walk its length. The two girls, who went with them, had to almost trot to keep up with the boys. They all walked fast, hoping to get away from the urchins who pestered them, begging and trying to slip a small hand in an untended pocket of the visitor. These little urchins had their tricks, too. They reached out holding some object, half hidden in their dirty little hands, and would say, "Wanta buy?" or "Did you drop this?" And just as soon as the tourist would take his hand out of his own pocket to reach out to that child, another little one would boldly delve into the unprotected pocket of the victim. Jay laughed to himself as he wondered how Sam would have reacted to these desperate children of all ages.

The one thing Jay had been unable to tell Sam was the problem of traveling in Wilbur's car. It was a coupe with a rumble seat. Naturally, Wilbur drove and the two girls rode in the front seat with him. Franz and Jay rode in the rumble seat. Along the highways, especially on mountain roads, they often got stuck behind a diesel truck that emitted a heavy black smoke that left soot-blackened faces on the boys in the rumble seat, as well as on their garments.

As their travel continued from Italy into Austria, Jay thought less and less about how he could describe the itinerary for Sam, and thought more and more about the short number of days that were left to enjoy the company of his German friends, Franz and Grenythe. With them, he especially enjoyed the music festival in Salzburg. He did not think again of Sam until they visited the salt mines. Sam, the engineering student, would have been designing or inventing another way to see the Salzkammergut (the salt chamber area). Jay, with the other tourists, was taken through them with a gunny sack under them, and the group, holding on to each other, went shooting down a slide into the chamber below. Jay wondered if a design by Sam would be as much fun.

When the five motorists stopped in Linz to watch the

river boats along the Danube, Jay thought again of Sam, the engineer. Would Sam have figured out the solution before seeing it happen, when a steamboat approached an auto bridge down river in Linz with a smokestack too tall to go under it? The bridge was not the type that split in the middle to raise up, or to swing aside. These five watched, spellbound, as the boat sailed right at the bridge — full speed ahead. But to their amazement, just as the boat reached the bridge, the smokestack on the steamboat was lowered by a hinge to lay flat along the deck, and passed right under the bridge. They had never seen this feat before.

Though Vienna had much of its old history to offer these five tourists, there was one thing Jay Fisk could not forget — Vienna was a poverty-stricken city! Men were on the street begging, some of them with emaciated children on their shoulders. The children were no burden for their fathers to carry — so many of them were only skin and bones depicting their pitiful starved condition.

Jay tried hard to concentrate on the historic old city surrounded by the Ringstrasse, the famous Hofburg Palace with its impressive Habsburg collection of the Habsburg emperors. The five traveling youths all enjoyed seeing the Spanish Academy and the performing Lipizzaner horses. Jay could almost forget the poverty he had seen in the streets when he saw the magnificent St. Stephen's Cathedral and the famous Opera House.

Riding in the rumble seat for many miles, trying to keep the soot from the diesel trucks off their faces and dust from the gravel roads out of their eyes, convinced

Franz and Jay that from Vienna they would take the boat down the Danube and meet Wilbur and the girls in Budapest. The trip down the river was an eight-hour cruise. The day Franz and Jay took it was cold and rainy. They were happy that they were sailing down river and not taking the much longer and harder return trip upriver.

"Which is worse — warm soot or cold rain?" Jay and Franz joked about their state of affairs — just another experience they shared together.

All too soon, the time slipped by and they were back in Munich. In September of 1933, the day came when Jay Fisk had to say goodbye to the friends he had made in Germany during his year there. The closest among those friends still in Munich, besides Franz Lubeck, were his landlady, Mrs. Weis, and his classmates, Grenythe Karlstein and Georg Blaich.

His last and hardest parting was with Franz Lubeck. Franz was uncertain about his future. Hitler was inducting all young males into Rohm's military service, and Franz did not know whether he would be forced into the armed service after his graduation in a year or if he could follow his own career plans in music, teaching and composing.

The two boys hugged each other and with tears in their eyes promised they would keep in touch, hoping a bright future would sometime bring them together again.

PART TWO

The War Years

CHAPTER FIVE

CHAPTER FIVE

December 07, 1941

"Wake Up! Jay, Wake Up!" Irene cried. She stood with her left foot on the floor and her right knee balancing her on the bed as she leaned across to shake the arm of her husband.

"Whazza matter?" he mumbled, half asleep, as he turned toward the voice that had disturbed him.

"Get up! Something's happened outside! The noise down on the street woke me up. People are running around and shouting, but I can't hear what they are saying."

Irene and Jay lived in a small and inexpensive apartment in upper Manhattan. They had gotten so used to the noise of the elevated trains running frequently right outside their wall, that it no longer disturbed their sleep. It was the unusual clatter in the streets below that had awakened Irene.

Jordan Fisk, Jr. was fully awake now. In his bare feet and pajamas, he walked across the cold floor to the window where Irene was standing. From the third floor, he could see young boys shouting and holding up newspapers. Jordan (usually called Jay) left the window, crossed the room and turned on the radio.

The words burst alarmingly into the room: JAPAN HAS BOMBED PEARL HARBOR!

In stunned silence, Irene and Jay stood right where they were — just for a moment. Irene ran to Jay and put her arms around his waist, "Does this mean we'll be going into war?" she asked.

"I'm afraid so!" Jay answered. They were standing there, still dressed in their night clothes when Jay moved out of Irene's embrace and said, "Let's get dressed and get out of here. Maybe we can get more information from the newspapers on what is going on."

"I wonder what ol' Damon will say to this?" Irene grinned.

"I expect the whole gang will be hurrying to The Village to talk about it. Let's go someplace and get breakfast, then we'll join them."

Times Before Pearl Harbor

Jay and Irene had been married four years. After Jay had graduated from college, he had gone to New York where he expected to find the best in the music world. He enjoyed operas and concerts, but it did not take him long to learn that classical music was not nearly as favored by the public as the pop variety and, therefore, would not be a source for a good living. With his knowledge of several foreign languages he had acquired while studying in Europe, he was able to supplement his income by working for an importing company, yet he kept up his contacts in a music club. One of the activities of the club was periodic dances.

At one of those dances Jay had met a pretty, dark-haired, brown-eyed girl that he enjoyed dancing with. He did not see her again, however, until the music club held its next dance. When a waltz was announced, Jay made his way through the sidelines to find the little brunette he had danced with before. Jay was a very good waltz dancer, having had much opportunity to learn and dance it often while he was in school in Germany. They made a handsome couple — he, tall and slender with blond hair and blue eyes, and she, not more than five foot, four inches in height, with dark brown hair and eyes to match. Jay found the little New Yorker girl was also good at waltzing. The two of them did not realize how good they were, until they found themselves alone on the floor, all other participants having retreated to the sidelines just to watch them waltz.

Jay saw Irene Gample often after that night. He took her to meet many of his friends in the music circles, and she in turn introduced him to a group of "debaters" who met regularly at The Village to argue (discuss) the affairs of the world — religion, politics, and anything else that came to mind. Jay listened most of the time, seldom expressing an opinion, since he as usual classified himself as apolitical about many things. As he became accepted in Irene's crowd, he appreciated the fact that Irene's views on the religious matters as well as political, more often than not, agreed with his own. That endeared her to him even more.

After two years of seeing each other they were married, and they made plans to buy a house. They had looked at property in Stamford, Tappan and Long Island. They figured that, with both of them working, in five years they could save enough to buy in a neighborhood of their choice. They could live in an inexpensive apartment in the meantime and save as much money as they could.

After Jay Fisk returned to the United States, he had kept in touch with his good German friend, Franz Lubeck. The first two or three years they exchanged letters every two or three months. As the time passed, they wrote less frequently, but still communicated now and then. Because of some of remarks that Jay heard in The Village group where Irene had introduced him, Jay paid more attention to a recent letter he had gotten from Franz. One sentence read: *There are more people in America helping Hitler than you know.*

Much of the talk at The Village these days was about the events taking place in Germany. There was still the constant extremes on the validity of the Bible — those who took it literally and those who thought it a propaganda publication for a certain cult. One of the group brought the Bible into the political affairs in Europe, "God will punish the evil doers in Germany!" she said hotly.

"But which are the evil doers?" She was challenged.

"The Bible says —" she began, but was interrupted.

"The Bible says many things, my dear, that are used to illustrate a point, not to be taken literally. If you will think about the times in which the Bible was written, you could understand why it can't be taken as fact. Many Christians today, and I mean good Christians, no longer believe in the Virgin Mary story. All the great leaders of Bible times were considered descents of the Gods. How could the promoters of the new Christian faith push Christianity without having their leader also of divine origin?

Think about it."

"Yeah!" another added. "Today when the locusts come, the farmers spray them with an insecticide to kill them. If they thought God sent the locusts as a punishment, spraying to kill them would be like telling God to go shove it." This caused enough laughter among the whole group that the religious aspect on the European situation was dropped.

Ever since he had come back from Munich, Jay had paid close attention to any European news that he could either hear or read. Jay remembered one of the more bellicose speakers in The Village arguing that the rumors about Hitler being unfair to the Jews in Germany was nothing more than propaganda, probably just rich Jews in America trying to wipe out their competition. Jay, at the time, did not dispute the statement, but had been amused, thinking to himself, "Just let him sound off — he doesn't know how silly he sounds." After he got Franz's letter, he wondered if he should take such remarks more seriously.

The discussions became more heated as month after month passed and the radio and newspapers were expressing the difference of opinions in the United States Congress. The headlines expressed the view that Hitler would *not* move outside Germany, even if he had ordered a blood purge of his enemies in Germany. When Hitler announced the reintroduction of military service on March 16, 1935, only small print in the United States newspapers suggested the opinion that Hitler would go beyond his own boundaries.

"Why do the papers keep suggesting that Hitler will

try to attack other countries? Are they just trying to get us all stirred up?" several of the members of The Village group said.

"Just wait and see!" others answered.

It was only six months later when anti-Semitic "Nuremberg Laws" were proclaimed. Opinions in the United States were getting more pronounced that something should be done to stop Hitler. That soon became the main topic Jay and Irene heard at The Village.

"I don't believe those stories about Hitler murdering the Jews. I think it is just this country's weapon makers wanting to get us into a war so they can make a million," a member of the group said.

"He's right, of course," Damon Hess said mildly, as he leaned back in his chair.

This brought about one spokesman after another disputing that assertion. The argument went back and forth until Jay Fisk, who usually was a listener instead of being argumentative, stood up. Everyone in the group had been seated around, arguing their various points. When Jay stood up, they all looked at him quizzically. This guy, they thought, wasn't used to arguing! They all became quiet and wondered what he would say.

Jay stood a moment, then spoke emphatically, "Hitler *is* dangerous and he *is* murdering the Jews. He will not stop in Germany — he'll try to conquer all of Europe." Jay remained standing. Before he could sit down, one after another were asking him why he believed Hitler was a threat to the rest of Europe.

"Don't you read what is going on?" Jay answered.

"What do the United States newspapers really know?"

a man called Damon asked.

"*I* know!"

"You're crazy! And just what would *you* know about it?" Damon sneered.

"I know because I was there!" Jay stated in a matter-of-fact way. Though Jay had been meeting with this group for some time, he had made no mention of his living and studying in Germany for nearly two years.

Jay's words were prophetic. In March 1936 Hitler occupied the Rhineland. When this news hit the papers, Jay said to Irene, "You know, Irene, when I was in Munich way back in 1932, several in our music class were at a beer hall arguing whether Hitler would take the Rhineland. One of the students said that land really belonged to Germany — that it was lost in the first world war, and it would make sense for Germany to try to get it back. Another of our group was a French girl whose home was in that area, and she said it was now a part of France. I wonder where she is now, and if she is in any danger."

"What's her name?" Irene asked.

"Her name was Helene Dolmet."

"Did you like her?"

"Of course, I liked her, she was my friend — oh, don't get me wrong. I didn't date her. She had a crush on one of the other guys."

"Was she pretty? What did she look like?"

"Umm, you're sure curious! To tell you the truth, she had hair much the color of yours and her eyes were like yours, too, beautiful!"

"Is that why you pay so much attention to me —

because I remind you of her?" Irene teased.

"No, not at all! The girl I liked was named Grenythe, and she had blond hair and blue eyes," Jay teased in return.

Jay and Irene continued to see each other, sharing Jay's interest in music and Irene's interest in the discussion group.

In March of 1938 Hitler invaded Austria and also issued what became known as the "Operation Green" against Czechoslovakia. The same differences of opinion that were being stated in Congress were also being argued among those who meet at The Village. And in both groups the feelings were becoming more heated with each passing month.

When Jay Fisk had not heard from his German friend, Franz Lubeck, for over a year, he knew that Franz had been inducted into the German armed service. He wondered if what Franz had written months before had kept his letters from getting through. In one of his letters he had written that he was serving under Field Marshal Erwin von Witzleben. He had written: *I like Witzleben very much. He is a kindly man, and like me, is horrified by the brutality and vulgarity of the Nazi rule.* That was the last letter Jay received for many, many months. Perhaps Franz was not given an opportunity to write again, or maybe Franz had not received the last letter Jay had written to him.

Then in October of 1938 he got another letter from his friend. Jay was delighted! The letter was written in German, of course, but Jay couldn't wait to read it. Irene, his wife, observed his joy on receiving the letter and she, too, wanted to know what was in it. Jay interpreted it in English as he read it to Irene. Then he stopped reading aloud in the middle of the letter! He read it again to himself before he read it aloud, in English.

> *"I am sure you know how things are progressing in this part of the world. I remember old times, the good times we used to have together. Do you recall that girl, the one with the blond hair that used to go around with us? You remember how I was always telling her she should take better care of her health. Since her brother died of that same disease, she is now following the advice I gave her so long ago, and she is now taking the care she should.*

Irene interrupted at that point and asked, "What health problem did she have?"

"Hitler problems!" Jay answered. His earlier happy attitude was now much more serious. When Jay read that paragraph, he knew Franz was sending him information in coded wording. He thought back through the years to when he and Franz had spent time with their associate students. He remembered the blond girl, Grenythe Karstein, always spouting off about Hitler's actions, and Franz always telling her she should shut up.

His thoughts were interrupted when Irene questioned, "What do you mean, Hitler problems? You mean Hitler has health problems, too?"

"No, I mean that Hitler kills anyone who opposes him. That's what happened to Grenythe's brother."

"How do you know who it was? He didn't mention anyone's name."

"I know! He's taking care of his own health as well as Grenythe's. That's why he wrote as he did. He wanted me to know that probably all incoming and outgoing mail in Germany is censored."

"Tell me about Grenythe. I remember that you said a long time ago, when I asked you about that French girl, you said that you liked Grenythe. Did you like her a lot?"

"Yes." But Jay was teasing and grinning as he pulled his beloved Irene close to him.

Articles in newspapers all across the nation of the United States were denouncing Hitler's action when information came about the thousands upon thousands of Jews who had been rounded up and sent to the death camps. It was no longer just rumors. Survivors who had gotten out of Germany, Poland, Austria, Czechoslovakia were telling their stories in France, in Britain and the United States. All these escapees were not Jews, but any person, a citizen of any invaded country, Christian or not, who had been caught helping a Jew, was also a target for assassination. Franklin Delano Roosevelt, President of the United States, appealed to Hitler, as well as to Mussolini in Italy, to stop their aggression of other nations. He asked them to sign a non-aggression pact, a pact to last ten years. Roosevelt promised that the United States would enter into a trade agreement with them that would be advantageous to all. Hitler refused and six months later invaded Poland.

In April 1940, when Germany invaded Denmark and Norway, and a month later began the German invasion of Belgium, Holland, Luxembourg and France, more and more Americans were thinking that the United States should do something to stop Hitler.

On June 10, Italy entered the war, siding with Germany. England appealed to Roosevelt, but any military help to England and her allies was denied. There were many American citizens who proclaimed that it was not their war and the States should stay out of it. Just as many felt the opposite — that if we let Germany go any farther, our allies defeated, it would be disastrous for us as well.

About a year before Germany's latest invasions, Damon Hess had brought a friend to the meetings in The Village discussion group. His name was Joe Klassen. He seemed a much more affable person than Damon, not nearly as argumentative. The members of the group had changed considerably since Jay Fisk first met with the group as a guest of Irene's. Those attending ran from ages of the late teens to the early forties, and most of them were singles. Many came to Greenwich Village just for a place to hang out and talk, a place where men could meet single women and the women to could meet eligible men. That was how the Village Discussion Group originated. As the years passed, so did the individual identities of the group. Most newcomers were single. When someone married, his or her spare time was more needed to raise a family. Jay and Irene were one of the few married couples still attending — perhaps because they had no children to absorb their attention.

As usual, most discussions in the group were on Germany's 1940 aggressions. Most of the attendants thought Germany was wrong and that the European allies were being unjustly attacked.

Joe Klassen, in his firm but in no way antagonistic voice, said, "The Allies brought it upon themselves. They defeated Germany in the war, then left a beaten, impoverished nation with nothing on which to rebuild. The Allies had it coming!"

"But I can't understand why the rest of the Germans would follow such a man, who has become a mass murderer," Hulda Dietrich asked. Hulda was a German American, yet she had no sympathy with what Hitler was doing.

The statement made Jay Fisk think of the first time he had heard Hitler speak in Munich, long ago in 1932. A very charismatic man had offered a starving, unemployed people a hope for the future. He had promised full employment and enough to eat. Was it any wonder that his listeners became followers. "Where else did they have to go? I can understand how they at first saw a resurgence of German prosperity, but Hitler has become a madman, and I wonder if the only reason they go along with him now is obey or face being shot," he said.

"What makes you say such a thing?" Joe Klassen asked. "Do you know something the rest of us don't?"

"I know that clear back as far as 1932 and 1933 that Jews were being oppressed," Jay answered.

"Did you just hear that or do you really know anyone that was persecuted?" Joe Klassen queried.

"I know of several —"

"Know of? Oh, yeah, but you can't really know. You weren't there!" Joe's voice had changed from a casual to one more litigious.

"Joe, I don't want to argue about this, but I *was* there.

The young son of my landlady had to leave the country for his safety. He was Jewish," Jay said quietly.

"What was his name?"

"Paul."

"What was his last name?"

"Weis. Why do you ask?"

"Oh, I just wondered. I guess you do know what you were talking about." Joe sat back in his chair and had dropped back into his affable mood. "I suppose there were others."

"Yes."

"Were they also Jews?" Joe asked.

The rest of the gathering had been silent as they listened to Joe and Jay exchange opinions. When the last question was asked, before Jay could answer, Irene popped up, "One of them was a French girl, her name was Helene."

Joe turned to Irene, "What was her last name?" he asked her.

"I don't remember, but I'll bet Jay knows," she laughed.

"Joe, she wasn't Jewish, and her name was Dolmet."

"Why was she escaping from Hitler?" Klassen asked.

For the first time, Jay was beginning to think Joe Klassen was asking too many questions. He wondered why, fearing he had already said too much. "No, she wasn't escaping from Hitler — she was just going back to her home in France," Jay said.

"Where did she live in France?" Klassen had not given up on the inquiry.

"I don't know exactly," Jay lied, "but I think it was in the central part of the country." Jay heard a gasp from

Irene, and he pressed down hard on her leg when she started to speak. She got the message and took another deep breath, trying to cover up her first gasp, but Jay saw the look on Joe Klassen's face and knew that Joe knew he had lied.

Irene immediately changed the subject and turned to her friend Joan, "Didn't you say that you had heard from your friend Mildred?"

"You all remember Mildred," Joan Smith said. Several of the group denied knowing her, so Joan went into more detail. "It was several years ago — some of you remember — she came to a few of our meetings to tell us what good the Communist party was doing in Germany and in Russia. You know I've been trying to promote Communism as a third party here in the United States. Mildred was born here in the U.S., but she felt she could do more good working in Germany. The Communist party is trying to defeat Hitler. I don't think many of you realize how great the Communist party is!"

"Now, wait a minute!" Joe Klassen exclaimed. "I know very well what the Communist party is doing! That Mildred Harnack is a spy for Soviet Russia, and she is not wanting to defeat Hitler because she doesn't like his policies — she and her Russian friends are conspiring to turn Germany into a Communist state, subject to Russian rule."

"You are crazy!" Joan shouted. "Mildred just married a German named Arvid Harnack. She is a Jew and she and her husband are just trying to stop Hitler from killing other Jews."

"Well, I think that would be a good —" Irene Fisk began, then stopped as Jay got up and remarked that it was time they went home. Jay knew Irene had Communist leanings, and he didn't want to get into any further arguments with her or with the group. Several others, in a lackadaisical manner, began moving away.

When Jay and Irene left, only Damon Hess with his friend, Joe Klassen, was still there arguing with the few of the group espousing Communism.

As they walked away from the meeting, on the way back to their apartment, Irene was upholding Joan Smith's Communist views, but Jay wasn't listening. When they were nearly home, he said, "I don't trust Joe Klassen. He was asking too many questions. Irene, don't say anything more about my connections or my time spent in Germany."

December 07, 1941

After hearing the startling and terrifying news flash that Japan had bombed Pearl Harbor, Irene asked, "I wonder if Damon or Joe will have some excuse for this?"

"We'll have to see, but I wouldn't be surprised." Jay and Irene dressed quickly, eager to get out and learn more about the Hawaiian situation.

On Sunday morning, they usually went out for a leisurely breakfast, read the newspaper, then spent the rest of the day on any chosen activity. Today their breakfast, in the little cafe nearby their apartment, was hurried. They had grabbed the EXTRA news bulletin to read what they could about the bombing of Pearl Harbor; then they rushed to Greenwich Village to see if any of their friends had shown up there. They wanted to know how others felt about this shocking attack.

The gathering at The Village was larger than usual. Many young men and women had hastened to meet their counterparts, wanting to discuss what might happen next.

"Will we be going to war?" several asked.

"We ARE at war!" came the answer from others.

As Jay and Irene Fisk joined their acquaintances, Jay remarked, "I wonder why Japan would pull such a dastardly trick."

He was supported by many others asking the same question, "Why?"

"Why, you ask," Damon Hess answered. "They must have had a reason."

"Japan *did* have a reason, a good reason," Joe Klassen asserted. "The United States has blocked off all oil deliveries from the South Pacific."

"That was to keep Japan from attacking any more of the South Pacific islands and countries," Jay said. "Japan was already making trouble there. The United States was doing the only thing it could to help maintain peace in that area."

"It was none of America's business," Joe retorted. Many of those standing around agreed with his opinion.

"We should stay out of what's going on in Europe and what's going on in the orient. It's none of our business." This judgment was expressed by several, the same ones, Irene and Jay noted, who had made comparable sentiments earlier.

"I will refuse to take any part in a war, if we are foolish enough to get into it," Joe Klassen stated.

"You are already in it, Joe," several friends argued. "The United States is at war, through no fault of its own."

"Not if it sits tight and doesn't do anything," Joe contended.

"We can't do that!" came from voices throughout the group, a decision signified the next day, December 8, 1941, when the United States declared war on Japan.

"Oh, Jay!" Irene cried, when the war news broke over the radio. "Will you have to go?"

"I don't know. I don't think so. At least I am not going to sign up. After all, I am thirty years old and I expect it will be just the young ones that will be drafted."

On December 11, Germany and Italy declared war on the United States.

Irene had heard about the declaration at work. She got home that evening before her husband. "The whole world is at war! Oh, Jay, I want you to stay out of it!" She was crying as she greeted Jay when he came home.

"We are all in it, either here at home or abroad. I don't know yet what I want to do," Jay told her.

"Don't know? You mean you want to join up and be a soldier?"

"Irene, I feel differently about Germany than I did about Japan. I know something of Europe. Perhaps I could help in that area where I couldn't in the orient."

"Surely you aren't going to sign up."

"I'll have to think about it."

"Let's go down to The Village. I don't feel like fixing anything to eat. We can get something to eat down there. Let's see what everyone else is going to do," Irene suggested.

Two very solemn people left their small apartment,

wrapped up in overcoats and boots to nullify the winter blast as they stepped into the sharp wind and freezing temperature of that December night. Neither of them were in a happy mood. Irene, in fear of losing her husband to the ravages of war, and Jay, torn between the comfort of riding out the uncertainty of being drafted into any division of the service, or the immediate action of signing up to go into the war theater of his choice — Europe.

Cold as it was, several of the group had assembled at The Village to kick around ideas on what the others planned to do. Damon Hess was there; he usually took the side of Germany. Jay, his chief opponent in days past, could not wait to ask him, "Now, my dear fellow, what do you plan to do?"

"I don't know. I don't think I want to sign up right away," Damon told the group, not answering directly to Jay.

"Where is your friend, Joe?" Jay asked.

"He's gone." Damon answered and turned away from Jay.

Jay persisted, "Gone? Gone where?"

Damon did not answer, but another of the group piped up with this information, "He left two days ago for Germany."

"You don't know that," Damon said crossly.

"Oh, but we do," Joan Smith said. "We've been watching him closely for some time. He's a German agent, and the Communist party intelligence in the Netherlands advised us about him and to watch him, which we've been doing for the last two years, ever since he got here."

Damon Hess got up and hurriedly left the building, while the others watched after him with perplexity.

Jay Fisk had been nervously clicking his nails. He put his thumb in his mouth and started chewing on the nail. He had never been in the habit of biting his nails, but what he had just heard greatly perturbed him.

That letter he had gotten from Franz saying that there were Americans working for Hitler among us of whom we were unaware came to his mind — he remembered the questions Damon and Joe had asked about his acquaintances in Munich, their names, where they lived, etc. He wondered if he had given out information that might endanger the lives of his dear German friends? Or even his French friend, Helene?

He couldn't sit still any longer. "Come on, Irene, let's get out of here. Tomorrow I think I'll sign up!"

The following morning Irene and Jay had just arisen and were dressing to go to work. Neither had said a word for the first few minutes. Irene broke the silence, "You aren't really going to sign up, are you?"

"I don't know, but I'm thinking about it," Jay replied.

"Damon, Joe and their friends were probably right about it — the gun makers brought on this war so they could make millions of dollars," Irene argued.

"You're not thinking, Irene. We, the United States, did not start this war — we were attacked by Japan and Germany declared war on *us!*"

"We probably caused them to do it. Why do you have to take part in it?"

"If you don't already know, I don't see how I can explain it. You see —" He stopped in mid-sentence as the thundering roar of a train right outside the wall of their apartment made his voice inaudible. For four years they had been used to these interruptions, and laughingly resumed their conversation when the loud clatter and screeching of the train had passed by. They were in the habit of treating these intrusions with a bit of humor, but not today.

"NOW you see what I mean!" Irene said as soon as the noise made it possible for her to be heard. "If you leave, how are we going to continue building up our down payment for a house, away from this awful noise. In a year or so we'll have enough to get out of this hell hole."

Jay, in the process of stepping into his trousers, stopped all movement, and with just one leg in his pants he stood up straight and looked at Irene, the hurt on his face showing, as well as the tone of his voice, when he said, "Irene, I didn't know you disliked our living here so much. I know this place is no paradise, but though it's a bit irritating at times, I thought we both agreed that it was a comfortable place for a temporary time."

Irene, halfway dressed, rushed over and embraced her husband. "Oh darling, I'm sorry. I just can't think about you going away to the war and maybe never coming back. I would live forever, in *any* awful place as long as you are with me."

Jay took Irene by the shoulders and held her facing him as he spoke, "Honey, believe me, I know how you feel. I don't want to leave you, either. But listen to me — I will probably be drafted anyway and will have to go to war somewhere, whether I want to or not. By enlisting I think I can have a choice of where I go, and what part of the service I want to be in. I know nothing about the Pacific area, except it is most likely hot and humid, and I hate that kind of climate. I want to go to Europe where I can speak the languages — and I know the country."

"What part of the service do you want to be in?" Irene asked in a defeated manner.

"I would choose the Air Corps. I want to enlist while I have a choice."

"I see I have no choice," Irene responded.

"I'm afraid not, honey. So let's fight the war against our country's enemies, not against each other."

"Much as I hate it, I suppose you are right, Jay. Together we'll see this war through." Irene gave Jay a quick kiss on the cheek and turned to finish her dressing.

A few days later, Irene had a smirk on her face when Jay walked despondently into their apartment and said, "I'm too old!" He sat down in a chair and continued, "They said that only the younger unmarried boys were being drafted now, and that I would be notified by mail if needed!"

"How lucky can we get!" Irene exclaimed.

"Lucky? We'll wait and see. If I just sit around and wait to be drafted, I don't know what will happen. I wanted a chance to make a choice of where I go and what service I wanted to be in."

"At least you'll be here with me for awhile. I think we're *very* lucky. If you are drafted, perhaps you can get what you want."

As the days went by, friend after friend got the note in the mail to appear at a certain draft board. Irene and

Jay's first thought upon reaching home after a day's work was reaching for the mail. Sometimes Irene would get home first and reluctantly go through the mail, dreading the appearance of a notice addressed to Jordan Fisk from the United States Government.

Jay's outlook was different. He expected the notice to arrive, it was just a matter of when, as the battles in Europe and the Orient raged on. One day, less than a year after war had been declared, Jay came home and found Irene crying. She did not say anything, just handed him the card telling him to appear at the draft board on a certain day.

Jordan Fisk, Jr. was enlisted in his choice of service — the Air Force in the European theater of the war.

CHAPTER SIX

CHAPTER SIX

THE ONLY GOOD THING about six weeks of basic training that Jordan Fisk, Jr. could recommend was that he was sent to New Jersey — not too far from home. Jay thought that he had kept himself in good physical condition by playing tennis, sailing, skiing and even mountain climbing, but he found all that was sissy stuff compared with the rigorous physical exertion he had to endure for six weeks in the service of the United States Air Corps.

He called Irene when he could and wrote often. In one of his frequent letters to her, he apologized for his handwriting, stating that even the muscles in his hands and fingers were so sore that it was hard to legibly scribble even a short note.

Once he wrote, *Irene, as I nurse my aching muscles, I wonder why I didn't apply for a commission, then perhaps I could have been an officer, instead of having to take all this crap from a sergeant. But I wonder if I could have handled that job very well. When I came here, I had never before heard all the foul language that is used here every day, as if it's necessary to train the enlisted guys. But I've learned! Now I know all of those words!*

After six weeks of the grueling physical conditioning in New Jersey, Jay was sent to Scott Field in Illinois for training in radio and communications. Scott Field was not too far from St. Louis, Missouri, and Jay realized he was living closer to his home town than he had in nearly ten years. He thought it would give him an opportunity to contact his father and sisters, when he had the weekends off duty.

Jay had written to his father occasionally during the past few years, but since Jay's mother had died and his father had remarried, he had not been as intimate with his father as he once had been. However, Jay had frequent communications with his sister Roxanne, who was just a little more than a year younger than himself. It was through her that he had kept in touch with news of his father and his younger sister, Rowena.

Jay and Roxanne had been close from their early childhood, and their relationship had not decreased through the years. While Jay was stationed at Scott Field, he called Roxanne who lived in Kansas City, hoping he could set up one weekend when he could get away to visit her and perhaps see his father and Rowena for a short reunion for all of them.

Roxanne had been married to an attorney for more than six years, and they had two children. Her husband, Richard Clark, had as yet not been drafted and was still practicing law. They hoped their having two little girls, five and two years old, would keep Richard from being called into the service.

When Roxanne got the message from her brother about setting up a weekend reunion, she contacted her father and sister immediately. Rowena, also living in the Kansas City area, was available for the visit, but their father, who lived in a small town in southern Missouri, could not make the trip because of the illness of his wife.

The weekend was set and arrangements made. Roxanne wrote Jay that she would meet him at the station when he arrived. When Roxanne and her husband, Rick, discussed meeting the train, they both decided to go to the station. The train was due in at six-thirty on Saturday morning. Thinking the little girls would be groggy from such an early morning arousal, they called the teen-age girl next door who usually baby-sat for them, but she decided it was too early for her to get up on a Saturday morning, the only morning she got to sleep late. It looked like they would have to take the girls with them.

"Rick, you could stay home with the girls," Roxanne suggested.

"Yes, I could, but I'd already be fully awake and so would the girls. When we talked about it yesterday, you remember that Jeanie said she wanted to go meet the soldiers. You know if we took her, Sara would be very unhappy. They will probably be so sleepy that they won't be any trouble."

"And they'll probably be so sleepy that they'll be cross, Rick. Is there some reason you don't want me to go to the station alone?" Roxanne asked.

"Yes. What if the train is late and you have a long time to wait there alone?" Rick replied, then grinning, continued, "or worse yet, I wouldn't feel comfortable with you in the station full of incoming and outgoing service men while you are waiting for Jay to come in."

"Okay, we'll both go and take the girls," Roxanne laughingly agreed. The problem on meeting the train was settled, but the plans for the weekend would have to wait until Jay's arrival. They would have to find out how much time he had, as well as when Rowena could meet with them.

Rowena had said that she would have liked to go to the station to welcome Jay, but since she had a baby boy and no baby-sitter, she would have to see Jay later. Rowena's husband, Jerry, was in the Merchant Marines, and he had sailed out of Seattle just a few months before. Being so lonely for these last few months, Rowena was looking forward to seeing Jay and spending as much time with him as possible.

The morning of Jay's visit arrived, and Roxane and Rick Clark rolled out of bed, dressed quickly and awakened the two youngsters. Roxanne took extra time dressing the girls — she wanted them to look especially cute, since Jay had never seen them before. She put them in little blue skirts with sweaters and berets to match. She had bought the sweaters and made the skirts and berets to match the blue color of the sweaters. She was proud of the way they looked and of her own accomplishment in their appearance.

"Are we going to get Uncle Jay?" Jeanie asked, fully awake.

"Yes, and you and Sara must be very good," her mother said.

Jeannie pointed to Sara, who was fully dressed but sound asleep with her head on her daddy's shoulder. "She'll be good. She's always good when she's asleep!"

They left the house shortly after five-thirty, a full hour before the train was due, but they didn't want to be late. If Jay arrived and they weren't there, he would worry and might miss them altogether.

Rick let Roxanne and the two children get out of the car in front of the station. Before he drove to the parking area, he told them he would meet them under the clock.

When Rick found his family under the clock, Roxanne was talking to Lucille Sanders. Lucille also had her two little children with her.

"Rick," Roxanne cheerfully exclaimed, "Lucille is waiting to meet her husband who is coming home for the weekend. I told her about Jay. I think they are both coming in on the same train."

Lucille was frowning a bit, and she did not seem in the same exuberant mood as Roxanne. "Rick," Lucille said, "don't mention Ned's coming home this weekend. He told me not to tell anyone."

"We won't say anything. We'll be too busy with our own company. Roxanne's brother is coming — and just for the weekend, too. Isn't Ned at Scott Field, Lucille?"

"Yes."

"Well, for goodness sake," Roxanne chimed in, "that's where Jay is, too. I wonder if they know each other. Maybe they will be coming in together."

"Let's go into the waiting room where their train will come in," Rick suggested.

"Yes, let's do. That's where I was heading when Roxanne waylaid me," Lucille said.

They visited awhile, waiting for the train to come. Ned Sanders and Richard Clark had gone from grade school through high school together. Though they had gone to different universities, they had remained friends through the years. Lucille and Roxanne had not met until they were married and were introduced by their husbands. They were friendly acquaintances, but had not become close friends. Most of the conversation in the waiting room was between the women about their children. The younger ones in both families were asleep in their mothers' arms, while the two older ones were running around, corralled and entertained by Richard.

The deep rumbling of the approaching train caught their attention and they sat up straight, closely watching the door through which the passengers would soon be coming.

One of the first ones coming through the gate was Captain Ned Sanders, spiffily dressed in his uniform. With a wide grin on his face, he rushed to his wife who had jumped up to met him, then looked quizzically at Richard Clark and his family who were standing not too far behind her.

"Oh, Rick, Roxy! I didn't expect to see you here. I told Lucille not to tell anyone I was coming," Ned said, the grin fading from his face as he frowned at Lucille.

"Don't worry, Ned, we're here to meet Roxanne's brother and just ran into Lucille," Rick assured him.

"I think my brother was due in here on the same train you were on. Lucille said you were coming in on the Wabash," Roxanne said.

"Yes, I came on the Wabash." Ned was tense when he said to Lucille, "I think we had better be on our way."

Roxanne touched his arm, "Wait just a minute, my

brother should be here any second."

When they had been ordered to postpone their forty-eight-hour free weekend from six o'clock on Friday until midnight Friday, Ned, an officer, had told his men that he, too, would not be leaving the barracks until midnight. The reason for the delay before anyone could be on leave was because of an unfinished project that had to be finished before anyone could depart. It happened that the project was done quite some time before midnight, but the restriction on the leave permission, for some reason or another, had not been lifted. Another important thing that had not changed was the Wabash rail schedule from St. Louis to Kansas City. The train still left at eleven fifty-nine. Ned had planned this weekend to see his family and did not want to change it. He had called Lucille when he found he could still get away from Scott Field in time to get to St. Louis and catch the train in spite of the restriction — but he wanted it undetected.

Almost in a whisper Ned asked, "What is his name, and what is his rank?"

"His name is Jay Fisk and he's an airman, Private First Class — not a big officer like you," Roxanne joked.

Captain Edward Jackson Sanders did not smile at Roxanne's attempt at humor. He should have been greatly relieved to hear that the other soldier coming in on the Wabash did not outrank him, but that was not so — Private First Class Jordan Fisk, Jr. was in the same unit, and Ned not only knew Fisk, but knew that Private Fisk also knew him

"Sorry, Rox, I can't wait to meet him," he said hurriedly. "Lucy, get the kids and let's go!"

Little Ned Sanders, Jr., holding open the entrance door to the trains, was watching the other five-year-old, Jean Clark, hanging on to the hand of a soldier and yelling, "Mommy! Mommy! Here's Uncle Jay — he looks just like the picture!"

Uncle Jay was resisting the pull of the tiny hand that was squelching his hidden position behind the door from the train into the waiting lobby. Jay Fisk had not been in the same car on the train, nor had he seen Captain Sanders moving ahead of him through the passengers making their way up the steps and into the station lobby. When he got to the door, he instantly recognized his superior officer just inside talking with his sister and her family. He jumped back, not daring to proceed until the Captain left.

Jay Fisk and his friends had been able to go into St. Louis for most of the weekends when they were off duty. The week before, while he was in the St. Louis, he had bought his train ticket to Kansas City for the long planned weekend with his sisters and their families. He had told his Sergeant of the problem when he heard about the leave restriction until midnight. But when time became available earlier than expected, Jay left Scott Field in time to catch the train in St. Louis. He was aware that the Captain knew he had to leave the base early to catch the train. If the Captain saw him, he could be arrested for being AWOL for a whole hour! He would have to stay hidden back of entrance door until the Captain left. He stood there, just waiting, until some passenger opened the door and a little boy held it open. Then a little girl, his niece, peeked inside!

Lucille and Roxanne both ran to the door to collect their children, and Roxanne to greet her brother. Jay did not look up as Roxanne pulled him out through the door. The nightmare of time in the brig for sneaking that extra hour was facing him now. His long-awaited weekend of visiting his sisters whom he had not seen for several years was gone! He knew of no way out of this predicament.

When he looked up, no Captain Sanders was in sight!

"Where's Ned?" a simultaneous query came from both Lucille and Roxanne.

"Lucille, he said something about meeting you under the clock — that he had to go to the men's room," Rick said.

Roxanne introduced Jay to Lucille and said they could wait with her for Ned's return, but Jay interrupted, "No, we must be going! I see Captain Sanders every day at the base — and officers do not fraternize with the enlisted men."

"Well, that's being kinda stuck up — after all, we're friends," Roxanne exclaimed.

Jay laughed, "Come on, Sis, that's the way it is!" And he rushed her along through the lobby, followed by Rick with the two little girls.

Jay was laughing because he knew his Captain was doing them both a big favor, making sure that they would not meet on this forbidden excursion.

Never again for the next three years did Jay Fisk ever try to extend his leave — not even for an hour!

In the days that followed, Jay was very conscious of the apprehending look he received from Captain Sanders every time he came face to face with him in the line of duty. Neither of them mentioned the weekend spent in Kansas city, to each other or to anyone else. The only time Jay ever mentioned their close encounter at all was in one of the letters he wrote to Irene. He wrote her about it the day after he returned to the base

Jay did not write Irene every day, but he came close. He was just as appreciative of the numerous letters she also wrote to him. One of the newsiest items that she had written was about her changing jobs.

There had been an announcement in the newspapers about help needed in the weapons factories and she had applied. She was making much more money that she had at her old job.

She wrote: *We had always put our savings for the house in your account. I am now putting the savings I have from my additional salary into a savings in my own name. Is that all right with you?*

Jay had said that it was right for her to put any savings she had in her own name — after all, she was the one making the money. The theme in all Jay's letters to Irene was how much he missed her. Every day he wrote a sentence or two, and when he had enough to make a letter worth sending he mailed it. Some days he felt that there was absolutely nothing worth mentioning, no happenings to write about, just everyday, the same old routine — *we got up, we trained, we went to bed. If someone fell and broke a leg, or got chicken pox, or broke into my lockbox, then I'd have something so tell you. The one thing that I can say always is that I love you.*

He heard from Roxanne now and then, telling of her

family and how Rick had been ordered to go to Fort Leavenworth for his physical, then sent home to await further orders. As yet no further word had come, so they were living their lives from day to day, never knowing what the future might bring.

The days at Scott Air Force Base came to an end. Jay wrote Irene and Roxanne that he did not know where they would be stationed next, whether it would be overseas or perhaps somewhere in the United States. He had heard that many would be going to the air base in Biloxi, Mississippi. He said he hoped he could be so lucky in this cold winter weather.

When Roxanne got that letter she hoped that Jay would be in Biloxi, because she and Rick were going to Mobile, Alabama, where Rick would be trying a case. They were going to be there at the time of the Mardi Gras. The attorney in Mobile who would be working with Rick had, along with his wife, extended an invitation to both of the Clarks to be their guests and to come prepared to attend the Mardi Gras ball with them.

Roxanne was very excited about attending the Mardi Gras ball. She had a new soft green velvet evening dress that she would wear with long gold gloves, and Rick had his tuxedo. They accepted the invitation and Roxanne wrote Jay about it, hoping if he were in Biloxi he would let them know before they left. While Rick would be in court, Roxanne thought she might be able to go to Biloxi and see Jay, if he could not get away from the base to see her in Mobile.

Roxanne had not heard from Jay by the time she and Rick left for Mobile. Since gasoline was scarce, they decided not to drive, but scheduled their trip by train. They would take the train to New Orleans, and there they would board a bus to Mobile. Since the bus would go through Biloxi on the way to Mobile, Roxanne wondered if they would see the Biloxi Air Force Base as they went through.

When they got on the train in Kansas City, they found they were outnumbered by the military personnel on board — civilian passengers were few. When they got to Memphis, their train was pulled over on a siding to let a troop train go by. Both Rick and Roxanne were asking questions about that troop train, where it came from, where was it going? It was a time of war and the excitement among the civilian passengers, as well as the soldiers, was notable.

Roxanne couldn't keep her curiosity in check. She asked one of the uniformed boys, "Are you going to Biloxi?" thinking that if he were, her brother Jay could be on this same train in another car.

"No, ma'am. That's an Air Force base. We are going to Fort Polk. That's an army base at Leesville, Louisiana," the soldier answered.

"Do you know where the troop train that passed us is going?"

"I don't know any more about it than you do, ma'am."

Another soldier entered into the conversation. "We don't know any more about that than we know about where we are going."

"We know a little bit about where we are going — we heard that the terrain is similar to the forests in Germany, so I guess we know where we are going next," a third soldier piped up.

"You talk too much!" a soldier with an MP band around his arm took the third soldier away from Roxanne and the other civilian passengers. The remaining soldiers all became quiet to any further questions from Rick, Roxanne or any others who asked anything.

It was nearly an hour before their train was back on track and headed south again for New Orleans.

The Clarks were comfortable in the home of the Grant von Boyles. Mildred kept Roxanne busy with sightseeing around Mobile, introducing her to friends and keeping her busy until Saturday night, the time of the most important ball of the season. Mildred impressed upon Roxanne that the original and most important Mardi Gras was in Mobile, not in New Orleans.

Roxanne, dressed in her green velvet gown, passed the inspection of her hosts, but when Richard came down the stairs in his tuxedo, both Grant and Mildred exclaimed, "You can't wear that! Where are your tails?" Rick was nonplussed. He didn't have any such other formal dress.

"You mean a tuxedo is not dressed up enough?" Rick asked.

"Not unless you want to be taken for one of the waiters. They all wear tuxedos," Grant informed him.

"Then I guess I won't go," Rick said.

"I don't want to go if you don't," Roxanne said, but her disappointment showed.

"How tall are you, Rick?" Grant asked.

"Almost six-three."

"Hold on for a minute!" and Grant rushed out of the

room. He came back a few minutes later and said, "Joe couldn't go, and you are about the same size. I called him and he said you could borrow his tails. I've sent Charles over to get them. He'll be back soon."

Richard, soon dressed correctly in borrowed tails, Roxanne in her green velvet and the Clarks attended the most sophisticated social engagement of their lives.

Mildred took Roxanne into a small room off from the ballroom where the dancing was taking place. There the women sat in chairs around the edge of the room and the men all stood at the end of the room at the bar.

After they had all had an alcoholic drink of their choice, Roxanne had her first dance with Rick. When he brought her back to her chair, he asked another woman to dance. A gentleman came over to Roxane and asked her if she would like a drink. Roxanne did not like much to drink and told him "No, thank you." He went across the room and said something to another young woman, and they went out onto the dance floor.

Soon Roxanne was sitting in the room alone. The women were all dancing, and Rick was dancing, too. One after another, the different men would come over and asked Roxanne if she wanted a drink, and after saying, "No, thank you" several times, she noticed all the women who were dancing accepted glass after glass of full drinks which they lined up on the narrow shelf behind their chairs. When the next gentlemen asked her if she would like a drink, she said graciously, "Why, yes, thank you," and when he came back from the bar with a glass of something or other, she mimicked the other women, placed the full glass on the shelf behind her chair and rose to accompany the man onto the dance floor.

When, once again, she danced with her husband Rick, she said, "I sat out a lot of dances because I didn't know the customs down here. If some guy asks you if you want a drink, he means do you want to dance. Rick, did you ask those gals if they wanted a drink, or did you just ask them if they wanted to dance?"

"I just asked them to dance, and only one of them said she wanted a drink first."

Intermission was over, and the evening had almost arrived at the exiting time of announcing the King and Queen of the Mardi Gras. The ball was held on the second floor of one of the larger buildings in the downtown area, not too far from the beach. Several guests at the ball had gone out on the balcony to take a break from the indoor activity. Soon they began shouting that there must have been some bizarre event to cause such a macabre happening down on the street. Some of those who had heard the clatter stopped dancing and tried to crowd out onto the balcony to see what was going on. But the balcony could hold a very limited number, and even those were not close enough to hear or find out the cause of the uproar.

Grant von Boyle and a few other men left the ballroom and ran down the stairs to find out about the procession of what looked like bodies being carried along from the beach, past the Mardi Gras ball building and on up the street.

By the time Grant returned to Mildred and the Clarks, several couples were dashing out of the ballroom, some running down the stairs, others waiting impatiently for the elevator. The other men, as well as Grant who had left the Ball to investigate the file of those marching by below, divulged the same information that Grant soon announced, "I'm so sorry to report this, but an Air force training plane returning to Biloxi from Florida got caught up in a storm in the Gulf and went down into the sea. We hear that there are no survivors. Since Mobile is the closest city to the disaster, they are bringing all the bodies in here and taking them to Smith's Funeral Service up the street."

Grant turned to Rick and Roxanne, "I am sorry that this sad affair had to interrupt our great party, but there are several people here who have sons or brothers stationed at Biloxi, and they are anxious to find out if their loved ones were on that plane."

Roxanne was pulling at Richard's sleeve. She whispered, "I'm worried, Jay could have been on that plane." Before Richard could make any response, Roxanne turned to the von Boyd's, "Grant, Mildred, my brother could have been on that plane. I don't know whether he was stationed in Biloxi or not. How can I find out? Will there be a list of those lost?" Roxanne was as nervous as any of the others at the ball. "Rick, can we go to the funeral home?"

"I don't know. Grant, what can we do?" Rick asked his host.

"I think we will just have to wait," Grant replied.

"I want to make a long distance call. If anything happened to Jay, Irene would be notified. I want to call her," Roxanne said.

"She couldn't have been notified yet, even if he were on that plane," Rick advised. "And if he weren't, you would really upset her."

"I suppose you're right," she agreed.

"Come on, Roxanne, let's dance!. This party is not over."

"I don't feel like dancing. You and Mildred go on out there."

"You know, Roxanne, Mildred and I have to stay until the ball is over. You might as well enjoy yourself." Grant gave Roxanne a pat on the arm as he turned to walk back into the ballroom.

Roxanne started to walk out on the balcony, but found the night air too chilly to be out there without a wrap. She retrieved her black velvet cape and returned to the balcony. She stood there alone as she looked down the street toward the beach and watched, as one body after another was brought up from the sea to be placed on a stretcher and mercifully covered before starting up the street, filing past the balcony and out of sight at the end of the next block. She slowly turned away, not waiting until the last one was carried by.

The following day, the list of those service men on the plane was in newspapers all across the nation. Jordan Fisk, Jr.'s name was *not* among them. When Richard Clark's case was completed, he and Roxanne Clark returned home telling each other that it was one week they would never forget.

CHAPTER SEVEN

CHAPTER SEVEN

THE FEBRUARY STORM that caused the disaster in the Gulf of Mexico was not the only storm troubling service men in the Air Force. Across the eastern half of the North Atlantic, another big storm was brewing, undetected at an Air Base in the United States when a certain troop carrier destined for the British Isles took flight.

The shortest flight mileage across the Atlantic between the States and Europe is following the northern curve over Newfoundland, the southern tip of Greenland, just south of Iceland and then on to Europe.

When it began its flight from the Air Base, the plane started out in cloudy, but stable weather. It was a C-47 aircraft carrying soldiers trained for service in the Air Force. A group of rowdy boys soon milled about the plane, after their original passive behavior on take-off.

There came a jolt and a few of the soldiers had trouble keeping on their feet as the plane pitched from side to side. Even though the plane became steady again, they heard the order from the pilot, "Take your seats, and remain seated until further notice! We are heading into turbulent weather." The stormy weather added to the discomfort of the bench-type seats that lined the sides of the plane. (The middle aisle was used for cargo.)

Pilots, navigators, radio technicians, mechanics, all airmen, were soldiers going to war in Europe. Among them was Jordan Fisk, trained in radio and navigation. As the airmen returned to their seats, Jay found himself seated next to Jade Browning, a friend he had made in training. When they had first met, Jordan told his new companion that all his friends called him Jay. Jade started laughing and said, "At home, all my family call me Jay, too, because I'm a John, Junior. How are we going to both answer to Jay?"

"What do most of your friends call you?" Jay Fisk asked.

"Johnny, or J.D. My middle name is Dayton. Several of us in our High School class began calling each other by our initials. There was a J.R. — his name was James Roland, and there was W.C. — he was William Charles, and then there was —"

Jay Fisk interrupted, "That's what I am going to call you — J.D."

Jay Fisk's addressing his friend as J. D. was soon taken up by others in their outfit, but before long the nick-name coined for John Dayton Browning, became J.D., shortened to Jade.

Jade and Jay's friendship had grown as they went through training. Now, on the troop plane, they sat quietly side by side and talked of their desire to be stationed together wherever it might be. Their conversation was often minimized by the gusting winds tossing the plane as it made its way eastward toward Iceland. In normal weather the flight was expected to take not more than eight hours to Keflavik International Airport, headquarters of the U.S. forces in Iceland, but the buffeting winds were slowing their progress.

The first quiescence of the troops that came with the bumpy and uneven flight through the storm soon gave way to the usual banter and horseplay among them.

One young airman, eighteen or nineteen years old, did not respond to the sometimes rough and ribald remarks of the others around him. Instead, he sat silently in his seat with his hands together and his head bowed, as if in prayer.

One of the more mature young men sitting on the bench next to him asked in a friendly manner, "What's the matter, kid?" Then jokingly added, as he tapped the boy on he shoulder, "Are you asleep or praying?"

The boy raised his blond head, looked first at his adjacent companion, at all those on the same bench with him, then across the aisle, as he very seriously answered, "We should all be praying."

"Whoa, there!" one soldier named Brad Wilson, without the empathy of the first boy's question, retorted, "Do you actually believe some mystic guy is sitting up yonder on a cloud, pulling strings on us creatures here below and listening to those prayers you are uttering?"

"Of course!" The young one sat up straight on his seat as he emphatically replied.

A few more opposing remarks were made by the two.

Brad, not wanting to continue a conversation he thought was stupid, said, "I just don't believe in that kind of God!" Then he turned away.

But the boy, Alan McMann, wasn't ready to give up

on his point of view. "Brad, you're on your way to Hell!"

Brad replied, loud enough for all the others around to hear, "No argument there, my boy, and you, too! Where did you *think* we were going when we got on this plane?"

As the troop plane approached Iceland, lights at Keflavik Airport were dimmed by the heavy rain and fierce winds. From the dimmed lights, long fingers of orange were reflected on the wet tarmac.

Coming in for a rough landing, the plane hit the tarmac with a jolt, but the gusty winds with less force brought uneven jolts of their own. The plane cast night shadows that looked like a dark and live monster waiting to pounce, which those on one side of the plane pointed out. On the other side of the plane, the young men looked out the windows and saw the cold driving rain, and one of them in a voice of protest said "Do we have to get out in this?"

"Yeah, and you'll get cold and wet!" another answered.

"Or you can stay on the plane for the night while the rest of us get a bed to sleep in," the teasing continued.

Alan McMann turned to the officer closest to him and asked, "We *do* get a bed, don't we?"

Lieutenant David Harvey stood up, balancing himself against the wall at the front of the plane. When he got the attention of the troops, he said, "Men, we'll be here overnight, and we'll refuel before we leave for Stornaway in the morning. In the meantime, you can get a good night's sleep here at the barracks, and while you're here, you can wash the chill right out of your bones with a nice hot shower."

How little they knew about that hot shower!

An ungodly shriek pierced the normal clamor that surrounded the service men from the C-47 who were settling in for the overnight stay at the Air Force base at Keflavik, Iceland. The shriek was followed by another and yet another, each as ear-splitting as the first one.

Half-dressed boys popped out of their sleeping quarters into the corridor, all intent upon finding the source of the shrill cries. They faced the lavatory from whence they thought the screams had come, just as those doors opened and naked, beet-red figures appeared, each grappling a towel and complaining, "That water is boiling hot! There's no cold water at all! How can we get a decent shower?"

By this time, fully dressed service men who where permanently stationed at Keflavik appeared and were laughing at the plight of the naked, red-skinned boys trying to cover themselves with towels. "Oh," they said, "didn't anyone tell you that all the running water in Iceland comes from the natural thermal hot pools and streams from the volcanoes?"

"Then how do you get a comfortable bath?" one newly arrived boy asked.

"You run the water in the tub, then let it cool to the temperature you want — then you take your bath," one resident answered.

"Or unless you are in a hurry," another added, "then you get a big chunk of ice and plop it in the tub."

"Don't they have any cold running water?" one of the half-scalded boys inquired.

"Not at the present, but that is one of the projects they are working on. They hope to build a big water tower to hold cold water, then they will have two lines, one of hot and one of cold water going into all the houses. Then people can choose what water temperature they want — but that is in the future."

The "red skins," the few who experienced the intense heat of Iceland's thermal running water, survived the near-scalding baths and the teasing from their fellow airmen. They were ready the following morning to depart with the rest of their outfit for Stornaway in the Hebrides. But the weather had not improved from the night before, and their commanding officers stated they would have to remain another day in Keflavik, with the order that they *could not* leave the barracks. The men (some hardly more than boys) took this news without any qualms, most of them happy that they would have one day less on the battlefields of Europe.

They found several ways in which they could entertain themselves through the waiting hours. Poker games were popular, as were even a table or two of bridge. Movies were available to watch, though most of those on hand had already been seen by the majority of the soldiers. The young eighteen-year-old Alan McMann thought card playing was a sin and would not enter into any of those games. Another young man, Willie Brandt, was a studious type and found reading a great pastime. Jordan Fisk spent much of his time playing his harmonica or writing to his wife Irene. He might have spent more time on his harmonica, playing known tunes or composing new ones, if some of the men hadn't said they were tired of hearing that "goddamned jew's harp" going on all the time. Jay grinned as he heard the disgruntled comments and told the complainers that if they would get him a clarinet, a coronet, a piano, a violin or any other instrument, he would be glad to give them a variety of music.

Thus the second day in the barracks at Keflavik was spent the same way as the first day, and so went the third day and the fourth. The weather had not cleared enough for them to fly out of Iceland to Stornaway, their destination. The soldiers protested about being restricted to the Air Force barracks, not being allowed to go into the city of Reykjavik, or to roam over the countryside of Iceland. They were given two reasons for their confinement to the barracks. Number One — they might be able to leave at any time, and they needed to be ready to go as soon as weather permitted.

The second reason was more threatening. In 1918 Iceland and Denmark had signed a mutual agreement to be sovereign states under a common king. In 1940 the Germans had invaded Denmark, and though the Iceland government broke off their previous agreement with Denmark, the American Forces that now occupied Iceland were not sure of the loyalty of all Icelanders. After Iceland broke with Denmark, it was soon occupied by the British, and a year or so later by the Americans. Out of their windows, the airmen restricted to the barracks could see lone fishermen on the beaches, fishermen often trying to initiate a conversation with the men in the barracks. Were these fishermen just friendly fishermen or were they German sympathizers? These were the questions the United States officers had to face. They knew it was important that soldiers stayed within the barracks.

The scenery from the barracks became boring after five days of seeing the same flat lands immediately out the door — barren brown grass, running streams of hot water giving off steam, a narrow road only wide enough for one car, yet used for the passage of two-way traffic. There were sheep, lots of sheep, eating the grass from the hillsides. Looking farther out in the distance, even through the fog and rain, a small shack could be seen on a rugged terrain. The shack was nestled between big rocks covered with moss, and not too far off a drift of snow not yet melted from the mountain tops. They could see a tiny white church, standing almost alone, away from all other buildings as if it was claiming its individual importance in the world.

Willie Brandt had read all he could find about the things to see in Iceland, and when the men were most vehemently protesting their captivity, Willie would start telling them about the two-hundred-foot waterfall at Skogarfoss, not too far from the airport, or the great spouting geyser or even a volcano waiting to erupt, all not a day's outing from the Keflavik airport.

"I don't know which is worse, you spouting off about what we can't see, or Fisk playing that damned harmonica," one airmen grumbled.

By the fifth day the rain had stopped, the air was clear enough for the planes to take off or land at Keflavik; yet these airmen were still delayed. Their destination was Stornaway, and though flying from Reykjavik or Keflavik was permissible, landing in Stornaway was impossible. It was not only the airways that were blocked by the storm, no ships were able to go into Stornaway either. The turbulent sea had waves rising twenty to fifty feet high in winds of hurricane force.

Five days restricted to the barracks in Keflavik had already produced a grumbling boredom among the airmen of the C-47. Further delay only added to the impatience building up as they waited, and waited, and waited.

Card playing was only fun for the good poker players, who had in a short time collected much of the money from the boys who knew little about the intricacies of the game. The losers soon quit and let the experts play against each other. The few bridge players after a few days were spending time teaching eager learners about that game.

Willie Brandt in five days had read everything he could find in the limited supply of material at the base. The pilots kept scrutinizing the skies, trying to judge the weather and arguing about whether it was acceptable for flying. Alan McMann read the tiny little Bible that he carried with him and took the razzing from a few others with good grace. Jade Browning, Jay Fisk's friend, was one of the losers in the poker games, and he had pleaded with the good bridge players to teach him that game. Through all these various activities, there were some of the stranded servicemen who found none to their liking. A few observed the natives who came into view around the barracks, arguing about whether they were German spies, British hangers-on, or just Icelanders, loyal or not to the Allied cause.

Jay Fisk did not play cards, but he did not spend all his time playing his harmonica either — he spent part of each day writing to his beloved Irene. The trouble was finding something to say, day after boring day, when nothing happened. One day he could say he counted fifty sheep on the hillside, the next day they had wandered down into the valley. He wrote about all the sightseeing possibilities that Willie Brandt had described. He did not tell her that they would have no chance whatever to see them. And always he told her of how much he missed being with her, and how much he looked forward to her letters. On the fifth day of their stay in Keflavik, he wrote that he should have something more exciting to tell her on the following day. Jay had nothing in mind that he thought would be of greater interest, but just hoped that such a suggestion might make Irene look forward to a letter that would not be as hum-drum boring as his last few.

When nothing seemed available to counteract the general boredom among the men, it was only natural that bickering between them became prevalent, if not about one thing, then about another. As the fifth day extended into the sixth and the seventh, the bickering intensified.

All around him, the bickering was going on about little or nothing, Alan McMann was reading his Bible. He looked up and said, "We should just be thankful that we are safe here. We are warm and have enough to eat. Stop bellyaching and be thankful!"

"You are right, Alan," Willie Brandt agreed, "and speaking of being thankful, did you know that all those costumes that people dress up in at Thanksgiving time are not the dress of the Pilgrims at all?"

"What are you talking about?" someone challenged.

"Oh, those costumes are the dress of the Puritans, not the pilgrims," Willie stated.

"They are one and the same thing, Willie boy!" an airman trained in the bomb squad said.

"No, they are not the same — the Puritans came ten years after the pilgrims, and they, the Puritans, are the ones where men wore those black high hats and great buckled shoes, and the women wore aprons," Willie answered. "The Puritans were not the ones who had the first Thanksgiving with the Indians, the pilgrims did."

By now every one had stopped his individual squabble and was listening to the discourse on Thanksgiving. Even Jay Fisk, who seldom took part in any of the spats, was giving his full attention. "Willie, why don't you tell us more."

Willie thoroughly enjoyed being the center of attention with a chance to exhibit his knowledge. "Well, you all know about Squanto, the Indian who brought about the first Thanksgiving with the pilgrims—"

"Who's Squanto? Massasoit was the Indian who made friends with the pilgrims," someone interrupted.

"Listen, please, for just a minute," Willie begged. "Squanto was of the Patuxet tribe which lived in what is today's Plymouth. His other name was Tisquantum. He was kidnaped by an Englishman in 1605, taken to England, learned English, got back and was then kidnaped by a Spanish Explorer who hoped to sell him as a slave, but he was rescued by a priest. He got back to Plymouth, found his whole tribe had been wiped out by smallpox, so he joined another tribe of which Massasoit was a member. Because Squanto, or Tisquantum, could speak English, he told Massasoit he could set up a meeting with the settlers, so that they could become allies instead of enemies. That's just a brief summary of the first Thanksgiving. Governor William Bradford, Squanto's closest friend, said that if it had not been for Squanto, who taught them how to raise corn, catch fish and various other occupations in this new world, probably they would have all died."

"Where did you get all that crap?" some dissenter contended.

"Oh, you can find it in any library under the history of Plymouth. You need to read it. There's a lot more to the story of Tisquantum, how he got rich and how he died."

A few were leaving the circle surrounding Willie and were resuming their own petty quarrels.

On the tenth day, an officer walked into the room where some bickering was still taking place. He observed the disquiet among the men and told them that they would be stationed here another day — restricted to the barracks. After ten days in confinement, tempers were on edge, whether these servicemen were draftees, recruits or volunteers. They did not yet know that this was their last day in Iceland.

"I know it's dull and tedious. I know you've all been arguing a bit, and that's good; debate is good for you — perhaps you can learn from some new ideas." The officer, walking out of the room, laughed as he turned his head and said, "Just stay away from religion and politics!"

That statement was a mistake! Whether it opened the door to those subjects or whether there was nothing else to argue about, religion and politics were topics most available for discussion. The door had hardly closed when someone called out, "Which one will we start on?"

"Democrats line up on one side, Republicans on the other —" another offered.

"What will we argue about — why we should be in this war?"

"That's no argument between Republicans and Democrats, there are as many of each party on both sides."

"Then what about us?" a quiet voice queried. "Does any one here think he should *not* be serving his country in time of war?"

Everyone looked around at a sandy-haired, blue-eyed man who had made that statement. He was about twenty years old, small of statue, perhaps five feet seven inches tall by stretching it, and weighing not more than one hundred and forty pounds. He was sitting on an arm of a chair and had been listening to the group looking for some subject they could argue about. Even though he was smaller than most of the others around him, no one even slightly offered to answer in the affirmative. If anyone felt an aversion to the duty to which he had been called, he did not admit it. When no answer came to the sandy-haired boy named Dee Horn, he said, "Then why don't we speculate on why we are ordered to go to Stornaway, and no place else, when the weather there is so rough?"

"Does anyone have any idea why that was our destination?"

After a few negative head shakes through the group, someone said, "Willie, since you know everything — why must we go to Stornaway?"

Willie, always ready to expatiate on any subject with which he was familiar or just as ready to joke about those of which he knew little or nothing, "Why, of course, we are sent to Stornaway to fight the giant." Willie held his hands high above his head when he got questioning noise from all around, "What Giants?"

Willie continued, "That great giant of Ulster in Ireland. He will fight with his enemy, the giant in Scotland."

"What are you talking about?" several asked.

By now, Willie was laughing hard. "Oh, maybe it's not the giant of Ulster that we'll fight — just fight for the privilege of crossing the few miles of sea to get to the whiskey at Bushmill."

"Whiskey?"

"Now you're talking!"

Several men were making these same statements, until one said, "Where do you get all that stuff you talk about?"

"I read."

"About whiskey?"

Brad Wilson got up from the bench on which he was sitting, looked around the group and said, "One of you the other day said he didn't like to hear Willie spouting off? Well, I want him to spout off more about that whiskey."

"Yeah! Yeah!" could be heard from several sources.

"I don't drink. I would like to hear more about the giants," Alan McMann said.

"You would!" Brad and several others, uttered contemptuously.

Willie Brandt was in his element. "I will tell you guys where you can get the whiskey, if you can get us off the base in Stornaway and, Alan, I will tell you the old-timers' story about the giants."

"Are you kidding about the whiskey?" several of the men asked.

"I don't know for sure what's goin' on since the war broke out, but before that there was a town called Bushmills in northern Ireland, where the oldest legalized distillery was in business for hundreds of years. Bushmills is not too far from the coast of northern Ireland, and on a clear day it is in sight of Stornaway, which is on the island of Lewis in the Hebrides. The Hebrides islands belong to Scotland. That's all I know about it."

"Where are the giants?" Alan asked.

"There aren't any giants, really. Down the coast of Ireland there is a peculiar geographic formation of column after column of basalt, mostly hexagonal, some just a step high, other as high as forty feet. Scientists say these column and steps were the result of volcanic eruptions, but the ancient Irish claimed it was the works of the giants, especially one giant called Finn McCool. They say this giant was a warrior from Ulster and was the commander of all Ireland's armies. He fell in love with a maiden on an island in the Hebrides, and he built these steps of columns as a highway to bring her back to Ulster. What I've told you so far is what I've read, but now comes the funny part — I didn't read it anywhere, but I heard it from an Irish storyteller.

"Giant Finn McCool had an enemy, a Scotsman in the Hebrides, who had a beautiful daughter that McCool wanted. The Scotsman was also a giant. McCool had not met him close at hand, but he had seen him across the way, just twenty miles, and old Finn figured he could whip the Scot giant, so he set out to get the girl. The Scotsman's wife saw him coming and told her husband about him. 'What will we do?' the Scot giant asked. 'Go get in bed, put on your nightcap, close your eyes and keep quiet,' his wife answered. The Ulster giant banged on the door of the Scotsman's house and the wife answered the door. 'Shush, be quiet,' she advised the visiting giant, 'you will wake the baby!' The big giant walked past the woman into the house anyway, looking around for the maiden. The Scotsman's wife told the giant that the maiden was not there, begging him all the time to not wake the baby. The giant, not believing her, went about the house searching each room. Then he came to the bedroom, saw the Scot giant in a big cradle with a nightcap on his head and his eyes shut. The Scottish wife was following him, keeping her finger to her lips, and whispering, 'Shush, don't wake the baby.'

"When the great Irish giant from Ulster saw the size of that figure in the cradle, he trembled with shock! He thought, 'If that is the baby, I wonder how big the giant father is?' and with a hurried goodbye, he rushed out the door and never came back."

Willie's story produced a good laugh among all the soldiers listening. It was the first time for days when they all laughed together. "Where do you come up with stories like that?" several asked.

"People believed those stories in years gone by. I suppose there are some who still believe them," Willie answered.

"How could anyone believe such tales?" Alan McMann asked.

"You should talk!" Brad Wilson countered, "You believe all those impossible stories in the Bible."

"That's different. The Bible is God's word!" Alan insisted.

"Not any more than stories by other ancients, Alan. The Bible was written by men who couldn't know what we know today, and attributed all things they didn't understand as caused by God."

"Brad, you are an atheist."

"No, Alan, I am not. I just have another conception of God. And I am a Christian and believe the way of life that Jesus taught. He came to dispute many of the ancient beliefs quoted in the Old Testament, the very things that you say are God's word."

"Like what?"

"Well, I think it is in Deuteronomy where the Hebrews say God told them to go into the promised land, kill all the men, women and children, but keep their possessions for themselves. That is NOT the God I believe in."

"That's different!" Alan protested.

"No it's not. You are a literalist, Alan."

"No, I'm not — I'm a Baptist!"

"Same difference!"

The rest of the men and boys in the room who had been listening to the giant stories were also listening to the controversy between Alan and Brad. As the two contenders had become somewhat belligerent in presenting their differences, one listener interrupted, "I thought we weren't supposed to argue about religion!"

"You are right," Brad said, "I just want to ask Alan one more question — that is, if he agrees."

"What do you want to ask me?" Alan said.

"I think it is in the book of Exodus where the people thought the locusts that caused a famine were sent by God. Do you believe that story?"

"Yes."

"If you believe that's what happened then, how can you not believe it when the grasshoppers (or locusts) descend upon the farmers of the Middle West today?"

"Well, I don't —"

"The only difference in these farmers and those of centuries ago is that long, long ago they didn't know how to kill the invading insects."

"Things were different with God then!"

"Oh? If those farmers of Bible days had killed the locusts — locusts that God sent — would they be sinners? Is that what today's farmers feel about God?"

"I don't want to talk with you any more. I believe in the Bible."

"I do, too, but as a history of the way people thought at the time — not as an infallible book. If you take the Bible literally, then you need a lot of props to keep up your faith, more than most people."

The conversation was no longer an interesting conversation, but a debate with bitter undertones. Jay Fisk noticed that Alan looked as if he were about to cry. He stepped into the center of the room and put his arm around Alan's shoulder.

"Let's stop this harangue!" Jay said. Then very seriously he added, "I think, before this war is over, all of us are going to need a lot more props than we now have."

CHAPTER EIGHT

CHAPTER EIGHT

FAR SOUTH of the Giants of Stornaway, a troop ship was leaving Sicily. One of the soldiers aboard that ship was Robert William Conway. He was not appearing on deck with his shipmates, but lay in his cabin suffering from another round of diarrhea, a scourge that had plagued him off and on after leaving the battlegrounds of northern Africa.

As he lay there on his bed, miserably staring up at the bottom of the bed above him, he wondered why he had been so eager to sign up in the army when he had a successful engineering business in St. Louis. He thought back and smiled to himself when he reviewed what he had accomplished through the years — he had come from the small town of Bluewater, graduated with honors from Missouri University's School of Engineering and had established a thriving firm of engineering and architecture with his university friend, Jerome Peel Ferguson.

When war was declared, the two young men, both thirty years of age, discussed their eligibility of being drafted to serve in the armed forces. Robert William was better known as Bill to his business friends and acquaintances, though he was still called Billy by his parents and everyone in his hometown. Bill wanted to volunteer and felt he could do so without abandoning his business. His partner, Jerry Ferguson, was diabetic, classified 4F, would stay at home and run the business until Bill got back. Lying abed on the ship, feeling sick, young and alone, he felt no better than little boy Billy, and should just be classed 4F. He felt he had contributed very little in the war effort in these last few weeks that he had struggled through — yet many of the other soldiers had physically fared no better, living on C rations much of the time as they fought their way through Africa and Sicily.

Africa, Billy thought of those days, months, in the heat of Africa — sometimes in his mind, they seemed to be something that happened a long time ago, and then it jerked back into reality and it was more just like yesterday.

Lying quietly, Billy's thoughts on Africa were suddenly squelched with the urgency to get to the latrine. On the way, the grungy matter of that emergency brought a touch of humor when it reminded him of General Patton's foul-mouthed speech back at Fort Bragg just before they shipped out.

Back in his bunk, Billy thought back to the confusion of the landing of his division in Algiers after twelve days at sea. They found the French causing a touchy political situation by not knowing who was in charge, the combat team that landed at Port Lyautey, or the one south of Casa Blanca. That problem was resolved when these two teams picked up a third team in Algiers, and they all made their way across Africa to Kasserine Pass, where Montgomery of the British Force had turned back Rommel's advance toward Cairo. On the way … Billy's mind lost focus as he became sleepier and sleepier as the ship rolled from side to side in a rocking motion ... a small historical village ... a nine or ten-year-old girl in a long white dress ... Billy's eyes closed in sleep, and the long white dress disappeared in a dreamlike vision. Suddenly a loud explosion! Billy sprang up shouting, "Bouncing Betty, Bouncing Betty!"

Across from Billy's bunk, another soldier was lying, his head held over the side of his bed, having retched violently onto a towel on the floor. Billy was fully awake now. "Oh, man, you really waked me up. I didn't know you were here."

"Why were you yelling 'Bouncing Betty'?" the sick man asked.

"I don't know. I must have been half asleep, and when I heard you vomiting, in my sleep I must have thought it was an explosion," Billy replied.

(The Americans had nicknamed one type of the German mines 'Bouncing Bettys' because of the way they were built. A can, about the size of a number two can, was filled with explosives and ball bearings, then buried along paths, rail tracks and road shoulders where people walked. When stepped on, the mine bounced four or five feet into the air before it exploded, so that the pellets went in every direction.) As Billy realized his error in judging the retching to be an explosion, he also knew that the long white gown was not a dream at all, but a funeral procession they had encountered near the small town of Tlemcen where a man, perhaps the girl's father, dressed in a formal black coat and tails, was slowly carrying the body of a young girl in long flowing white dress down the street.

After hearing Billy's explanation about the "bouncing betty," the other sick man spoke in a weak voice, "I would laugh if I didn't feel so sick. Aren't you seasick, too?" He lay back in his bunk, saying no more.

"I don't get seasick," Billy told him, "I just can't get rid of the trots. One guy said I had dysentery and another said I had diarrhea. I didn't know which — the medic told me dysentery was a disease and that none of us had it. Dysentery can cause diarrhea, but so can a lot of other things."

The sick man across the way said, "I had diarrhea, too, I think all of us did at one time or another."

"Yeah, from that 'C' ration!"

"No, I don't think it was *our* food, I think it was something several of us got in Sicily from the water or food we picked up somewhere on that trek."

By now the seasick man was feeling a bit better and had entered into the conversation, "You remember when we got that 'C' ration in shiny tin cans? When we were through with them, we made the mistake of pitching them out of the foxholes. One of the German prisoners told me that the circle of glistening cans gave them our location and a target to shoot at."

The ship was pitching and rolling a bit heavier now, and Gary Draughn, the seasick man, threw up again.

"Can I help you?" Billy asked.

Gary just shook his head and made no answer. Billy decided to go upon deck and get some fresh air. Maybe he himself would feel better then. He still wondered what good, if any, he had done for his country in the year that had just passed, especially after being sick half the time in this last few weeks.

There were few men on the deck, only those who had the task of getting this ship safely through the rough waters and avoiding German submarines. He met his superior officer, Major George R. Huff. When Huff asked him if he was feeling any better, Billy answered in the affirmative, then asked the officer the same question that he had been asking himself, "After fighting for over a year, I wonder what good have ***I*** done, in the over-all picture, to help my country?"

"You're alive, aren't you? That, in itself, is an accomplishment, soldier! And you are a good engineer — you were a big help when I coordinated that engineering movement of our water purification units. We had to get them in the best position for ours and other troops. If you have any further doubt, think, just think about all the battles we have won so far in this war!"

Seeing so few fellow soldiers on deck, Billy went back to his bunk. He found Gary Draughn sound asleep. Billy lay down and thought about what Major Huff had said, "Think about all the battles we have won." In thinking about their military movements, he understood why Huff, Assistant Division Engineer, became a Major.

While the British were chasing Rommel westward toward the American army in southern Tunisia, the Germans turned north along the east side of Tunisia, bypassing the American army in the south, but one night all of one American division, the one including Billy Conway and his superior officer Huff, moved from the south end through the supply lines of all the American and British troops in Tunisia to the north, so that when morning came the Germans, heading for Biserte, were facing an American force unexpectedly cutting their progress.

Near Biserte, engineers were working on a road in a valley in preparation for the approaching forces of the French, British and American. The engineers got pinned down by shells from a German 88. A car carrying an officer and a driver came from the front ridge of battle to draw the fire from the Germans, which gave the engineers a brief respite.

With the battle to recapture Biserte, the Engineer Colonel was wounded by a mine set by a trip wire across a walking trail. In his place, the officer who took over the Engineer Battalion came on with such a blustery and dictatorial manner that he was soon replaced, and moving up the line, the Assistant division Engineer Huff became Major Huff.

Soon after, as the Allied advance toward Biserte took place, the German and Italian forces began to crumble. It caused a rapid change of duty — instead of *fighting* the enemy soldiers, the Allies soon had over three hundred thousand of them as prisoners.

Conway and his engineering division did not stay with the prisoners — they were moved across to the edge of the desert south of Oran in Algiers at the headquarters of the French Foreign Legion. The reason for being sent to Oran was to train for the invasion of Sicily, along with the 39th Infantry Regiment. One night after being bombed, the taunting voice of one called Axis Sally came over the air enticing the weary soldier to surrender so that they could go home and be with their families. The soldiers listened to her. Billy Conway thought it was funny, but he wondered if any of his comrades were tempted.

Most of the bunks around Billy Conway were now filled with his shipmates, and the talk among them was of the many various experiences they had undergone to be now on a British ship on their way to England for further training for the European theatre of war. They talked mostly of their latest battles in Sicily. Under the command of General Patton they pushed swiftly up the east and central coast, while the British Montgomery was plodding up the west coast, both armies fighting to cut off the Germans and Italians as they were retreating toward the Strait of Messina trying to escape to Italy. Patton was a good field commander, who operated with a tank commander's approach — break through, move fast, and get the enemy off balance. Montgomery was more methodical — move fast, all right, but not until everything was precisely planned. This difference in command in Sicily was perhaps the beginning of Patton's and Montgomery's distaste for each other.

"When we get to England, who's going to be in charge, Montgomery or Patton?" one soldier asked.

"Because we are on a British ship, do you think we are under British control?" another asked.

Billy Conway had been listening to the many such questions going around and had said nothing until those last two remarks. "I don't think Patton will be in charge of anything," he said. "Remember, it was just while we were in Sicily that he slapped that GI in one of our evacuation hospitals and the medics reported him. That could be the end of his command."

"Yeah, a lot of things happened in Sicily," another soldier said.

"I think it was a lot better there than that hell-hot African desert!" one soldier observed.

The sea had become calmer and the few who had succumbed to seas sickness had found temporary relief. As the night wore on, they talked of their experiences, and many of them couldn't say enough in praise of the island of Sicily.

"Did you see those magnificent old Greek Temples?" one boy asked.

"I wasn't looking for temples — I loved it when we appropriated all those mules!" another laughed.

"Shame on you! I felt sorry for the people when we took their mules from them," someone protested

"Well, we had to do it!" another spoke in defense. "You must remember that vehicles weren't any good in those rugged mountains, and we did have the cooperation of the town mayors before we took any of them."

"How many mules did we take, do you have any idea how many?"

"Oh, we had several hundred — that is, to start with, but many of them were killed or died during the fighting. It was too bad we couldn't take all of them back to their rightful owners," Billy told the group. "When we returned the ones we could to the various villages, the people were most grateful."

"I liked the fruits, not the mules and, Brady, how did you find time to visit the Greek temples?"

"Well, we did get some time off for rest — occasionally! I enjoy the history of the ancient churches and the old ruins. I like the narrow streets and the people who seem to live out on their streets as much as in their houses. I liked to give candy to those little kids. They were begging just like the kids did in Africa. And they weren't that poor — each family had at least one mule, or did until we took it away."

"You'd think from the way we're talking that we weren't at war in Sicily at all. We sound like we all want to go back," Billy Conway said.

"Maybe I will, someday, when this war is all over and I am rich and can bring my wife over here."

"I didn't know you were married."

"Not yet, but I expect to be sometime."

Billy Conway, who had been listening to all the conversation, jumped from his bunk, again making a hurried trip to the latrine. When he got back, before he lay down on his bunk he said, "I don't ever, ever want to come back to Sicily. What I remember most is that camp on the north coast that became contaminated with flies. I'll never forget how the medics covered the latrines with a cheesecloth netting. I think that could have been where so many of us got sick and why there were a lot of desertion cases. I heard they tried fifty-four cases at the General Courts."

"Do you want to desert, Billy boy?"

"No! I just want to get rid of the trots so I can fight a good fight."

"The medics say that when we get to England we'll all be given a good health check before we are sent on any more fighting assignments."

The conversation died out as the boys, one by one, fell asleep for the night, each with his own dreams. Billy Conway did not fall asleep before he thought about what the others had said about Sicily. He seemed to be the only one who disparaged the beautiful little island. It made him think of one incident that he wouldn't forget. It happened in one little village where they had appropriated the mules. All the animals were not mules; some were donkeys, and the one particular little animal was called a donkey by the servicemen, yet it was smaller than most others and might easily be called a burro. When the American officer asked the owner if they could take the little donkey, the owner was very obliging. But a little girl standing behind the man, evidently her father, was crying. As they were prepared to take the animal, the little girl dashed around her father, put her arms around the little donkey's neck and kissed it goodbye. At that time Billy almost felt like adding his tears to those of the little girl. Billy remembered his own, as well as the joy of the little girl weeks later, when they were able to return the little donkey to its owner. Billy went to sleep with a smile on his face — maybe Sicily was not all bad!

All the soldiers on the ship were aware that their division was on its way to England to prepare for the invasion of the continent. Their division was one of the few divisions with combat experience. Since no one got off, many of them wondered why the British ship stopped at Algiers after its departure from Sicily. From there it headed for an outside course around the European continent. The rough seas of the Atlantic and the undisclosed routing helped to avoid the German U-boats that were known to lay off points where regular sea lanes converged. The ship was scheduled to go around Ireland, come in the north channel past Scotland before docking at Liverpool, England.

The long route to England did get them safely past the German U-Boats, but it did not bring relief to Billy Conway from the bug that had infected his intestine, a relief he needed badly.

Little did Billy Conway know what Fate, the Goddess of Destiny, held for him as she brought him a deliverance from the Sicilian scourge.

CHAPTER NINE

CHAPTER NINE

AFTER SPENDING ten uneventful days in Iceland, the airmen arrived in Stornaway, on the Isle of Lewis in the Hebrides. They had no time to make their way over the twenty miles of sea to northern Ireland to visit Bushmills and sample the whiskey of renown that been described to them by Willie Brandt. Nor did the more adventurous men have a chance to view the Giant's Causeway, that spectacular geographical phenomenon along the coast of Northern Ireland.

There were two very good reasons why they were not permitted to visit Ireland — Ireland was NOT united or cooperating with the Allies in the war, and the servicemen did not have the available time anyway. Almost immediately after their arrival in Stornaway, they were dispatched to England. Most of them were sent north and east of London to the Norwich area, where there were six hundred or more airfields.

The group of airmen who flew together to England did not stay together — they were scattered over the many different fields, seldom, if ever, to see each other again. Jordan Fisk felt at great loss in being separated from his friend, Jade Browning. Many others, too, were sorry that assignments did not coincide with the ones with whom they had bonded in training.

Jay Fisk had one bright side of the situation — now in England, he felt that he had something interesting to write to Irene. The only problem was getting the time to write it. During the ten days when he was confined to the barracks in Iceland, there was more than enough time and nothing to write. Now that he was in the war zone, there was much more to write, and so little time to do it.

Jay and Irene had made a game of those letters during the last ten-day period while he was in Iceland. Jay wrote every day, saying he could make his letters more boring than Irene could make hers. Jay wrote in one letter: *This is the most boring letter I think I can write and the most appropriate of what goes on here. I get up, I eat, I do nothing, I go to bed. Can your days be any more boring than that? Did I forget to tell you I love you!*

Irene wrote back: *Yes, my days are boring, too. I got up, went to work, went home, went to bed — oh, yes, I ate when I thought about it. I love you.*

Jay found England a new and interesting experience. Seeing it for the first time was in itself fascinating to him. Another fascination was watching the people in time of war when disaster, day after day, seemed only hours away. Jay could not write anything about his location in England. What he was allowed to tell Irene did not include the scenery or anything about the landscape — what he could write about was the people, and he hoped she would find them as interesting as he did, but writing her about them was another thing. What could he say?

Jay was part of a group of four assigned to fly cargo

planes, delivering supplies to the fighting ground troops on the European continent. The type of plane they flew was called a C47 in the military. In civilian use, that same type of plane would be the Douglas DC3. The four men in the plane's crew were the pilot, a lieutenant; the co-pilot, also a lieutenant; the crew-chief or main mechanic,a sergeant; and Jay Fisk, the radio operator and navigator, a corporal.

Jay wrote Irene that he was the low man on the totem pole, but still had his own little cubicle up front, right behind the co-pilot. He also wrote that he did not have to fly every day and had time off once in awhile to visit different places in England.

As he had these more interesting things to write to Irene, she also had more interesting things to write to him. She had quit the job she had held for the years since their marriage and had taken a position in one of the weapon factories at a much better wage. Through all the turmoil of training for their flights over war-torn Europe, his letters from Irene were the bright spots in his existence. He hoped his letters would make her days brighter, too

Following the arrival at their first base in England, the boys in Jay Fisk's division spent many evenings at the pubs. Because of the war, the pubs were open only from seven o'clock in the evenings until ten o'clock. Often, long lines of servicemen were waiting at the doors before opening time. The line was made up from various branches of the service, as well as from servicemen from all the different allied countries.

One night standing in line at one of the pubs in Oxford, Jay Fisk met a Scotsman and they fell into a conversation while they were waiting for the doors to open.

In a very Highland Scottish brogue, a boy in a Scottish kilt standing right behind Jay asked him, "Have you been to Scotland?"

"No, but I hope to before I go back home," Jay answered. "Tell me about your Scotland, so I will know what to expect."

"One of the first things you should know is not to call a Scotsman or a Scotswoman, Scotch. Scotch you drink! You can call us Scots, or Scottish, but not scotch."

Jay told the Scotsman a bit about his growing up in the Midwestern part of the United States, before settling in New York. Their conversation was often interrupted by others talking with them and asking questions of them both. Before the doors opened, Jay had given his name and learned that the Scotsman's name was Dan MacDougal.

Jay asked him if he had heard the story of the Giant's Causeway, the feud between the Irish and Scottish giants. When Dan told him that, yes, everyone's heard that story, and though some people really believed it, most thought it was probably just a bit of someone's imagination.

Jay agreed with him, and then remarked, "Now, the Irish are fighting among themselves, the North and the South, the Protestants and the Catholics."

The Scotsman thought a minute, and said, "There's more to it than that. Rural Scotland is a pretty hard place to make a living, and back a hundred years ago many farmers were driven off their land by wealthy men who wanted the farmers' small plots for their own use. With the additional land they would have larger pastures for their sheep, thereby increasing their profitable wool trade. Thousands of Scots emigrated across the North Channel to northern Ireland, only about twenty miles away. Eighty percent of the people in northern Ireland are of Scottish descent and are of the Protestant faith. Though they call themselves Irish now after so many years, the root of their feud goes back to more than just religion — it's economic and nationality as well.

"It seems they should be able to work out a peaceful situation, acceptable to both groups." Jay said.

"Yes, just the way we are trying to work out a comparable situation with Germany now!"

"You think there's no other way?" Jay questioned in surprise.

"Who knows?" The Scotsman answered.

Jay Fisk was glad when the doors of the pub opened. He felt he would enjoy a beer right now, for the Scotsman had left him with a perturbing thought about the friction in Ireland.

On one of the visits Jay and his companions made to a pub, they were entertained by an accordion player. Jay Fisk was intrigued with the music. He himself played many instruments, but he had never tried to play an accordion. The entertainer was an especially good performer, which made Jay even more fascinated with the instrument.

When the first break came in the music, Jay made his way immediately to the musician. "Where can I buy an accordion?" he asked.

The musician told him the address of a music shop where he could get one, then asked, "Do you play the accordion?"

"I've never tried, but I think I could," Jay answered.

"I think you better take some lessons first before you buy an instrument," the entertainer laughed as he shook his head at Jay.

"Okay," Jay agreed. "Do you give lessons?"

The musician looked askance at this American serviceman who wanted to buy an accordion, yet had never played one, whose stay in England *might* be a matter of months, but possibly it could be just days — or hours, on whether he would be among one of those who were lost every day in this war.

The accordionist sighed, and feeling a pity for Jay, told him to come see him when he had a day free.

"I don't have to fly tomorrow! Where can I reach you?"

The next day, Jay bought the accordion and surprised his teacher with how little instruction it took for him to play the new instrument. The teacher found that Jay had a perfect ear for tone, and soon was not surprised to learn that Jay Fisk was an accomplished musician and played several other musical instruments. The instructor found out quickly that all this American needed was the opportunity.

In the spare time of the days that followed, while many of Jay's buddies were playing cards, reading, telling stories or whatever, Jay was practicing on the accordion. He wanted to play as well as the man at the pub. After a good many evenings of hearing Jay's practice, one card player said, "Turn it down! We can't hear anything. Don't you have anything to do but play that damned music box?"

"Well, you got tired of the harmonica," Jay laughed. "I thought you'd like a change."

Another came to Jay's defense. "I like to hear the music. I even like it every morning when Jay whistles. I always liked to hear my Dad whistle when he got up every morning. That's why I like to have Jay around."

The days in England seemed to be always rainy. One day as they left from their base flying supplies to the ground forces in France, Jay remarked to his fellow flyers, "Why is it always foggy and rainy in England and the minute we reach the French coast, the sun comes out?"

"Why, didn't you know that the Germans control the weather — they keep it foggy in England so that we can't find our way over here," the pilot joked.

"No, that's not it," the mechanic Stockard chimed in, "they just turn the sunshine on when we get to France, so they can see to shoot us down."

A sudden silence engulfed the four — the lighthearted chatter that had begun shortly after take-off was supplanted with recollection of the ground fire they had previously evaded, to the dangers that lay shortly ahead of them now.

Their destination today was not the same as yesterday's, nor likely would tomorrow's be familiar — they waited from day to day to see where their orders would take them. Corporal Jordan Fisk, the navigator and communications officer, studied the routing they were now on. He looked at the two lieutenants; the pilot, Quentin Peterson; the co-pilot, Ray Goins, sitting in front of him, and then at the mechanic, Sergeant Shelby Stockard, with a certain fondness. The four of them had flown together since their arrival in England — they did not fly daily, but had days off intermittently. They often enjoyed each other's company in that free time.

They were flying over the green pastures of France as they took this load of supplies to the troops on the ground. They were still high enough in the air that they hardly noticed that the green pastures were speckled with the ruins of fire, bombs and other ravages of war. As they neared their target to drop their cargo, their decreased altitude made them fully aware of the proximity of the war to where they must fly. With no sign of any enemy offensive, they followed the usual routine and made their return to home base, ready to report "mission accomplished."

Routine! Yes, routine, nothing special, just their usual task in doing their part in the war. Jay had these thoughts as the C47, minus its cargo, entered the clouds and rain hovering over its landing base. He hoped there would be a letter from Irene, maybe a handful of letters. It had been over a week and he had not had any word from her at all. But that wasn't too unusual. There had been times before when he did not receive any mail, then there came a whole bunch of letters at one time.

Checking the mail was the first thing Jay did when he was back at the barracks. He was delighted to find a letter from Irene! There was just one, however, when he had visions of there being several, one for each day that he had not heard from her. He had written to Irene every day that it was possible. Perhaps there were days when she couldn't write either.

He tore open the letter immediately, not waiting to get back to his bunk. He read it while walking across the grounds, not noticing the rain, the fog or fellow soldiers as he bumped into them. He read it again after he was seated on his bed. The smile on his face increased as he reached into his locker for pen and paper, for she had given him a great idea for subject matter he could write in his letter to her! She told him about the different people she had met at her new job, and how she spent some of her spare time with them. She wrote also about their old mutual friends, the ones that were still around, with this third year of war depleting their number.

He read the last paragraph again: *Jay, darling, I have been putting as much saving as I can into an account for our house. I have not been putting it into your account, as we used to do, but have opened a savings account in my own name. What about putting my name on your account? I hope you won't mind— after all, I'll keep building up our house account. Don't you think that is a good idea?*

Then Jay re-read it. He had a good-sized savings account of his own before he and Irene had ever married, and they had put their mutual savings for buying a house into it through the years. Neither one of them had thought of putting her name on his account. Irene was right, of course, she should have her name on her new account — all the money in it was hers, she's the one who had earned it. He also sent her as much of his pay checks as he could, keeping only spending money for himself. She was probably putting that into their joint account, too. He might ask her in one of his letters.

He got settled, ready to begin his letter, first, to agree that she should put her savings in her own name, and then he would tell her about his flying buddies. Flying as he had with them these past few months, he had not told Irene very much about them at all.

There was Quentin Peterson, who everyone called Pete — no one was going to the trouble of saying Quentin. Pete was twenty-five years old, unmarried and came from Beaufort, South Carolina. Pete was of medium height, medium weight, with light brown hair and brown eyes. He had a Southern drawl when he talked and he loved to talk. He took great pleasure in telling about the sightseeing tours that were available in his town, how some of the guides took great pleasure in shocking a few ultra conservative puritanic tourists by telling them they wanted to take them into the *Tabby House*. Pete would laugh and laugh as he told how some of those tourists would huff and puff and say they didn't want to go, thinking Tabby house (cat house) meant a house of ill-repute — and there were other very sheltered conservative oldsters who had never heard about the expression "cat house," and it didn't affect them one way or the other. Pete laughed even more when he had to explain to some of the servicemen that tabby was the kind of building material that was used in construction of some houses.

Ray Goins was older, married, and came from Columbus, Ohio. Jay, one day in talking to Ray, said, "My sister, Roxanne, has a friend that lives in Columbus. I don't suppose you would know her. Her name was Molly Rogers. I don't know whether she ever married or not, so I doubt —"

"Molly Rogers! Of course, I know her. We live in the same apartment building. My wife and Molly are good friends."

"Wait until I write my sister about that. I know she keeps in touch with Molly all the time. They were such good friends when they were little," Jay said.

"Molly is one smart girl. She is a CPA and does taxes for everybody in our building, as well as holds an important position in an auditors firm," Ray informed Jay.

That night Jay wrote his sister, Roxanne, that one of the pilots in his plane lived in the same apartment building as Molly Rogers and knew her well. In his letter to Irene, he wrote even more about Ray. He told her that Ray was the father of two children and would not have volunteered to be in this war except that country was badly in need of pilots in the service, and he was already an experienced pilot with a major airline.

Jay wondered what he could tell Irene about Shelby Stockard, except that he was an excellent mechanic. He was younger than any of the three others, only nineteen. Blue-eyed, blond hair, tall and skinny. Jay said that Stocky, as they called him, was anything but stocky in build. In fact, he was about the same size and coloring as Jay himself. Stocky was a born mechanic. His father was a mechanic for a car service station in Kansas City. Stocky said that people from all over the city came to have his father work on their cars, because his dad was the best mechanic in town. He said his father taught him many things about fixing engines, things that most mechanics never learn. He finished his letter to Irene in just two more lines.

"How can I be so lucky as to be with these three, day after day in my flights. Don't worry about me, I have one of the easy jobs. Love, Your Jay"

When Jay had finished his letter, he was surprised how much he had written. He wondered if he had sounded too satisfied with his effort here in the war, and didn't let Irene know how much he missed her. But the letter was already written and some of the guys were yelling at him to come along, they were ready to go to a great pub. He forgot to say anything at all about putting her name on his own savings account.

CHAPTER TEN

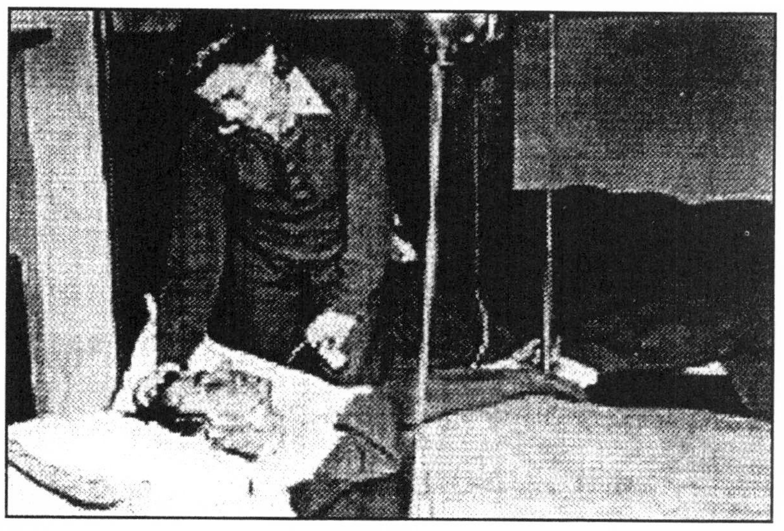

CHAPTER TEN

WHEN HIS DIVISION of the Army engineers arrived in England from Sicily, Robert William Conway was taken immediately to the Army hospital. His diarrhea and vomiting had left him extremely dehydrated, and he had developed a high fever. In the occasional hallucinatory moments he would yell out, "Get behind that bush or down in the gulch where the Germans can't see you." Then he would continue, "This damned hot sand!"

A tall, blond and extremely good-looking nurse met the Major as he accompanied the sick soldier to the hospital. "Nurse, get the best doctor here," the Major said. "I want you to take good care of this boy. He's an excellent engineer, and we need him."

"I'm Nurse Carter, and I'll see that he's properly cared for. What is his trouble?"

"He picked up a bug in Sicily and has become feverish and dehydrated. He hallucinates and is still fighting the war in Africa."

"I'll get the doctor right now." The nurse left the Major with the sick man as she hurried from the room, crowded with row after row of other wounded and sick servicemen. The Major, hoping to brighten the patient's spirit, leaned over the bed and whispered, "You'll be all right, boy. You've got a good-looking nurse to take care of you."

The next time the Major called at the hospital to enquire about Conway's health, he talked with the doctor who had cared for him. The doctor told the Major that the powerful drug that they had administered and the IV had given him for dehydration had proved very successful and the boy would be out of the hospital in a short time — not yet ready for battle, but he would be fully recovered in a few weeks.

"No more rantings about fighting in the hot sands, are there?" the Major said, half jokingly.

"No, but right after he got here, his ravings were not about fighting in the desert, but he kept saying, 'Anna Mae, I'm sorry! I didn't want to hurt you,' and he said it several times. The head nurse, Amy Carter, said he must have had something in his past that troubled him, because when he was no longer feverish, he calmed down and never mentioned it again, nor did he say anything about the African battles."

"Good, I'm glad that he is getting well. I hope that he'll be up and about soon, and it won't be long before he will have his strength back."

Though the early morning fog had lifted and the rain clouds had moved on eastward toward the continent, the blackout left little light for the troops to make their way into London. The troops who had the next day off thought it was a good time to go into the big city. The evening stars broke the darkness a wee bit, providing a pleasant atmosphere to enhance their limited time to explore the part of London where they might meet some lonely girls looking for company. Together, perhaps they could forget the terrible hours of war.

Jay Fisk, accompanied by several of his buddies, arrived in London by train from their base and made their way to the first pub they saw. They had just entered one and found it already crowded with other Americans, soldiers from all branches of the armed service. To Sergeant Shelby Stockard, who was standing next to him, Jay remarked, "It's too packed in here. There must be another place where we can go."

"Let's get one drink here, then we'll head off to another joint," Stocky proposed, and the others with them agreed.

Their group pushed its way through other uniformed bodies, standing three-deep in front of the bar, until they got close enough to put in an order. It wasn't hard for several to get in front of Jay, who wasn't in any hurry to quench a questionable thirst for a foreign liquor. When he reached the counter, Jay asked for a beer. The American boys had already found out that Britishers' favorite drinks are beer and whisky (spelled whiskey if you are in Ireland). If you order whisky in England, it will be Scotch. Bourbon is not always available. Jay ordered beer, but had forgotten that lager was the closest thing to American beer. He thought of Guinness, the famous Dublin stout, but he had tried to order that once, and learned since the war started, Irish liquors were not too popular here in England. He had also learned that Irish drinks were much stronger than the Continental liquors. He stood at the counter, hesitant in making up his mind what to order. Stockard and some of his other friends had already obtained their drinks and had moved near the door, away from the crowd. The army boys in back of the airmen were trying to hurry Jay along, telling him to do something — just order anything and get done with it — they wanted to get their drinks. Jay turned to face the infantry boys, ready to back off and let the impatient ones take his place, when one of them, standing in back of the others, called out, "Aren't you Jay Fisk?"

Jay, startled, nodded as he peered through the dimly lit room to get a better look at the man who spoke. The uniformed man pushed his way to a space beside Jay, and said, "Let me buy you a lager." He plopped down some change and held up two fingers to the clerk behind the counter. Then he turned to face Fisk.

Jay looked closely at the man — saw a face that looked familiar, yet not immediately recognized, "I know you," he mused, as he studied the man, and when a grin appeared on that face, Jay gave a whoop, "You're Billy!"

Billy Conway gave Jay a slap on the back and said, "Jay, how are you, how many years since we've seen each other?"

"I left Bluewater in 1928, Billy. When did you leave, or do you still live there?"

Several of the soldiers in back of them were trying to push the two aside, some of them yelling, "Pick up your drinks, guys — move along!"

"Call me Bill. Only my folks and people at Bluewater still call me Billy. We should have a chance to talk. I would like to hear about you — and Roxanne. You remember I always liked your sister. Where is she now, and what is she doing?"

"You didn't answer *my* question, Bill. Do you still

live in Bluewater? Tell me about yourself," Jay insisted.

As these two acquaintances of old times stood chatting, Jay's Air Corps buddies were calling him to come along — they were ready to leave this joint and wanted to try another one. Bill's friends were cutting into his conversation with Jay, too.

"I don't know when we can see each other again. If you don't have any specific arrangements for this evening, why don't we drop everything, get out of here and find a place where we can catch up on old times," Jay suggested. Billy Conway liked the idea, so they each told their companion that they would see them later, and the two of them left together.

As they walked the streets, they talked of their different positions in the service, what they had already experienced, and what might lay ahead. One of the first questions Billy asked was, "Are you married?"

"Yes, and very happily married to a wonderful girl named Irene. We've been married for nearly seven years. I write to her almost every day, and she writes to me often, but I don't get the letters every day. It is probably the difficulty in delivery. Are you married?"

"I was, but it only lasted a year. I've been divorced for a long time. And that brings up another problem. I am head over heels in love with a nurse. She is the most beautiful thing you've ever seen. She has blue, blue eyes and blond hair. I was in bed at the hospital, my eyes and face all red and swollen, leaning over the side of the bed, vomiting, and this nurse sat down beside me. She was so kind! I told you about the chronic diarrhea I got in Sicily. Our commanding officer said I had to get over it before we invaded France, so he sent me to the base hospital as soon as we got to England. That's how I met this gorgeous nurse."

"What's her name?"

"She says her name is Amy Carter. But she looks so much like someone else. Do you remember Anna Mae Cowan?

"Of course! I don't think anyone would forget Anna Mae," Jay laughed as he said it, and then he added, "especially you."

"Oh, Jay! Don't throw that up to me. I've regretted that whole ugly incident all these years. To tell you the truth, that's why I got married to that girl I was going with, Jay. Peggy wanted to have sex, and I wouldn't do it without getting married. Believe it or not — that's the truth! I was young and still hurting over the harm I had done to Anna Mae a few years before."

"Did you love her?"

"Who? Anna Mae?"

"No! Peggy!"

"I don't know. I know I did not feel the same way I feel about Amy Carter. You must see her, Jay, and you'll know why I'm so in love with her."

"Billy, how long have you known this Amy? A week?"

"No, I've known her for months. I was in the sick bay and saw her every morning for ten days, and now I just keep on going back to see her. I always say I need to get another check-up."

"Then what's your problem, Billy? Doesn't she like you?"

"It's strange, Jay. When she was first helping me, I

was leaning over the pan, so I didn't even look up to see her, but I heard her tell me that she was nurse Carter, and was there to help me. She was very kind and solicitous. Then when I lay back in bed, I got a real good look at her. The minute I saw her, I thought she was someone else, and I couldn't help but say, 'Anna Mae?' She turned around to look at me. But I want to tell you something funny about that. She took a look at my chart — I was registered in the Army as Robert W. Conway — then she moved on to the next bed without saying another word.

"The next day another nurse took care of me. I asked her about the other nurse. The new nurse said Miss Carter had asked her to take over my case. That's when I saw this gorgeous creature walking past my bed again. She didn't even look at me, so I called out, 'Nurse, what's your name?' That's when she stopped and told me her name was Amy Carter, that she thought she had told me that when she was sitting beside me the day before.

"I soon got better. They have a new medicine now that they tried out on me. It's a drug called sulfa. That medicine made me sick at my stomach, at least I think it did. But it also made me completely well of the diarrhea. I asked Amy Carter to go out with me, but she very kindly refused. The other guys in the beds around me at the hospital told me to save my breath, that she had turned them all down. They said that she was a cool one, and probably wouldn't be much fun anyway."

"Well, Billy, I think I better meet this love of your life. Now don't worry about me cutting in. I told you, I am a very happily married man, and I would never, ever be unfaithful to my Irene."

In November it is cold and often rainy in England, and the two walkers, even without the rain, felt the chill. They soon expressed the desire to find a place where they could warm up from the damp, dark streets of London.

"Let's go to the base hospital — maybe Amy will be there," Billy proposed.

The two Americans, one in an Army uniform, the other in Air Force habit, took the underground rail to the closest station to the hospital where Bill Conway had been treated. Billy guided Jay through the aisles of wounded soldiers, looking for Amy Carter. As he passed by, Billy spoke to a few of the patients he had known, surprised that they were still there.

"Bill Conway, are you still trying to make out with that nurse?" one of them teased.

"I just want to see her. Is she on duty?" Billy replied.

"I haven't seen her today. Maybe she's got time off." Two or three of the patients agreed with that statement.

When it was evident that Amy was not available, the two men left, discussing when and if they could meet again. Jay was stationed north and east of London in the Norwich area, two hours or more by train from London, while Billy was just a short distance west, less than thirty minutes from London.

Neither knew when they would have free time to meet again, or how best to contact each other.

"I'm so close here, that I will come in to see Amy as often as I can. "

"Billy, I've got an idea," Jay spoke enthusiastically. "Why don't I come as often as I can, too, and try to see Amy. I'll ask her to be our go-between. I can leave a note with her for you — you can give her a note for me. That way I'll get to meet her, and you will have many excuses for her to talk with you. What do you think?"

Billy seemed to burst with excitement. "Great! I'll have an excuse to come in almost daily to see if you have left a message."

"Billy — you want me to call you Bill — why don't you let me see her first. I have tomorrow off and I'll come in to see her first. That way it won't look like such a put-up job."

The two men, ready to part company, shook hands — it was more like a clasp of hands that held for several moments. "What a coincidence, that we should see each other after all these years. I am so glad to see you again," Bill Conway said.

"It's been at least fifteen years. I guess we've both changed," Jay replied.

"I hope I've changed for the better, a little less swagger, but a lot more sense — I hope. Goodnight, Jay!"

"Goodnight, Bill, and look for Amy in a day or two with a note from me."

The next morning Jay Fisk arose early, slipping around like a mouse avoiding a hungry cat. In spite of his concern for his sleeping companions, a few of them awoke. They could not understand why he would get up at seven o'clock in the morning when he had the whole day to just stay in bed if he wished.

Jay continued to be reasonably quiet in his movements, so as not to disturb those who were still asleep. A man named Seth remarked, "We do appreciate it, though,

Jay-boy, that you didn't get up and start practicing on that accordion."

Jay put his fingers to his lips and in a moderately whispering voice said, "*Seth-boy*, your early morning talking is just as disturbing as my night music is at night. Just go back to sleep and I'll be out of your way."

"No offense, Jay," Seth whispered, I'm just curious as to why you're getting up so early."

"Going sleuthing in London!" Jay whispered in response.

The whisperings had drawn more attention than the earlier normal talk, especially Jay's last bit about sleuthing. Shelby Stockard, lying a few beds down from Jay, heard it and said, loud enough for all to hear, "Is it about that Army guy you were with last night?"

"Could be!" Jay tossed back as he hurried out the door. Jay had learned the night before that he could get a fast train that left at 8:52 a.m. and would be in London at 9:06. He would get to the hospital base as soon as he could and look for the beautiful *and* mysterious Amy.

Remembering the route he had gone with Billy Conway the night before, Jay Fisk made his way through the rows of beds, looking for Nurse Carter. He saw at the end of the room, a blond-headed nurse, her face turned toward a patient. He thought about waiting until she came toward him, then changed his mind. He would go up to her and introduce himself, hoping that she would be Billy's heart throb.

The nurse left the patient she was attending, and did not notice Jay as she stopped to check on the next patient, but Jay had seen her face when she turned in his direction. She had to be the right one! She looked so much like the Anna Mae Cowan, the young girl he remembered in years long gone by. It did not just look like Anna Mae, Jay felt that it *was* Anna Mae, but he mustn't let her know he thought that. He approached her, "Nurse," he said, "I am looking for a friend of mine. He was here in this hospital —" Jay stopped saying anything, for when the nurse looked up, he had caught an instant flash that came over her face — he felt sure that she had recognized him.

In just as quick a flash, the look had disappeared, and a very calm young woman said to him, "Can I help you, sir?"

Jay's mind was racing — what do I say now? He recovered his composure just as quickly as she had, and said, "I am Jordan Fisk, better known as Jay to my friends. A long time ago, I lived in a little town in the Midwest and this friend of mine did also. I heard he was hurt in the war and was sent to this hospital. His name is Billy Conway. Do you know how I can get in touch with him?"

"He comes to the hospital regularly. You might call at another time and find him here."

"Nurse, you must know, a soldier's time is not his own in times of war. I don't have any idea when I can come back. I am in the Air Force and am stationed quite a ways from London. Could you take a note from me, and give it to him when he comes in?" Jay hoped he had pulled it off just right, that he had given no indication to Amy Carter that in his own mind he had identified her as Anna Mae Cowan. He felt sure of it, that in an unguarded moment when she first saw him a look of recognition had lighted her eyes and expression.

When the nurse did not immediately answer Jay's request to handle the note to Billy, Jay continued, "What is your name, miss?"

Jay noticed that in those moments when she did not answer him, she had been studying him intensely. When he asked her name, she seemed to come out of her reverie and said, "I am Amy Carter."

"I am glad to meet you, Miss Carter. It is Miss, is it not? I see you are not wearing a ring."

"It is Miss Carter. I see you are wearing a ring," she answered, and Jay noticed a defensive tone in her voice as she mentioned his ring.

"Yes, I am very happily married to a wonderful girl named Irene. I write to her every day. I am one lucky man."

Jay thought Amy Carter seemed to relax a bit when he told of his marriage. "I hate being away from her for so long in this war. I wonder if you could have a cup of coffee with me. I need someone to talk to. It makes me feel less lonely if I can talk about Irene."

Amy looked at Jay intently and said, "I am very busy here with these many patients, and —"

Jay interrupted, "I understand, Miss Carter. I would like a cup of coffee, and I need a place where I can write my note to Billy. Can you tell me where I can go, and where I can find you when I finish the note?"

Amy Carter gave Jordan Fisk directions to a spot where he could get coffee and where a little table was available for writing his note. She told him not to look for her, that she would come to him at the coffee table as soon as she found time — would he just wait for her there.

Jay sat at the small coffee-stained table, sipping at a cup of very strong, hot coffee. He had become acquainted with English habits of making strong coffee, then diluting it with milk. Jay preferred his coffee black, but was slowly getting used to the bitterness of the undiluted brew. It was one of the things he wrote in his letters to Irene, telling her how much he would love to have the mornings with her and her coffee. He did not gulp it down, as he might have if it had been what he was used to; this liquid had to be sipped, and taken in small quantities. Wasn't this an American hospital base? Wasn't the cook here also American? He sat there wondering why supposedly American made coffee was taking on the aspects of the native brew.

While he was muddling over the quality of the coffee, he was trying to compose his note to Billy. Should he tell Billy what he thought about the identity of Amy Carter, or not. He decided he would skip that for the time being, until he was sure that this Amy Carter would not read the notes he gave her to deliver. He wrote that he would wait for word about when the two of them could meet again, that he would talk with Amy as often as he could to see if she had word for him.

He had not finished the coffee, but had the note written and sealed when Amy Carter came by the table. Instead of just asking for the note she was supposed to deliver, she sat down at the table with a cup of coffee in her hand — milk-diluted, which made it look like dirty water to Jay.

"Corporal, I have a few minutes. Sorry I couldn't give you more time earlier," she said.

"Well, tell me how you happened to be in this war," Jay asked.

"Probably for the same reason you are. It was my wish as well as my duty to serve my country," she answered.

A few more platitudes in their conversation, when Jay said, "I will tell you what I know of Billy Cowan; then I would like for you to tell me what you think of him, since you have seen much more of him in recent times than I have.

"I have known Billy all my life. He was in my class at school, and we came from a small town where everybody knew everybody else. Billy came from a good family. He chummed around with another boy who wasn't as high-principled as Billy, nor was his family, but in a small town, there are few other kids the same age — you take what is available, I guess. Anyway —" Jay was about to tell the story of how Billy got in trouble, but thought better of it. If Billy wanted to tell Amy, then it was up to him. "Anyway, Billy got his education — he was a smart boy, and he became an excellent engineer. I heard that he has a very successful engineering business in St. Louis, Missouri. That is the reason that he is a Lieutenant in the Army." Whoops! He didn't mean to tell that! Amy Carter would wonder how he knew that Billy Conway was a Lieutenant. Time to let someone else talk. "You probably know more about him than I do. Tell me what you know about him. Is he as good-looking as he used to be?"

"He wasn't good-looking when they brought him into the hospital. He was sick and too thin. When they gave him the medicine, he must have been allergic to it because his face and eyes were swollen and he was sick at his stomach." Amy didn't say any more.

"Is that all you know about him?" Jay probed.

"I know he comes in here almost daily when he isn't on a war maneuver and keeps hounding me to go out with him."

"Do you?"

"No! I won't go out with any of these soldiers!" Amy was very abrupt.

"Why not?"

"Because I don't trust them. There are lots of English girls who do go out with them, and they say American boys all want the same thing." Amy's cheerful and pleasant mood had become curt and defensive.

"They aren't all the same. I know of some married soldiers who say they are happily married, yet I know they go out with girls here. But I don't. I wouldn't do that to Irene. I like talking to you, but that's as far as our relationship would ever go. I think you will find Billy Conway is like that, too, and he would never hurt you."

"What makes you so sure of that?"

"I make no promises — I'm just expressing my opinion. How has he treated you when he comes in here? Can't you tell what he's like?"

"He tells me he loves me." Amy gave a little derisive laugh and said, "Isn't that a riot? I have to take that with a grain of salt, since he doesn't know me and I don't know him."

"Then get to know him! I don't know why I'm saying that. I just want you to be our go-between. You will do that, won't you?"

"Yes."

Jay handed Amy the sealed note addressed to Billy Conway, no further identification, just his name. He pushed his half-empty cup of cold coffee to the side, and told Amy he would come in as often as he could, hoping she would have a note from Billy for him.

When Jay was watching Amy as he made these last remarks, she raised her head and looked directly into his eyes. Meeting her unswerving gaze, he had the uneasy feeling that she knew his visit was not just to get in touch with Billy, that she thought he was probing. It was time to leave! Jay immediately said as he handed her the note, "I want to see Billy. Please give him this."

Jay Fisk had planned his activities for a full day in London before he left the air base. He would first call on the nurse called Amy, who Billy Conway claimed to be his life-long love. Then he would visit at least two of the art galleries. He would like to study the techniques of the Masters. Besides his love of music, Jay also liked to paint, but in spite of the fact that his training in that field was limited, he enjoyed it. He thought the perfect ending for the day would be a night at the opera. He was happy to learn that the Royal Opera House had not closed down during the war.

Jay left the hospital on the Tube, (or the Underground as the subway was most often labeled) with his destination being the National Gallery and the National Portrait

Gallery on Trafalgar Square. Covent Gardens, within easy walking distance, was near the Royal Opera House. He could spend the rest of the day in this area and be happy. But when he had been in the art gallery only a short time, he began to find his attention wandering from the paintings back to the nurse, Amy Carter. He felt so sure that Amy Carter was none other than Anna Mae Cowan, the young girl who had been in the same high school with him in the little town of Bluewater in the foothills of the Ozarks.

He remembered a letter he had gotten from his German friend, Franz, several years ago, stating that there were many Americans who were supporting Hitler — that they were unknown to most of the United States citizens. Could Anna Mae be working for the Germans and using an assumed name to cover her identity? If so, how could he expose her? And what if he was wrong? Perhaps this girl was not Anna Mae Cowan at all. It had been sixteen and a half years since he had seen her. Then he remembered the startled, yet fleeting glimpse he had seen on her face when she first saw him. He was so sure she recognized him before he had told her his name. And he felt she knew Billy Conway, too, and that was why she was avoiding him like the plague.

Jay felt he was looking at the paintings in the gallery without seeing them at all. He took a deep breath, opened the little guide book he had bought, and tried to concentrate on each painting. He finished touring the National Gallery in an hour and noticed his stomach was rumbling. He would find a pub close by before he did any more gallery visits. When he got outside, he stood looking at the Nelson Column and the pigeons, still thinking about Amy Carter instead of looking for a pub. Should he tell Billy to back off in his courtship of that girl — she might be a spy?

"I have to stop imagining things," Jay thought to himself. "This day I must enjoy London, its great art galleries, its many other attractions and tonight the opera. In war, it's one day at a time — I may never have this chance again. I will forget about Amy Carter for the rest of this day."

Jay Fisk did not get back to London the next day, or the next. His division was moving. Over six hundred different air bases northeast of London, and the airmen stationed at any one of them had been preparing for the big move that was to come. They all knew they were training for the invasion. The airborne would probably be the first troops to go, the navy would take the foot soldiers to land on the beaches, and the airmen flying the cargo planes would follow them all, delivering the supplies they needed to press on. Yes, they all knew the invasion was in the offing, but they did not know where or when. During all the maneuvers practiced, Jay looked forward to the day when he could get back to London and contact Billy Conway. He also wanted to interview Amy Carter again, to see if he could find a break to prove a false identity.

Billy Conway was just as busy in preparation for the invasion. He would be one of the foot soldiers, a Lieutenant with men under his command. He was doing some special training with classes right in London, giving him a convenient proximity to the hospital where he could call often to see Amy Carter. When he had finished his training for the day, he set out for the hospital, hoping to find that Amy would still on duty. He arrived there just one day after Jay Fisk had met her that first time.

Amy saw him coming down the corridor between the rows of beds, and she thought what a handsome man he was, how he walked with such confidence, such a happy attitude, as if all life was a breeze. What she couldn't understand was why she was beginning to feel a lift in spirits every time she saw him coming. Of all people, she mustn't, under any circumstances, let herself become involved with that happy-go-lucky Lieutenant.

When the Lieutenant spotted her, the brilliant smile that lighted his face made her smile, too.

"You look as gorgeous as ever, Amy, Queen of my life," he said, as he made a sweeping bow in front of her.

Amy laughed, "Stop all that folderol, Lieutenant."

Billy Conway became serious, "It's not folderol, Amy. I love you and I want you to marry me."

Amy was shocked when she heard the proposal. Just the proposal itself was enough to shock her, and to come when she felt she looked like an old harried 33-year-old nurse at the end of a difficult day. She just stood there with her mouth open, and for a moment she didn't say a word; then, "Billy, don't joke with me!"

Billy took her by the arms and held her firmly as he looked her into her eyes and said, "I mean it. Oh, Amy, please say 'yes.' "

"I can't, Billy. I can't do anything like that until after this war. You understand that, don't you?"

"Yes, I know we have the war in front of us, but I feel

I could *survive* it, if I knew you were here waiting for me."

"Okay, Billy, we'll talk about it after the war."

That was as far as Amy would go in answer to Billy Conway's proposal of marriage. She did go out with him that evening, and they saw a movie before Billy took her home. Before they said goodnight, Amy remembered to give him the note from Jay Fisk.

Jay got back to London a few days after his first meeting with Amy Carter. He had been moved in the Norwich area to an air base nearer London and could make the trip after training hours. He was hurrying to get to the train, hoping he could have as much time as possible in London. Another airman decided he wanted to go to London, too, and asked Jay to wait for him. Since the man had not planned the trip, he was wasting time getting ready to go.

"Ward, you're flopping around like a chicken with its head off. Get what you need and let's go!" Jay urged him.

Ward grabbed a few things and said, "Where'd you get such a silly expression about a chicken with its head off?"

"Didn't you ever see a chicken with its head off?"

"Of course! All the ones you buy in a store have their heads off."

"Ward, did you ever chop a chicken's head off?"

"Of course not!"

"Well, I have!" Jay told him, as they jogged out toward the train station. "You chop off their heads and they flop around for a while before they lie still. That's how the expression started."

"Ugh!" Ward grunted.

Jay got a kick out of Ward's reaction and continued, "That's what we had to do before we had chicken for dinner. I had to catch the chicken and chop its head off, and my sister, Roxanne, wouldn't touch it 'til it lay still; then she picked it up by the feet, dipped it into boiling water, after which she would pull out all the feathers."

"Ugh, how could you eat it?"

"No problem," Jay laughed.

Ward and Jay had just gotten off the train in London, when the air raid sirens started shrieking and the bombs began raining down on the city. Ever since spring had come, the Germans were sending their buzz bombs over England. They were timed to run out of fuel at a certain point — usually over London; then they would explode. Tonight they were coming over regularly. Jay and Ward could hear distinctly the rather slow putter of the motor. They knew what was coming when it stopped. They raced into the nearest subway for protection, just as the ground above them swayed from the explosion, leaving them both shaking with the same fear they noticed in all those others around them.

In the underground where Jay and Ward had made their way, they saw, as they had in other Tubes (subways), that they were crowded with people, some seeking refuge from the air raids, while a large number of others lived there, a make-shift residence since their homes had been destroyed by bombs. The subways became their homes. Bunks lined the walls of the stations.

After the explosion above them, as Jay and Ward watched people approaching the train, they saw people walking along toward some destination, just like the two of them. Yet right beside them were others sitting on a cot, drinking their tea, as if the bomb was nothing. Nobody paid any attention to anyone else — it had become so commonplace. Little children played with one another along the side of the tracks as if it were the best playground in the city. Jay watched many grandmothers, sitting close by watching over these children, their parents seeking shelter somewhere else in the city or away fighting in the war, perhaps never to return.

That scary night, Jay did not get to see Amy Carter or Billy Conway. He became separated from Ward in the crowded subway and did not see him again until he was back in the barracks the next day.

Air raids came frequently over England, usually targeting London, but it did not keep Jay Fisk from going there. The raids did not make him forget that he must warn Billy Conway of his suspicious thoughts about Amy Carter.

CHAPTER ELEVEN

CHAPTER ELEVEN

NEW TROOPS from the United States were pouring into Britain by ship and by plane. They trained daily, preparing for the invasion of European continent. They knew the invasion was coming — they just didn't know when or where. All they could do was just train and wait.

An apprehensive atmosphere hung over them all — including Jay Fisk and Bill Conway, as the spring of 1944 progressed. Jay had made an effort to have another visit with Amy, hoping he could find out more about her, as well as to ask if he had gotten any word from his hometown friend, Billy Conway. Surprise awaited him when he found Amy — she was not alone, Billy was with her!

"Well, my friends," Jay sang out, "I won't have to ask if I have a word from Billy, will I?"

"No, and I have, well, almost have, news to tell you, Jay," Billy exclaimed.

"You sound like it's good news. What is it?"

"Amy hasn't said 'yes' yet, but she hasn't told me 'no' either."

When Billy paused, Jay asked, "About what?"

"I asked her to marry me." Billy Conway stood beside Amy Carter and reached to put his arm around her shoulders, but she shied away.

Jay looked at the young, tall, blue-eyed Lieutenant standing there. "One very good-looking young man," he thought, "and Amy Carter, a blond, blue-eyed, beautiful woman. What a handsome pair they make." Jay then thought about another blond, a blue-eyed girl of years gone by. That girl of long ago was Anna Mae Cowan, and her hair was lighter, more of a yellow blond than the ash blond hair of the woman calling herself Amy Carter. Perhaps he could be wrong — maybe they weren't one and the same girl, after all. His thoughts were interrupted.

"I told him we would talk about it *after* the war." Amy looked first at Billy, before she spoke to Jay. She didn't tell either of them her thoughts — about the wounded she tended, those that were brought in every day, many who were beyond saving, about the cries she heard of the ones who had lost their buddies. She had a sinking feeling that neither she nor Billy would survive this war. Amy felt she was safe in saying they would talk about it after the war — and that she would never have to tell Billy Conway that she could never marry him.

The three of them went to a pub for some drinks and a bite to eat, Amy made sure that they were in public places and other people were around them all the time. She did not want to be completely alone with Billy Conway, or with Jay Fisk either, for that matter. Billy wanted Jay to leave, so that he could have some time alone with Amy — and Jay wanted some time alone to talk to Billy.

Amy sensed the latter situation quickly and announced that she needed to get back to the hospital. She was tired since she had had such a busy day, and she expected an equally hectic day on the morrow. They were at a pub not too far from the hospital, so Amy insisted that they not accompany her back to her quarters — she could make it on her own.

She struggled with her thoughts as she walked the few blocks back to the hospital. What was she doing, spending time, any time at all, with Billy Conway! She remembered how she felt the first time she saw him in the hospital. He was the last person in the world she would want to marry — no, that wasn't right — he was the *second* last person she would ever want to marry! That had been over six months or more ago when she got her first glimpse of him, and she was now aware that her heart gave an extra beat every time she saw that tall, handsome man with his captivating smile approaching her day after day. What had happened to her? How had she let her stupid head be ruled by an incorrigible heart? And what was she fearing most now? Could Corporal Jordan Fisk say something to Lieutenant Robert William Conway that would make him think less of her? For the first time in her life she really cared what another man, a boyfriend, really thought about her. She had seen and been courted by several men in her thirty-two years, several that she liked, but never one she honestly cared enough about to even think of marriage. How could she feel differently about Billy Conway? Was it really love?

Amy got into her bed, just one in a room full of beds for many other nurses, all serving their countries in this time of war. She didn't say anything to anybody, just got in bed and buried her face in her pillow. She tried to stifle her sobs, so as not to wake or disturb any around her. But the nurse in the next bed heard her whimpers.

"Amy, what's the matter? What happened to you tonight?"

"Nothing, Mary, I just have the sniffles."

"Don't tell me you're getting a cold?" Mary agonized. "We are so overworked now, what would we do if you can't help?"

"I'll be all right tomorrow," Amy assured her, as she turned over in bed to face the other way.

This was not the most popular pub in London for the American servicemen, but there were a few coming from each of the different branches of service, with the members grouping with others of their own unit. Only at one table, a variation caught the attention of other soldiers. A man in an Air Force uniform was talking seriously with an Army man. An enlisted man with an officer. The Army man was a Lieutenant, yet he seemed to be kowtowing to the Corporal in the Air Force. What could be taking place? And they wondered what could be the reason. Did it have something to do with that gorgeous nurse that had just left them?

When Jay and Billy saw that they were attracting too much attention from other customers in the pub, the two men got up and left. Once outside, Jay said, "Billy, I still think she is Anna Mae."

"So what! I don't care if her name is mud — I love her and I want to marry her. And call me Bill."

"Okay, Bill, but don't you think we should find out why she changed her name?"

"What if Amy isn't Anna Mae, Jay?"

"What if she is?"

"I told you — what difference does it make?"

"Bill, I'm a little paranoid, I guess. When my German friend, Franz, wrote me that there were many Americans sympathizing with Hitler in this war, I couldn't believe it at first; then one acquaintance of Irene's and mine left New York to fight with the Germans *against* the Allies."

"Are you kidding?"

"No. That's why I keep wondering about Amy Carter. I feel so sure that she is Anna Mae Cowan, even if it has been nearly fourteen years. I know her hair is a little darker than I remember Anna Mae's, but mine's darker, too. We were both very light blond when we were in high school."

"I don't believe Anna Mae would ever do anything to hurt her country."

"I don't, either, Bill, but don't you think you better check it out before you up and marry her?"

"How the hell would we check it out, except just asking her?"

"Then ask her! I haven't any better ideas, Bill. You are the Lieutenant and know all the answers about checking people out, don't you? Knowing the big shots in the Army —"

Billy interrupted, "Yeah, yeah! I know just the one to see. He's a Major and he's an Engineer. We worked and fought together all across Africa. I think he's up for a promotion to Colonel."

"I don't know how much time you have. The invasion is coming soon."

"I don't know when, do you?"

"No, but I know the Air Force is doing something down around Dover across from Calais. But you better contact your Major and get started soon with the investigation.

The two men said good-bye, and each went in his own direction, neither of them making any mention of when they would meet again. Jay was eager to get back to base. Surely today there would be a letter from Irene.

Billy was thinking about a check-up on Amy, how he would do it. And how could he do it? He thought there was no way he could ask the Major to check out *Amy*, the head nurse at the London hospital. If they found out that Amy was really Anna Mae, then the Major could find out too much about himself, Robert William Conway — things Billy would rather the Major not know. Or even worse — it might get Amy in trouble! He just couldn't do it!

Jay was eager to get back to base. Surely today there would be a letter from Irene. He hadn't heard from her for over two weeks. Jay was delighted when he got back to his barracks to find that he had, indeed, gotten a letter from Irene. As usual he couldn't wait to read it. It wasn't quite as thick as many of the letters he had received in the past, but at least he did have news from her. She wrote about the work she was doing in her new job, manufacturing war weapons. She told him about the new song, "Rosie the Riveter," that everyone was singing. She said that the girls at work were calling her "Reenie, the Riveter." Then Jay came to the last paragraph: *Jay, dar-*

ling, I hope nothing happens to you, but I read all the time about the war getting worse and worse. Just in case you never come back, don't you think it would be a good idea for you to sign over your savings account to me, now?

That was the second time she had mentioned that. Jay knew how the English people around him felt about their loved ones who were already fighting on the continent, and he knew they dreaded the coming invasion, yet knew it was a sacrifice they had to make. It was no wonder that Irene was frightened. He had no idea what difficulty she might have getting his account signed over to her in case he was killed, especially if there was no identification of his body, and he knew this was happening often. Of course, he would write to have his account signed over to her. He smiled to himself as he re-read the letter, and started his reply to "Reenie, the Riveter."

It was several days before Jay Fisk thought again about Billy Conway or Amy Carter, or even about his getting into London again. Training was getting more intense, the certainty that invasion of the continental coast was coming soon filled the thoughts of all the servicemen. Threads of both excitement and dread occupied their minds — glad they were going to do their part in this war, yet knowing their lives were at stake in the endeavor.

When Jay thought again about Billy Conway, he reviewed their last meeting and realized that neither of them had spoken of a future appointment. Jay grinned when he thought that an agreed date and place was absolutely unnecessary. He knew exactly where he would find Billy — as close as he could get to Amy Carter at every chance available. No doubt about it, Billy was nuts about that girl! The grin left Jay's face as he felt sure that Amy Carter was none other than Anna Mae Cowan, a girl from his home town of Bluewater. She was just the right age and though her hair had darkened a bit, she looked so much the way he remembered her — not too different from the way she looked now, fifteen years later. He needed to get back to London at the first opportunity he had.

The first day that he did not have to fly, Jay took the first train available to London. He headed straight for the hospital, hoping that Billy would be there. He wasn't sure that Billy would be in London, for Jay knew the ground forces were in just the same rigorous activity as the Air Force, preceding the great push. But Jay wanted to know what Conway had found out about Amy Carter's background.

When he arrived at the hospital, he went to the section where he usually found Amy, but Amy was not there, Billy was!

"Glad to see you, friend. Where's your gal?" Jay asked.

"Jay," Billy frowned as he answered, "I think she is avoiding me. The last time I was here, I saw her leaving when she saw me coming. I have the funniest feeling — I think she likes me, but doesn't want to get involved."

"Billy — Bill, if she is Anna Mae Cowan, you know why she is avoiding you, don't you? She probably hates you."

"Jay, when I was real sick, I thought she was Anna Mae, and I kept saying I was sorry, that I didn't want to hurt her, and the nurses told the doctor that I was hallucinating. I wasn't! I really thought she was Anna Mae!"

"Well, then, what have you done about finding out if Amy Carter is really Anna Mae? Did your Major say he could help you find out?"

Billy Conway hemmed and hawed a bit before he replied, "Jay, I want to tell you about the Major."

"Okay, I'm all ears," Jay said as he pulled Billy aside, anxious to know what the Major said. "Let's go find a place to sit down, and you can tell me all about it. Maybe Amy will show up before we leave."

"You should hear the talk going on in our division about what the Major got to do. He and another major and a load of generals were invited to meet the King and Queen and the rest of the Royal family. It seems our Major Huff got all dressed up in his finest uniform and went to Buckingham Palace, where he was taken to a waiting room. There he was introduced to Mrs. Antony Eden, Mrs. Churchill and Lady Astor before being escorted into a large room close by. In that room he stood in line to meet the King and Queen and Princess Elizabeth and Princess Margaret Rose. And then —"

"That was quite an honor! Your Major must be very important. But I want to know what he said about Amy Carter," Jay interrupted.

"Aw, Jay, first I want to tell you about how important my Major is. Okay?"

"Okay." Jay leaned back in his chair, wondering if Billy had spoken to his Major at all. But his Major was an important man, if he got to meet the King and Queen. No wonder Billy was so enthusiastic about it.

"Our Major and his companion, another Major, wandered around a bit after they met the king and queen and found the table of eats. It was while they were helping themselves there that Lady Astor came up to them and said they weren't getting much attention with all the generals around; she thought they would like to meet some young ladies. She told them to just wait and she would bring them along. She was off through the crowd. Our Major remembered that he was married and did not know what Lady Astor had in mind — well, at least he could talk to whomever she might bring around.

"When Lady Astor returned, she had with her Princess Margaret Rose and Princess Elizabeth. The Major said that no one could have been more charming than those two young women. Elizabeth was about sixteen, and Margaret Rose about thirteen." Billy took a deep breath, then continued, "Isn't that something?"

"Yes, it is. Now tell me what Major Huff said when you asked him bout Amy Carter?"

"I want to tell you something funny about Lady Astor. The Major said he heard the story. Mrs. Astor was up in years, but she was full of life and made clever conversation. She had a sharp tongue and once told Winston Churchill that if she were married to him she would put poison in his coffee, and he replied that if he were married to *her*, he would drink it."

"Billy Conway, you haven't said anything to the Major at all about Amy Carter, have you?"

"No!"

"Our time is short! You could be shipping out any day. There is no way I can find out anything about her, except just ask her. Why don't you ask her, if you won't talk to the Major?"

"All she would say is that her name is Amy Carter."

"You are in love with her, aren't you?"

"Yes."

"Then tell your Major that you are in love with Amy Carter, and want to marry her — tell him that she reminds you so much of a girl you knew back in your home town, years ago. See what he says — that couldn't hurt Amy."

Billy became quiet, pulled at the neck of his shirt, and the frown on his face showed his indecision. At first he shook his head, then said, "Maybe I will."

"I've got to get back, Bill. I know we'll all be moving before long and I haven't heard from Irene for days. Maybe I'll get a whole bunch of letters at once. That's what happened to Quent — he's the pilot on the plane I'm on most of the time. He got nine letters at one time after not hearing for several weeks." Jay seemed to have lost interest in Bill's and Amy's love affair for the moment and stood staring off in the distance. He got up from the bench on which the two of them had been sitting and started walking away.

"Jay, I know something is in the offing. I may not see you again. I just want you to know that I have been delighted that we met. I don't know why, but seeing you reminded me of our early years way back in Bluewater more than fifteen years ago, and has made these last few war weeks seem like fun."

"I think the fun is about to be over, Billy. I wish you luck, and hope everything with Amy turns out for the best." Jay patted Conway on the shoulder as he said goodbye, then turned and left the building.

Robert William Conway stood, his back straight, his eyes following the other man as he watched him disappear. He suddenly slumped and tears came to his eyes, as he once again felt like the young teen-age boy, Billy Conway, seeing a another classmate walking away, not on a street in London, England, but down a dusty road leading out of a small town.

Amy Carter had come from the sick bay just in time to see the erect shoulder of the handsome Lieutenant sag, his hand brushing away a tear from his face. Her first instinct was to go to him to see if she could help, but she caught herself quickly — she mustn't see Lieutenant Conway again. She turned to retreat, but the soldier saw her and called out, "Oh, Amy!" as he immediately straightened up and faced her.

Though he tried to present his usual composure, Amy couldn't help but hear the crack in his voice. She delayed her departure and moved slightly toward him as she spoke, "Is something wrong, Lieutenant?"

"I just said goodbye to my friend, Amy. I may never see him again."

"Was it Jay Fisk?"

"Yes."

"Well, from what I gathered in your conversations with him, you hadn't been in touch for years on end anyway. Why the sudden grief?"

"Amy, you wouldn't understand. We were never close friends, but he brought back memories of years long gone by, days when I secretly knew he was one of the best persons alive. He was what I would liked to have been."

Billy Conway now stood directly in front of Amy. He reached out and pulled her into his arms, holding her close.

"No! Let go of me!" Amy almost shouted, as she jerked free of Billy's grip.

Billy was so shocked at her sudden ejection that he jumped back a step or two himself. "I'm so sorry I upset you, Amy, I just want you to know that I love you so much. These last eight months that I have known you have made my life full of hope and desire. I have never touched you because I could tell you were afraid of personal contact. But I've wanted to hold you in my arms, day after day, and kiss you, let you feel how much I love you. I think you like me, too, Amy. Please say you do!" Billy reached out his hand to her, but did not touch her.

Amy took his hand in both of hers, and looking into his eyes, said, "Yes, Billy, I do like you. I like you a lot, but that's as far as we can go with this war. Like I told your friend, Jay, a few weeks ago, we'll wait until after the war."

"Oh, Amy, I believe the time is close when we'll be invading the continent. Today may be the last time I'll ever get to see you." He paused a bit before he continued, "Until after the war." He paused again. "Amy, darling, will you kiss me goodbye?"

Amy suddenly took Billy's face in her hands and kissed him hard on the mouth. By the time Billy had his arms around her, she had hers around him. He held her to him and kissed her on the mouth, then on her forehead, and on her cheeks, until she broke away.

"Goodbye, Billy. Until after the war!" And Amy was gone.

CHAPTER TWELVE

CHAPTER TWELVE

WHEN JAY FISK GOT BACK to his barracks after leaving London, he found most of his airmen friends packing up all their personal belongings. Jay gave little thought to what they told him about getting his stuff together, that is, all that he wished to take with him, for they might be moving out soon. Jay's only thought was finding out if he had gotten any mail from Irene.

He put down the little package he had bought in London with a loving pat. It was a scarf he had bought for Irene, and he smiled as he envisioned the happy pleasure on her face when she opened it. He would have to get it off to her immediately if they were moving again. Right now he wanted to run down the mail carrier and see if he had a letter. He had a premonition that this could be the last time he would be able to send her anything. It was getting late in May, and now seeing the guys all packing, he thought it would not be long before he and his mates would be flying supplies, if not troops, into France, Belgium, Holland or wherever they were ordered. And it was possible that his own unit might be stationed on the continent — he didn't know.

He rushed out the door yelling good-naturedly at his mates that he would be back in a few minutes. He returned very shortly, shoulders drooping and his eyes focused on the ground. He dragged into the tent, flopping down on his bed, and just stared at the ceiling. No letter for him from Irene! It had been days since he had heard from her!

His tent mates sensed his disappointment and made an attempt to get his mind on their own situation right here at the war front.

"Get goin', Jay," the soldier next to him remarked. "Something's going on, a lot of cargo was moved away today. I'll bet we'll be starting our sorties into France soon. That's the reason we all started to get our things together."

"Yeah, Fisk, you can leave that accordion here," one friend teased.

"Better yet — why don't you sell it?" another added.

The bantering did bring Jay up from his bed. He opened his locker and took our the accordion and started playing popular tunes, but played them loudly and grinned at his tormentors. After a few minutes he toned it down, then quit playing and asked, "Where do you think we are going?"

"Not very far — anywhere in England is not very far," said Shelby Stockard, who had just joined the others.

"We haven't received any orders yet, so why don't we get some card games going while we're waiting," one soldier suggested.

Jay still had not been able to forget this intense disappointment in not getting a letter from Irene. He looked around at the others and asked, "Did any of you guys get any mail today?"

Only one airman answered in the affirmative. "I got a letter from my mom and it was written two weeks ago. So don't worry if you haven't heard, Fisk, none of us have gotten a lot of mail recently. I think all our letters are being mulled over long before we ever see them. If your gal said anything that the censor didn't like, you might never see her letter."

"She's more than my gal — she's my wife. What could she say that could not pass inspection?" Jay protested.

"Something big is coming up," another boy a few beds down added to the conversation. "Remember a few days ago, when Brad's box of cookies from his mother had been opened before he got them?"

"I don't think that was inspection," Brad argued, "I think some S.O.B. just wanted to sample those cookies!"

While the uniformed men were bitching about the mail service, their CO came in and announced that they would be moving out before dawn the following morning.

"Can I take my accordion?" Jay Fiske asked.

"No! No! No!" shouted voices from around the group, yet all of them were laughing as they yelled.

"You better leave the accordion," the Lieutenant advised.

Some of the boys were getting out cards; others had split away from the group to seek other activities, and Jay Fisk sat on his bed, playing the accordion softly. After a short time, he put it away and told Stockard that he was going for a walk.

Jay, being in a depressive mood, hardly noted the skies getting darker as he walked way from the barracks toward the town; neither did he pay much attention to his surroundings as he walked farther and farther from familiar signposts. His thoughts were entirely upon his disappointment in not hearing from Irene. He wondered if she was all right, if her new job was too hard for her — more than she was physically able to do. Jay had walked around the town before and, in spite of the semi-darkness, continued his trek away from the barracks, on through the town.

Because of the stormy weather approaching, it had become darker than customary at this time of day. With the lengthening of spring days, darkness of night usually came late in the evening, but with the heavy clouds, the light was fading quickly. Jay knew the blackout would come, but thinking about Irene, he had forgotten all about it and continued walking — and walking. When all the artificial light had disappeared, together with the blackness of the storm clouds, Jay found himself in total darkness, not aware of his exact location. He seemed momentarily shocked into his situation — no street lights, car lights, house lights — all were suddenly dashed into oblivion. Jay was surrounded by blackness! There was not the light one could expect from a clear night's normal sky, for the heavy clouds shut out any illumination whatever. All artificial light had abruptly disappeared.

Jay stopped abruptly and knew he must turn around and get back to his camp. He considered his plight, knowing he had paid little attention to where he had walked, or how far he had come. He turned and started to retreat in the direction that he thought he had come, but in the absolute blackness he became disoriented. He couldn't see the street, the curbs, or know when a block ended.

He needed to get back to the barracks as soon as possible, but he didn't know which way to turn. He reached out his hand to touch the wall of the building next to him, feeling his way along, hoping he was going in the right direction. Even though he was moving slowly, soon his hand met an empty space — the wall had ended. Was it the end of the block? He stepped cautiously forward and found the curb drop-off. Should he reach back to touch the building, keeping his hand on the wall and turn the corner, or go straight ahead?

Jay, for the first time in his life, knew the utter hopelessness that a blind person must often face. But he wasn't blind! He could see if there was one bit of light. Through the tiny slits in covered windows, a tiny ray of light might give him direction, but he could see none. Looking in both directions, around the corner to his right there was no glimmer of light, nor was there one ahead. He remembered the wall he had sidled along must have been a business building where all lights had already been extinguished long before the blackout, so he could expect no bit of light from those windows. He decided to turn the corner while he could still keep his hand against the wall and see how far he could go until he could spot a glimmer, any tiny glimmer of light.

Cautiously he moved ahead, staring into the blackness, searching for a small flicker, a spark, anything to give him guidance. The blackness obliterated his seeing, but his ears were sharp to the least little sound. He listened for the sound of footsteps, but they had vanished along with the illumination.

The darkness wasn't the only obstacle for Jay; the

dark clouds were just a forerunner of the rain that was starting to fall. A late May evening in England did not have the warmth Jay was used to at home. The dampness and the chill of this night made him want to get back to the barracks at once — but which way? He was lost!

When he looked about him, he could remember only one occasion in his life when darkness had so engulfed him — years ago he had traveled with his family to Carlsbad Caverns in New Mexico. On the tour through the caverns they had reached one large cave room where the lights were turned off, and they sat in total darkness. But he wasn't lost then. While he sat with his family for those few minutes, the guide told them they were in complete darkness, not one shred of natural light could reach down into this underground room. It was fun then to experience the blackness, for he knew where he was and that the lights would soon come back on. Jay thought of that happening so many years ago as he slowly shuffled blindly, one step at a time, along a street that he couldn't see, into an unknown quandary.

Jay listened. He was sure he heard footsteps, light footsteps that were ahead of him, and coming in his direction. The footsteps were not as guarded as his had been — they sounded as if they belonged to someone who knew exactly where he or she was going. With the lightness of the steps he assumed that they belonged to a woman. He wondered how that someone could manage so well in this blinding rain and darkness.

He heard the footsteps slow down, as a tiny piercing light appeared. It did not light up the figure behind it, but it dropped down a notch as the walker stepped down from the curb, and a moment later the light shifted a bit as the walker stepped up. The light went out and the walker was now on the same level and on the same block with him. With the light off, she was coming right toward him. Jay wondered if the walker had heard his steps. He had moved so slowly, shuffling along, that he doubted he had made any audible sounds. He was wondering how to get his or her help in finding his way back to the barracks. As the footsteps neared, he stepped out in the middle of the sidewalk, put out both arms, so that no one could get past him.

The thud came, but Jay was ready, because he felt the presence of the person before contact. He felt now that it was a woman, because she was much shorter than he, and he knew that she had been walking with her head down, since her head had hit his chest. She had probably been protecting her face and head from the driving rain. "I beg your pardon, Miss, I need your help."

The woman sprang back, "Get away from me!" She almost screamed.

"I am not going to hurt you, Miss. I—" Jay's plea was cut short as the woman turned to run. Jay caught her by the arm and held her with a firm grip as he continued, "Miss, I am Corporal Jordan Fisk from the United States Air Force, and I am lost in this darkness. I need to get back to my barracks. I saw you had a little light. Please — I need your help."

While he was talking, the tenseness went out of the woman's body, and she emitted a soft sigh of relief — to Jay's consternation.

"Why didn't you say so, Jay?" she said, lightly laughing. "I couldn't see you; that's why I was so frightened. Jay, you can't see me either, but I'm Amy Carter."

"Amy? Amy Carter, what are you doing this far away from your work?"

"I had the day off and came out here to visit my mother's cousin. I should not have stayed so long in this threatening weather. We are just a block over from the underground. I was counting my steps, using my little flashlight to see the curb. I didn't want to fall and break a leg." She took Jay by the arm and pulled him with her as she led him back in the direction from which he had come.

"Where does your cousin live?" Jay asked.

"About two blocks back. When I wrote my mother that I was stationed in London, she asked me to visit her cousin whom she had never seen. The cousin I visited is Paul Carter and his wife Maude. My Grandfather Carter came to America years ago when he was a young man."

While they were walking, Amy was telling him about the visit with her English cousins. Though Jay was listening, his mind was questioning his previous judgement about this young woman. He had been so sure that the nurse, Amy Carter, was none other than a girl who had grown up in his own home town, a girl named Anna Mae Cowan. Yet here she was, visiting relatives named Carter, the same name she also claimed as her own. His thoughts were interrupted as Amy turned on her small flashlight and said, "Watch your step."

They crossed a street and with the help of the tiny light from the flash located the entrance to the underground. Cold and wet, Jay was shivering. Amy was dressed to protect herself from the rain for the few blocks she had to walk to the underground, and had not gotten wet and chilled like Jay.

When they got out of the inclement weather into the underground, Jay for the first time knew where he was — this was the station where he always came to catch a train to London! Though he now knew his location, he continued to shiver.

"We don't want you getting pneumonia, Corporal. This might help you warm up a little bit before you catch your train," Amy said, as she took off her raincoat and wrapped it around Jay's shoulders.

Jay did not tell her that he wouldn't need a train, but he went along with her into the underground to get warm before taking the familiar walk back to the barracks.

The underground here was not as crowded with the homeless as were the subways of London, nor were there as many travelers. A few women and children were waiting for a train. An old man was sitting on the platform, leaning against the wall, as limp as a half-filled sack of flour. Jay recognized some of the people, for he had seen them often, even the old man, when he had come this way en route to London. There was one little girl that he always said "Hi" to. He looked around for her, expecting to speak to her again, but she was sound asleep in an old woman's lap. Other waiting passengers paid them little heed as Amy and Jay walked on past, concentrating more on what they would say to each other.

Jay's thoughts were confused about this woman who called herself Amy Carter. For a fleeting moment he wondered about the family she had been visiting — were they contacts she was scheduled to make for some ulterior purpose and not relatives at all?

"What is the name of your relatives again?" Jay asked.

"They are Paul and Maude Carter, their address is — " She didn't finish the sentence; instead she pulled out a letter from her purse. Jay asked to hold her purse while she was opening up the letter. She handed it to him as she perused the page, then pointing to a line, she continued, "Here is their address. Do you want to copy it down?"

"Yes, I will. Thanks, Amy, but I don't know how or when I can use it. We are shipping out first thing in the morning. I have no idea where we are going." Jay made a note of the address, wondering if it should be checked out. Amy had been very above board in offering the address to him. Did she know he would have no chance to verify the address, or was everything on the up and up?

"Amy," Jay said, after he had written down the name and address of Amy's relatives, "did you tell Lieutenant Conway about your relatives?"

"No. I thought it best not to."

"Why?"

"I can't let myself get that involved with the Lieutenant."

"Again, why? Did you not want him to meet your relatives?"

"Oh, Corporal! Don't ask so many questions. Bill Conway wants to marry me and I cannot marry him. Why then would I want to get him involved with my family?"

"He's very much in love with you, Amy. Of course, you don't want to marry him if you do not love him. I can understand that. Why don't you just tell him so?" Jay was looking Amy straight in the face as he spoke. He couldn't help but see the tears forming in her eyes. "Amy, I believe you do care for him, don't you?"

Amy turned away and said very quietly, "I can't!"

"Why? Amy, why?"

"There's too much about me he doesn't know, and I don't want him to ever know."

For the first time, Jay felt that his suspicions might be true, but he knew she was not carrying a gun in her bag, so he felt safe in blurting out, "Amy, are you a traitor to our country?"

"WHAT!" Amy shouted. The shock on her face was instant. There was no fear in her eyes, just total appall and astonishment.

"Amy, I think you are Anna Mae Cowan and I am puzzled on why you are posing as Amy Carter."

The beautiful face in front of Jay became very solemn. The clear blue eyes, looking into his own, showed intense sadness. Amy Carter said firmly, "Jay Fisk, I am not a traitor to my beloved country, and *I am* Amy Carter." Jay stood there, still looking at Amy with a puzzled look on his face, not knowing what to reply. Amy, too, was silent for a moment, then spoke softly, the sadness in her face reflected in her voice, "I could tell you the story of a girl who was raped long ago, a poor girl whose reputation was ruined, who left the town where she was born and moved into a city where she legally changed her name to Amy Carter — Carter, her mother's maiden name. Never again would that ravaged girl bear the malicious repute, nor be connected to the town where she was labeled a 'slut.' " The emotion in Amy's voice increased as she spoke. "No longer is there any Anna Mae Cowan."

Remorse! Jay Fisk felt welling up inside him, the same pity, the same sympathy he had sensed about that young girl long years before. Tears were gathering in his eyes as he listened to her story. How could he have ever doubted the patriotism and the loyalty of this super nurse who was risking her life for the good of her country. And he should have understood why, at first, she had shied away from the handsome Lieutenant Conway. He was one of the boys who had raped her!

But that was no pitiful young girl standing before him now! Amy Carter was not only a strong young woman, poised and well educated, but strikingly beautiful.

"I am sorry I misjudged you, Amy. No wonder Billy Conway is so in love with you!"

They could hear the rumble of a train approaching. It was the one Amy needed to get back to her hospital. Amy spoke hurriedly, for their time was limited. "Now you know why I cannot marry him."

Jay removed the wet raincoat from around his shoulders and handed it to Amy, not knowing whether she wished to put it back on or to carry it with her on the train. As he gave her the coat he made answer to her statement, "No, not unless you don't love him."

"And what if I did, that would make no difference."

"I believe you do love him, don't you, Amy?" Jay called out as she rushed to get on the train. "You should tell him so, just as soon as you get back!"

"It's too late — too late. He's already ... left ... for ... the ... front." Amy's voice trailed off, as the train pulled out and she waved goodbye.

CHAPTER THIRTEEN

CHAPTER THIRTEEN

JAY WATCHED the train leave, musing about what strange things this war had brought about — such as meeting *on foreign soil*, two of his high school classmates that he had not seen or heard from in years. Strange that they would be stationed in fields of battle so close together. He stood quietly for a moment before he turned to go up the stairs of the underground. He was still cold and wet from the downpour and hesitatant about going out again into the storm, but he had to get back to base and soon.

Now, at least he knew where he was. He felt he could make his way back to the barracks with his eyes closed — was relieved to see that the black cloud had lightened a little and so had the rain. He took the customary route of his frequent junkets, his thoughts again returning to days of long ago, nearly seventeen years, when he had lived in a little town in the foothills of the Ozarks.

Billy Conway, though a year behind him in school, was well known, as were all the students in the small town high school where the enrollment was a little over one hundred students. Jay had never been close friends with Billy. Billy hung out with one boy in particular,

Eugene Smith, an unsavory character, in Jay's thinking. Jay remembered his mother's occasional remarks — that she couldn't understand why a good family like the Conways would let their son, Billy, associate with the likes of Eugene Smith. And then came that uproar when those two boys raped a farm girl. That incident split the whole town in half on who was to blame.

Billy, just sixteen years old, was just driving for fun on the road south of town. He was accompanied by his friend, Eugene. A short distance out of town, they came upon Anna Marie Cowan, a school mate who, after basketball practice, was walking home, a distance of four miles south of town. They offered her a ride, which she accepted with pleasure, since she was tired from basketball practice, and she was also carrying a heavy load of books. Eugene was the first to attack the girl. People often wondered why Billy also became a rapist.

As Jay walked through the dark and the rain toward his base, he still wondered about it. From that day, years ago, Billy and Eugene were never quite as close as they had been before, and Jay remembered what his sister Roxanne had said; somehow after that Billy seemed to change for the better. Roxanne had always disliked Billy because he always teased her about her red hair, but she said when Anna Mae was shunned by many students after that rape episode, Billy talked with Roxanne to let her know that Anna Mae was in no way to blame for what happened, and that the town should not frown upon her. He even asked Roxanne and her pals to befriend Anna Mae and help her become adjusted to the ridicule that was heaped upon her by judgmental people.

Jay realized that he was now thirty-three years old, and that Billy Conway would be about thirty-two. A young, handsome man, a Lieutenant in the army, and in private life a well adjusted and successful engineer in St. Louis. What a success that boy had made of his life after a grievous error he had made in his youth. Jay laughed to himself, as he reminisced on his mother's remark, "He comes from a good family."

The rain was letting up and Jay was nearing the base, but he couldn't put the thought of Billy Conway out of his mind. Amy Carter had said, "It's too late, too late!" Did she mean she had dismissed him from her life entirely, or that he had been assigned to the front for the invasion, and his chances of coming through that battle were slim.

Jay felt he would have liked to further his acquaintance with Billy Conway, even to become good friends after all these years. But there was little chance — their vocations and interests had taken them far apart, one still in the Midwest, the other in the coastal area. And what about Amy Carter? She made her home in Chicago and would probably go back there when the war was over. Jay remembered her aloofness to the young Lieutenant when he first started paying close attention to her, and how over the eight or nine months her reserve seemed to break, and bit by bit he had noticed the light in her eyes when Lieutenant Conway appeared in the hallway of the hospital. Jay felt that she, in spite of herself, had fallen in love with the tall, good-looking officer who kept professing his love for her. Too bad that they had not been able to express their mutual affection before the war had separated them.

Jay's musings came abruptly to an end when he got back to his tent. All his thoughts now were on getting out of his soaking cold, wet clothes and getting warm again.

"Where you been?" greeted him from every bunk in his tent.

"I met a friend in Nottingham, and we talked awhile," Jay told them.

"Was it the talk or the friend that kept you out in that rain so long?" Brad quizzed.

"You would have been in trouble if you had not reported for lights out," Ray Goins advised him. "You would have been AWOL!"

"I got here, didn't I?" Jay shot back. Jay got into his bunk and under covers, thankful that it was not yet time for lights out when he returned, but glad there was no time to explain to his buddies why he was so late returning — that he got lost in the dark!

Tension filled the atmosphere of the whole tent with the knowledge that early tomorrow they were moving! They knew the time had come for a major action in the progress of the Allies! Sleep was needed, yet it was slow in coming to them all.

Miles across England, Lieutenant Robert William Conway was pondering his own situation. He was in the Engineers Battalion of the Ninth Infantry Division, and an advance party of his outfit had come to Liverpool, England, after fighting the Germans across the sands of Africa and the mountains and valleys of Sicily. From

Liverpool they went by train to southeast of London where division headquarters were set up in an old school building in Winchester.

Most of the troops were scattered in towns, estates and in military installations throughout the area, but the Lieutenant was taken immediately to a hospital in London upon their arrival in England, suffering from fever and diarrhea. It was at this hospital where he met the attractive nurse, Amy Carter.

In good health now, Bill Conway was remembering his last few moments with Amy. He came away thinking that she really did care for him. It had been eight months or more since he had first started seeing her, and he couldn't remember the times he had told her of his love. For so long, she had brushed him aside, but he persisted in his attention. Her last words, "After the war," were accompanied by a kiss of warmth and affection. He felt for the first time that he and Amy had a future together.

But first there was a war to be won!

The British and the Americans were arguing (better phrased — discussing) the procedure of the invasion of Europe. Eisenhower, of the United States Army, was trying to keep his own top generals satisfied, Montgomery of Britain, though sanctioning Eisenhower, secretly felt that he himself should be the one to handle that command, because of his own strong and experienced leadership. The British people strongly supported Montgomery in anything he did. They held a little contempt for the Americans — the common description of the American GI — "overpaid, overfed, over-sexed and over here." The Air Force Generals disagreed on the bombing procedure. The British wanted to bomb cities only at night — the Americans wanted to use daylight to better hit exact industrial targets.

General David Eisenhower had become the supreme commander of the Allied Forces on December 24, 1943. There was a serious question on whether General George S. Patton should be given a command after the "slapping" incident in Sicily. Patton, labeled "old blood, guts and glory," was known for his extravagant exhibition. He was quoted as saying in one address to his troops, "No bastard ever won a war by dying for his country. You won it by making the other dumb bastard die for *his* country." Patton, in an uncontrolled mood in Sicily, slapped a GI in one of the evacuation hospitals, and that brought about his undoing as being a top General, but he was a good field commander. His style was break through, move fast. This was what brought about the dislike between him and the British General Montgomery, who was more conservative and precise in command. But Eisenhower recognized Patton's ability on the field of battle and decided to keep him, but he put him under General Omar Bradley, instead of above him as he had been before the incident.

This was the American/British situation around Lieutenant Conway on this June day in 1944. All southern England was full of service men, both American and British, readying for the push across the channel into France. It was decided that the Fourth Infantry Division would follow the first invasion by Airborne troops. The Fourth Division was inexperienced and was to be followed by the experienced Ninth Division, their command to cut off Cherbourg, thereby splitting the peninsula.

Because the Fourth was an inexperienced division, several officers from the Ninth were sent ahead with them to brief and advise where they could. Lieutenant Conway was one of the Ninth chosen to go with the Fourth group. Conway, with a few accompanying officers, embarked on an LST at Plymouth and sailed around to a small port full of ships of various kinds. On the night of June 5, they started across the channel with the other boats and barges. The small boats were towing barges loaded with equipment. The following morning, June 6, a mine-sweeper working on one side of them and with a navy cruiser firing guns on the other, they moved toward the opposite shore, landing through shore bullets and air strafing the next day

The Fourth Division was fighting its way toward Cherbourg, trying to reach Ste. Mere Eglise. Billy Conway, following them, side-stepped land mines and kept coming upon the dead bodies of those who had not made it moments before. The airborne troop landing must have surprised the Germans, for Billy and his comrades found the enemy living quarters just as they left them, with food on the tables, camouflaged vehicles and the remains of the Allies airborne parachutes on trees and houses. One paratrooper had landed on the roof of a house and had used the ropes of it to slide down from the roof to the ground.

As the Allied Airborne troops moved ahead, step by step, they found streets and roads blocked by broken equipment, logs from fallen trees and other debris that their gliders had penetrated. The Fourth followed close behind. Conway would lean down to some of the bodies he found lying in the battle path, whether it was a fallen American or a German. If the prostate soldier was still alive, he wanted to give aid. He found it hard not to feel sympathy for the German boys, too, when he saw their young faces.

After several days, some of the airborne troops who had led the way, weary and worn, were straggling back to join the soldiers of the Fourth. Along with Billy Conway, they found an old barn where most of them dropped off to sleep almost immediately.

Billy wanted to ask these paratroopers if they knew Jay Fisk in the Air force, but he was too tired to ask, and they would have been too tired to answer. Bombings and bullets were routine, shelling was all around them. He wondered if Jay had survived the flights he made. Was Jay flying only cargo, not troops? As his exhaustion took over, the frown on Billy's face faded as he dreamed of Amy Carter's smile, and his tired mind and body fell into deep slumber.

The Ninth Division arrived and Lieutenant Conway and his men were back with their own, having served their purpose in the first few days with the Fourth. They proceeded with their assignment, in the black of night — cutting through fragments of German units, through hedge rows, past anti-tank guns.

Hardly a week had passed in the Allied invasion operation of Europe, before Germany launched their first V-1 rocket on England. But it did not hinder the Allies' determination to proceed in their assignment to capture

Cherbourg. Their goal was not accomplished in days, but it was three full weeks of intense fighting before the Germans abandoned that city.

When Cherbourg fell to the Allies, Lieutenant Conway, along with some other Americans, was able to obtain some radios from captured Germans. They eagerly listened to what news they could get of the war. The news all came from the British Broadcasting Company, praise leveled mostly toward the British, even though the Americans far outnumbered the British soldiers fighting on the continent. Much attention was given to Montgomery's advance on Caen, though he didn't get there until after the Americans had run the Germans out of their way.

On September 8, 1944, the first German V-2 Rockets fell on London! The Allied troops all heard the news, not just from the radios they had acquired, but from the soft voice of the persuading German temptress, telling them to surrender, as that was the only way they could save their loved ones at home. Lieutenant Conway and his men knew that death and destruction were left by that rocket, and Conway's thought was of Amy Carter, and he wondered if she had survived the devastation. He had no way of finding out, and he and his men fought even harder against the unrelenting German Army. Paris had been liberated, and Brussels was freed by the British eight days later. Surely the end must come soon.

The cold and fog of the autumn season was approaching, and some days were already chilly. Billy wondered if they could get this war over before winter set in. Their next assignment was called the Ardennes Offensive. Through forest and underbrush they advanced, digging trench holes in hard ground, fighting fatigue as well as enemy soldiers.

In early June Jay Fisk's Air Force group moved from their location northeast of London to a southern coastal area, and practice flights were carried out, preparing for the eventful day of the invasion. The Airborne troops would be flown in first. Some would go in on gliders, other dropped from troop carriers. Jay was not assigned to the troop carriers, but stood by to follow with cargo to provide supplies for the troops.

The crew of the C-47's were given thin cloth maps of France, showing the areas where they were to drop the supplies. The cargo could be ammunition, food, medicine or any other kind of equipment that was needed. Jay never knew from day to day what they would carry or the target for their drop.

He had been in the south of England a few days before he received mail. He heard nothing from Irene, but he did have two letters from his sister, Roxanne.

In the first letter, she told him about her brother-in-law being shot down in the ocean near Tokyo. He was not killed, but was recuperating in a hospital in Hawaii. When he was patched up enough, he would be ordered back into the service. Jay read again the story of his injury:

> *Clay was stationed on a ship in the Pacific and was in a plane on the way to drop a bomb on Tokyo, but before they reached their destination, their plane was fired upon. It caught fire, and the crew members that were still alive bailed out. Only four of them made it to the ocean, and they only*

had one little boat that they inflated. One boat would hold only two of them, so they took turns, while two were inside, the other two were in the water hanging on. Sharks were thrashing around near them, and one attacked Clay while he was in the water. It left a big slit in his left leg.

They were picked up by the rescue team before any further damage would come to them, but Clay said he could never get over seeing his buddy burning to death as he fell from the plane.

Jay stopped feeling sorry for himself because he had not heard from Irene and knew how lucky he was to be where he was and not in any trouble at the present. And he did not have to fly every day.

He opened the other letter and was surprised the news it held about someone who was fighting in the European theatre. Roxanne told about news of one of her acquaintances who was serving in the Third Division.

Our friend is a First Lieutenant and writes his folks about battles in Africa and Sicily. He and his Division were especially noted for their victory at Anzio. ________________

____.

Jay wondered what Roxanne had written that had been blacked out. He knew that American soldiers fighting in Italy were waging war against a great number of German soldiers, and that it was making their own task less impossible.

The Italians had declared War on Britain and France

in 1940. In September 1943 they surrendered to the Allied Third Division, and a month later joined the Allies, declaring war on Germany. But the Germans still held positions in Italy, and the Third Division, having won a fierce and deadly battle at Anzio in January, was invading southern France. While Billy Conway was fighting with the Ninth Division for the break-through at St. Lo, the United States troops were closing in on Paris.

Jay continued with the rest of Roxanne's letter, which told of her two little girls doing well and her additional responsibility in caring for their sister Rowena's little boy while his mother worked. Rowena's husband was in the Merchant Marines.

Jay got ready to respond to Roxanne's letter. He wanted her to get in touch with Irene, to be sure Irene was all right. He couldn't understand why he hadn't heard for a couple of weeks, when she had been so good, writing every day or two.

"Be ready, Jay," Quentin Peterson tapped him on the shoulder, "we fly out tomorrow."

"Have you told Ray and Stack?"

"Yes,"

"Do you know where we drop?"

"Not yet. We'll be given our cargo and destination in the morning."

Early stirrings in Jay's tent the following morning were raunchily interrupted by an airman who poked his head under the flap, and announced, "Go back to bed, you fly boys — you aren't goin' anywhere!"

"Don't give us that crap; you're just trying to get us

in trouble, aren't you?" Shelby Stockard shouted back.

His head still inside the tent, the messenger said in a more serious voice, "No, no. I just heard that you won't be makin' the trip."

"Now where did you hear that?" Jay asked.

"Why, a little bird told me!" the messenger grinned as he replied.

"Naw, tell us where you heard that!" the pilot, Ray Goins insisted.

"I'm not kiddin' you guys. I just heard it a few moments ago, and when I asked where the Major got that information, that's what he told me."

"Told you what?"

"That a little bird told him!"

By this time the tent full of airmen were dressed and ready to report for active duty. They pushed their messenger out of the way and headed for their assigned planes. As soon as they got to their cargo loaded planes, they noted that the *troop carriers* were still on the ground.

The procedure was for the troops to fly to the destination where they would be dropped, and the cargo planes would come later with the necessary supplies.

Jay Fisk and the other two in his flight crew followed their pilot, Lieutenant Quentin Peterson, as he looked for their commanding officer.

After Peterson found him, he saluted, as did the others, and the pilot said, "We were told that we were not flying as scheduled. It is a clear day, and the only explanation that nut gave us was that a little bird told him!"

The Major laughed hard, and replied, "Yes, and be thankful for that little bird!" Several other airmen had gathered around, and the Major continued. "See all these troops lined up to take off on their mission? They were ready to go when that little bird," and he pointed to a pigeon that was perching atop a birdcage close by, "flew in with the message that the Germans had news of our plans and were waiting to ambush us. That little bird has saved many lives today!"

That day, the American Air Force boys named the homing pigeon GI Joe.

All the airmen and troops were asked to stand by for further orders. Jay and his companions returned to their tent wondering when they would be called and where they would be sent. They knew the missions they had already flown through the last weeks, even months, had been dangerous, but as the intensity of the war kept increasing with the German bomb blitz over London, along with the number of the dead and wounded of their own being returned from the continent, they could never cease to wonder about the good fortune that "little bird" had brought to them.

The good fortune brought about by the homing pigeon was welcomed by all those whom it affected, but within hours after the gaiety had subsided, rumors were circulating around among the airmen, including Jay Fisk, that that "little bird" had brought more news to the military authorities than was written in the message. The written message had told them to hold up their flight plans because the Germans were lying in ambush. What was not in the note was how did the Germans know what the Allied flight plans were for that day!

Somewhere along the line in Britain someone had leaked the information to the enemy, just as on the continent, the Allied handler of the pigeon had obtained information to warn the Air force to hold the flights on that certain day. Where was the leak in the Allied forces? Was it just an unintentional leak, or was there an enemy infiltrator in their midst?

Jordan Fisk, Jr. was of an easy-going, tranquil disposition, and he had even surprised himself when he first entertained the thought about Amy Carter's identity being a mask for perhaps some undercover activity. After the meeting he had with her on that dark day in the little town of Eli, he had immediately forgotten what suspicions he had previously held. He didn't feel happy with himself at all when again his thoughts reverted to doubting her. But he said nothing to his buddies, nor did he enter into the talk that was taking place around him. He just listened.

"Why aren't the Big Shots disturbed about German spies over here?"

"Who says they're not?"

"You'd think they'd be around here questioning everybody, wouldn't you?"

"Okay, Brad, then where were you when you went out the other night by yourself?"

"I was in the first pub at the end of Main, and I wasn't alone. Check it out. I was drinking with that buxom lass with the big blue eyes," Brad explained.

"And who are you to question?" Lieutenant David Harvey asked Shelby Stockard, who had posed the first question.

"Maybe it's my fault," the young airmen, Alan McMann, said. "I went to the church when I found out we were going to fly that day, and I told the minister, priest, or whoever was in that church that I was afraid, and I wanted to pray and be blessed."

"What's wrong with that, Alan. We all knew we were flying out, but none of us knew where we were going, so what could you have told the minister that could hurt?" Jay finally broke into the conversation.

"I just said that a lot of us were heading out the next day."

"That couldn't have hurt anything. Everybody knew that," several of the men spoke together.

Jay's thoughts were again about Amy Carter. He didn't say anything to the other airmen around, but he somehow felt he had to get to a higher authority and tell about Amy being in that little town of Ely, so far from London, and saying she was meeting cousins. He wondered if he would have that opportunity before they got their orders to fly again.

Before the men in the tent were finished talking of the "little bird" and the message it carried, they got the order to be ready to fly out the next morning.

Jay, in flight uniform, the small cloth map of France tucked into his pocket, watched the troop planes take off. As they flew into the distance, Jay thought of the "little bird." only these weren't little birds, they were big birds, and they reminded him as they got smaller and smaller in the blue skies of a flock of Canadian Geese flying south for the winter, and he knew that he, too, would be following shortly.

But he could never imagine his own fate, or that of the "big bird" which he would navigate across enemy territory.

CHAPTER FOURTEEN

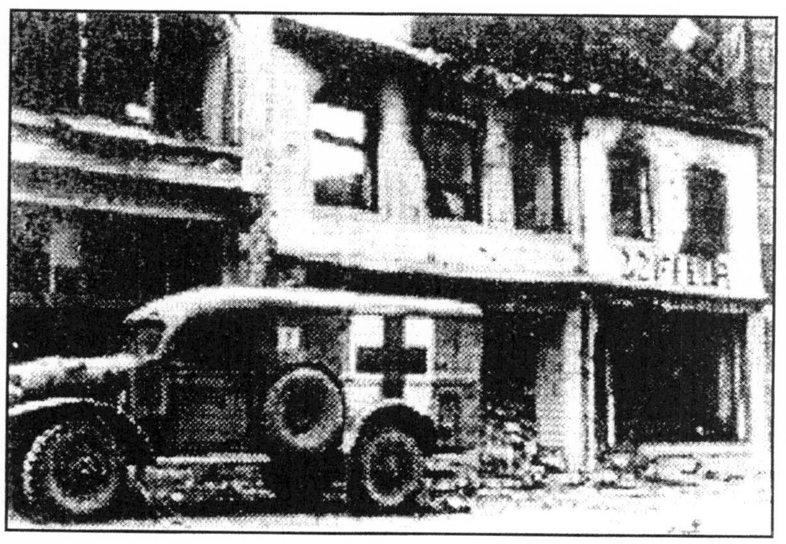

CHAPTER FOURTEEN

THE BLUE SKIES on that day made the prospect of flying a pleasure, not a chore. The four airmen talked of the unusually clear skies as they looked up into the heavens before boarding the plane they had nick-named Fat Charlie. Quentin Peterson was the pilot and Ray Goins, the co-pilot, sat next to him. In back of them were the mechanic, Sergeant Shelby Stockard, and the navigator, Corporal Jordan Fisk, who was also in charge of communications.

They had flown across the channel many times, always just as a lone cargo plane, not part of a squadron. Their plane had encountered gunfire on various occasions, but had been fortunate enough to receive no hits.

"The skies are so blue —" Ray's praise was cut short by Quentin.

"The better to see you with, my dear."

"Oh, the big bad wolf," Jay Fisk laughed.

"Don't laugh about it, Jay," Shelby shook his head, "That big bad wolf is behind a German gun."

"Do you think they know we are heading right at them?" Ray wondered.

"If they have any sense, they know we are! They know that our troops landing ahead of us have to have supplies," Quentin remarked, then in a more brooding tone continued, "I wonder how many of them made it."

"Do you guys think the leak that our 'little bird' uncovered is the same leak who may notify the Germans of our coming?" asked Ray Goins.

"Has there been any news that the leakage was discovered?" Quentin asked.

"I have not heard any such news on the radio," Jay told the others, "but leak or no leak, I expect the Germans are waiting to shoot us down, no matter where we fly. They need these supplies as much as we do. The last word I heard, the Germans are in short supply of food, ammunition and all other kinds of equipment." Jay said this to his companions, but he didn't mention the other thought that kept creeping into his mind — Amy Carter, and the question on what was she doing in Ely, so far from her work assignment!

The four airmen were silent for a few minutes before Jay, as if thinking out loud, said, "I wonder what kind of weather those troops found when they landed. The autumn months can be cold in this part of Europe, especially if they get in the mountains."

"I don't think the weather will be their problem," Stockard told him.

"I think they were dressed for any kind of weather — weren't they?" Quentin's statement was also a question, as he looked down on the uniform he himself was wearing.

"I expect they had more substantial clothes for cold weather than what we have, since they have to stay over there. We get to go back after our delivery, so we aren't supposed to be exposed to cold weather," Ray said.

"But we do have good warm jackets with us," Stockard said, just before they heard the first gunshots from far below.

Conversation ended immediately as each airmen's attention went quickly to his task. Since they were some distance still from where they were to drop the supplies, Quentin followed the flight pattern they were given but soared ahead to a higher altitude.

Once outside the realm of gunfire, the conversation among the four men again became trivial, almost frivolous.

"In France, they speak French, in Germany they speak Deutsche." Stockard laughing, turned to the communications expert, "Jay, what do they speak in Belgium — Belge? Belgie?"

"Okay, funny guy! The Belgians have two official languages, Flemish in the northern section and French in the southern region, but they speak German and English, too, so if you get caught in Belgium you can undoubtedly find someone who will tell which way to go to get away from the Germans — just don't ask a German soldier."

"You're behind time, boy! Have you forgotten that the British are in control there now?"

"The British took Brussels last month — that doesn't mean they have the rest of the country. I'll bet there are plenty of German snipers still around, so you better be careful!"

"Listen, you guys," the pilot, Quentin Peterson, said in a much more serious tone, "We are going to have to fly lower very soon to drop this cargo. If we get enough flak, we may have to bail out. You know the rules we've talked about before. If any of us are together when we bail out, we can stick together, but if we find ourselves alone, we are not to spend time looking for one another — each of us must be on our own trying to reach safety. Understand?"

"I would hate to be alone. I think I would try to find one of you," Shelby Stockard said.

"I know just how you feel, Stock. I feel more antsy today than I ever have before, but you heard me, Stock!" Quentin answered, "We've gone over this before. You can't succumb to panic — nor to any juvenile heroics either. We have to fly across enemy territory. If we get badly hit, keep in mind what I said!" A few minutes later, with information from navigator Fisk, Quentin called out, "It's almost time to drop our load. We're on our way down!"

Almost as soon as the C-47's descent began, flak around them increased. Within minutes there was a burst of fire ahead of them. Peterson yelled out, "Be ready to bail out if we get hit!" He pulled up on the yoke to get the plane above the stream of fire, but it was too late to avoid all the shots headed their way.

"I smell smoke," Jay yelled, "can you see any fire?"

"I think we were hit back there. Stock, take a look around," Ray turned to look back as he shouted.

"We haven't too many miles to go before we drop this cargo. Hang on back there," the pilot instructed. Another burst of fire hit their plane and Quentin called out, "Bail out! Bail out! We're on fire!"

Shelby Stockard was the first to bail out. With the

speed of the plane, it had gone miles farther before Jordan Fisk had time to follow. Shortly before his descent into a forest of evergreens, he saw in the distance their plane plunging downward, engulfed in flames. Jay saw no indication that either the pilot, Quentin Peterson, or the co-pilot, Ray Goins, had been able to get out in time. Had they bailed out before the plane was a ball of fire? Taking the necessary steps for his own landing, he wasn't watching to see if either of them had escaped before he saw the flaming plane. And where was Stock? He hadn't seen him landing either.

Jay was alone, alone and slowly dropping down into enemy territory! His slow landing, he knew, was visible to the gunners who had shot them down. He wished he could hurry the parachute's progress, so he could get out of it quickly and do what he could to find some point of safety before the German soldiers were upon him.

He wanted to get down and have time to bury the parachute. He wanted to get into hiding before the enemy had time to catch him. Whether the wind came from nature or its velocity increased by the passage of descending plane, Jay didn't know, but he was thanking his lucky stars that it had been strong enough to blow him into the forest. The forest was located on a series of hills which helped cover his visibility. His moment of gratitude was short lived, however, when he found that he and his parachute were tangled up in the limbs of a tree, high above the ground. On impact, his left foot had broken a small limb, and Jay felt a stabbing pain as the sharp edge of the broken limb pierced his left thigh.

The minutes were flashing by as he tried to untangle himself, get out of the parachute harness and reach the safety of the ground. Though he could feel the pain where the broken limb had slashed his leg, he paid little heed — his thoughts were to get himself out of the parachute quickly and to the ground. After he had clambered down the tree, he took time to look at his leg. Though he had felt the smarting from the moment of injury, for the first time he noticed the gash in his left thigh was bleeding. He glanced up at the tree and saw that he had left a trail of blood on his climb down. He knew he had to stop that bleeding before he could go on. He mustn't leave a trail of blood to be followed. What could he use? He couldn't take the time to climb up the tree and cut a piece of the parachute to bind up his wound. He quickly removed his shirt, took off his undershirt and used it as padding to wrap around his leg. For the first time he was sorry he wasn't wearing a tie. It would have come in handy for a tourniquet, but he used his belt instead. He placed the belt on the outside leg of his pants so he could readily adjust it if necessary to keep it firm.

He looked forlornly up at the parachute snarled up in the tree and knew there was no way he could get it down. All he could do was just leave it, and try to find a hiding place. But hiding would have to be temporary — he couldn't hide forever — he had to get out of this area, try to get to Allied territory of some sort. He listened to the popping of gunfire, which helped him select the way he should go. It being a sunny day, he could figure directions, and he knew which way they were headed to drop the cargo. Using the sun to point the way, he moved as fast as he could toward where he thought their cargo should go. He had not considered any immediate hiding until he heard sounds of the approaching enemy.

It wasn't long before he recognized the faint sounds of German voices, probably at the site of the tree and entangled parachute. Had they seen or captured Stockard? There was no way he could risk his own safety to find out! He hoped the Germans would take time enough to remove the chute from the tree — that would give him time to put more distance between them. But as he knew, those soldiers weren't stupid — they were searching for him, not trying to retrieve a mangled chute. The voices were getting stronger by the second, and Jay wondered what he could do, how he could avoid capture. The brightness ahead made him aware that the woods were getting thinner and open ground was not far away. Where could he go, where could he hide?

He had passed a small stream several yards back. He saw that it ran away from the direction he wanted to go, but there was no other terrain around that could offer any form of shelter. From what he could make of the search going on behind him, even as distant as it was, he believed the German soldiers had spread out in many directions in their search for the airmen from the downed plane. Again he was wondering about Stockard — had he gotten away? Jay prayed, if you could call it prayer, that Ray and Pete had gotten out of the burning plane before it went down.

He came to the edge of the forest and could see a village in the distance across the open stretch of land, but he knew he had no chance whatever of getting across the open fields without being seen. Nor did he know how people in the village felt about the war, whether they favored the Germans of the Allies. He wished there had been more leaves on the trees, perhaps then he could have just climbed a tree and the leaves would have shielded his presence from the line of searchers passing by, but it was autumn, and many trees were already bare. Only the evergreens had given him the cover he needed this far.

He didn't have time to stop and think about what he could do. Any action he must take immediately; he hoped it would be the right one. He could see a line of brush and small trees ahead in an open field. From his long ago boyhood experience on a farm he knew that kind of growth had to be along a stream. Perhaps that was the stream he had passed awhile back. He hoped he was far enough ahead of his pursuers to get to the stream before they were out of the woods in time to see him. He hunched down, half crawling, half running across the meadow. The long brown grass gave him cover as he kept close to the ground, making his way for the last few yards to the line of trees. As he expected, those trees and the brush did line the sides of a creek. The bank was muddy, and Jay hesitated to get into the water. He lay there, hidden by the tall dried grass, examining his wound. It had not yet bled through the bandage, in spite of his vigorous activity. As he thought about climbing down into that cold water, it made him shiver all over.

Through this whole escape attempt, his leg hurt, not a lot, but enough that he worried about an infection if he didn't give it proper care, but he had no time to do anything about it now. He didn't think he had left any sign of his passage through the grass, no broken-down trail, and no drops of blood. He had already moved beyond the tree line to the edge of the water before he heard the commotion in the forest. He dropped quickly into the water and found a place to hide behind the roots of one tree where the ground had washed away. He hoped he could squeeze in and stay quiet enough until the search party had passed. He hoped his shaking from the cold would not be heard. When he crawled in, a little animal dashed out of the hole. Jay was worried the trackers would hear the splash and rush to the spot. He tried to crawl back farther into the space behind the exposed roots of the tree, hoping there would not be another little furry creature to give away his hiding place.

The mass of voices that Jay heard were from German soldiers as they came out of the forest and gathered near the stream, and it frightened him. He felt they would find him if they looked around the stream at all. About that time a man in a row boat came paddling up the creek. The Germans approached him and flooded him with questions. Jay was glad that he could understand what they were asking.

"We are looking for an enemy soldier. His parachute is back in the woods. We shot down his plane and he seems to have disappeared. We can't let him escape. Have you seen him in this area?"

"No, I have been a little ways down the stream fishing. I hoped to get something for our supper. This is where I tie up my boat, to the roots of this old tree."

"If you see anyone that you don't know, you must come to us immediately," the soldiers warned the man.

"Of course!" the man answered.

Jay could hear the German soldiers retreating. He kept his breathing as quiet as possible, hoping the man, still standing in the boat, could not see him huddled in the dark behind the roots. Jay couldn't hear the soldiers parting remarks as they moved on, but he did hear the boatman's answers as he tied up his craft to this particular tree. He explained that he used this tree because it was closer to his farm house than the dock upstream near to the town.

He laughed as he told the soldiers, "One of these days a heavy rainstorm or wind will topple this old tree and I'll have to find another anchor for my boat." The soldiers laughed with him, and their dying laughter was the last thing Jay heard from his pursuers. The man called after them that he would report immediately if he saw any enemy soldiers in the area.

After his last words to the soldiers, the man, still standing up in the boat, took much more time than Jay thought necessary to carefully check the rope and the knot where he had tied the boat to the root of the tree. Then he shook it, as if to check again to see that the boat was well fastened.

When the man shook the root, a bit of dirt filtered down over Jay's head and shoulders. Jay wished he would move on. His leg was hurting and he felt cramped and cold, tightly curled up in this skimpy space. Instead of moving on, the man started talking in a low, matter-of-fact voice, as if he were talking to himself. "You can come out now, but don't follow me, nor go anywhere near our village. Go in the opposite direction. Our village is near Strasbourg, and the Germans are all over this area." He did look into the sprawling roots as he spoke, but kept his eyes looking upward as he mouthed the words. He moved toward the middle of the boat where he stepped up on the largest bare root and hoisted himself out of the boat and onto the bank.

The heavy step on the root caused much more soil to fall from around the stable roots of the tree. Jay's legs, as well as his head and shoulders, were covered with the loose, brown soil. At first Jay almost cried out when the dirt hit his face. The last thing he needed was to have his mouth and eyes filled with mud and dirt. When it first started falling, he was a bit disgruntled, but suddenly he noticed a respite in his chill — that layer of warm loam around his shoulders was like a blanket, warding off the cold of the air around.

When he was sure the man had gone, Jay crawled out of the hole, climbed into the boat, avoiding the water as much as possible to keep from washing off any of the dirt. He hoped there was enough brown soil to camouflage his uniform, if not close up, at least if seen by anyone at a distance. He looked around and decided he could not move anywhere until after dark. He pulled loose some of the tall withered grass near the bank and put it in the boat. He could use it, if necessary, to cover himself as he lay in the boat. He did not want to cover himself yet, because the few hours of the remaining sun could help dry out his clothes and perhaps warm him up a little. As he lay there, he fought sleep. He dared not go to sleep! He must keep awake, listening for any sounds that came near. As soon as night fell, he would get moving, away from the village he had seen in the distance. He was so tired and hurt that he almost dozed off anyway, but thoughts of the whereabouts of his companions kept creeping into his mind and brought him back to consciousness.

After a short time of lying dormant in the boat, Jay felt it was foolish to remain here. He would fall asleep in spite of himself and would be spotted by anyone coming this way. He could not be sure any approaching noises would wake him in time for him to quickly hide behind the roots again. The boatman had spotted him, so it wasn't a very good hiding place. The only reason he could be sure that the Germans hadn't found him was the word of the fisherman that no one had been seen in the area.

Jay was so nervous, he was biting his nails and he couldn't lie still. He carefully peeked out from under the dead grass with which he had covered himself. He peered through the thin leafless trunks of the bushes and small trees to see if there was any movement across the field beyond the forest. He couldn't detect any motion of any kind, not even a farm animal. He wanted to get over to the other side of the creek, but he didn't know how deep the water was, and he didn't dare to get any wetter than he already was. He had been able to get behind the roots without getting water above his waist, and he had been able to keep his gun and ammunition dry. If he waded across the stream now, it might be too deep to protect his weapon. But he couldn't go back toward the forest from which he came! He would just have to borrow the boat and paddle across the stream, tie the boat to a little tree on the other side. He hoped the boatman would understand his problem and not be too upset. If the Germans came back, however, and noticed that the boat was on the other side, they would know that someone other than the boatman had crossed. But he had to take that chance. Again he was debating whether he should go now or wait until dark. Likely the Germans wouldn't notice the boat's position until the next day, so he could wait until dark. He wished he knew whether his trackers had returned to the forest or had progressed onward across the field.

He was hungry and thirsty and his leg didn't feel good, though it wasn't as bad an injury as he first thought. He looked at his watch and was happy to note that it was still running, even though it had gotten a little wet when he had slunk under the tree roots. It was nearly four o'clock in the afternoon and he knew it wouldn't get dark as soon here as it did in England, but at this time of the year it would be dark in a couple of hours, even dusk before that time. He would be safer waiting a little longer, waiting for the enemy searchers to get farther away. He knew the search would not stop, not until they had captured him, dead or alive. He wondered, if they found him, would they take him as a prisoner or just shoot him. And he thought again of his companions — what had happened to Stock, Ray and Pete? He must quit fretting about them, for there wasn't anything he could do to help them. He must think of something pleasant — IRENE! Dear Irene!

It was always pleasant to think of Irene! In those

pleasant thoughts, he now understood why she wanted to have his account put in her name, and he agreed, it was a wise move, for he wasn't sure he would ever get out of this precarious situation. As he thought of her, he wondered how she was getting along — what was the weather like in New York. Was it as cold there as it was here in France at the end of October? He shivered as he thought about it. He needed to move about just to keep warm. That was when he noticed that the sun no longer was giving him any comfort as it had a short time ago. A cloud had appeared, not a big one, but it had cut out the warmth he had first enjoyed. Maybe that wasn't all bad. Without the sun, the clouds would hasten the darkness of evening and he could get moving sooner.

The appearance of clouds was not the only thing that expedited Jay's departure from the creek and the boat. It meant that there might be rain, and he couldn't stand to get soaked in a cold rain — he had to find shelter somewhere. Then there was the danger of dusk, for that was the time when farmers in the area would begin to appear to care for their flocks. At first Jay thought he mustn't be seen, then it occurred to him that it wouldn't matter too much — he would be just another being moving about at this time of day, and if he kept his distance from anyone, his uniform would not be noticed. He untied the rope that fastened the boat and used the paddles to propel him across the stream. Tightly fastening the boat to a tree on the other side, Jay jumped out, looked in both directions and crouching in the meadow grass, hurried on his way toward the west and away from the boatman's village. He wondered which way Stock, Ray or Pete had fled. What was his chance of running into one of them?

He slowed down when he remembered that the boatman had said his village was close to Strasbourg. That couldn't be! Strasbourg, France was a long distance farther than where they were to drop the cargo, and he felt sure it was twice the distance they had flown. He must have misunderstood the name of that village in the distance. Maybe he should try to get to whatever town or city it was. His Munich school friend of years ago, Helene, Helene — what was her other name? Helene Dolmet! She lived in Strasbourg, or in a suburb of that city. But he was sure he was a long way from there. Why had the boatman said Strasbourg — to confuse him, to get him to make the mistake and wander into a German stronghold?

As he lay in the boat, he kept remembering Helene. She had fled Munich to get away from the Hitler regime. He wondered if she were still in Strasbourg or had she been arrested with the rest of her family. But he couldn't dwell on that now, he had to find help, but not in that little town, nor in Strasbourg — for he knew he just couldn't be in that territory. Strasbourg should be miles and miles away from where he had dropped down. Whatever town it was, the boatman said it was infested with the Germans.

Jay wished he knew which direction to go to get away from the danger. If he could come across a highway with markings, he could learn from the signs which way to go. But the main roads were all traveled by the military, and the military in this region was German. Jay didn't know whether he would be safer trying to get to a town, or heading out into the hinterland — and which direction to go. He thought he was at least two or three miles or more from the boatman's town, and after dark he would have several hours to get away from there. He didn't know anything better to do than continue in the direction away from the town the boatman had called Strasbourg. He wondered what city it was — where in France was it located?

He looked everywhere as he walked, keeping a safe distance from anyone he saw, not knowing if they were of the French Resistance or German sympathizers. What he needed to do was to get rid of this uniform, then he could pass as French or German — he hoped. How well he could speak French was dubious. He could read it very well, because his job at home had kept him up to date in reading many languages. He felt his German was perfect, because he had kept in touch with German-speaking Americans for years.

Through the next few hours, Jay looked for signs that he hoped would help him find the way to a city, *any city or town*. He had turned his jacket inside out, hoping to disguise the United States uniform, should he be seen by anyone, though he kept out of sight as much as possible. After a while he sighted something ahead of him. It was after nine o'clock at night and he could barely see lights ahead, coming from a few windows and dimmed street lights. He kept to the edge of the settlement, sneaking his way from street to street. Skirting the activity around the area was much harder than what he had expected. He dodged in and out of one edifice to another until he could get a glimpse of a huge residence.

It was the most lit up of any house in the block, but all the houses on both sides of the street were showing signs of much greater activity than the other places he had already passed in the town. He listened to the people speaking as they passed his hiding place in a corner garden. They were not speaking French; they were speaking German! The mansion looked as if it had become the headquarters of the German Army in this place.

"Poor, poor French residents!" Jay spoke lowly to himself, hardly a whisper. He wondered what had ever happened to them, or were they German sympathizers? Had they been arrested, or had they acquiesced and become a part of the ruling invaders. "Poor people —" but that thought was quickly replaced by "Poor Jay! And how am I going to get out of this mess?"

Moving slowly so as not to attract any attention, Jay moved out of the area as soon as he could. He took just a block at a time, being sure no one could see him move from one dark spot to another. He had to get out of the city environment and into the country. He thought about the total darkness in which he had gotten lost back in England. If he got lost here, he had no hope of ever reaching safety.

It was after midnight when he found his way into the countryside, and Jay drew a sigh of relief when no one else seemed to be moving. Working his way across fences and fields, he finally saw a farm house with a good-sized barn in the distance. It looked very inviting. If he could get to it, perhaps he might find something to eat and drink, and also have a place to hide and keep warm. He moved slowly as he approached the barn. He didn't want to set any dogs barking or disturb any other animals that might awaken the farm owners.

Jay slipped quietly into the barn. He had good eyes and knew he could see well in the dark outside, but was surprised how well he could make his way in the night's blackness in the barn. His entrance startled two cows that were separated in individual stalls. The cows made sounds that signified they were aware of his intrusion. He moved even slower as he passed by them, then cautiously looked for a ladder or any other means he might need to reach the loft. There were a few chickens on one side of the barn, but they were closed off from the cows. If he got them cackling, the whole household would be aroused!

He was very tired, but before he climbed into the loft for rest, he needed to find a drink. His mouth felt as if it were full of cotton. He was hungry, too. The candy bars he had started out with had sufficed him a little, but his mouth was dry — as much from tension as from lack of water. He found a watering trough outside the barn and dipped his helmet in it. He drank from it, and hoped the water was not contaminated. When his thirst was quenched, he made his way back into the barn, past the cows until he found what served as a makeshift ladder that led to the hayloft. It was above where the cows were stalled, not on the side of the barn above the chickens. He climbed up, felt his way to the very back corner, covered himself with hay and fell asleep.

Jay didn't know which had awakened him first, the crowing of the rooster down below, or the rumbling of his own empty stomach. He listened carefully to be sure the farmers had not yet begun their morning chores. When he heard no further sounds, he slipped down the ladder, carrying his helmet. Using it as a bucket, he sidled up to one of the cows, patted her on the flank, talked soothingly to her and squatted down to milk her, taking just the amount of milk he thought he could drink. He did not want to take too much milk from just one cow. The farmers would know something was amiss. He divided his attention between the two cows. When he had drunk what he had obtained, he ventured over into the chicken abode. He felt in the nests for eggs, but found only two. Evidently the eggs had been gathered the night before, and the hens had not yet started their day's production, but he had these two. He had never liked raw eggs, but he had no way of cooking them, so he broke the end off the shell and sucked the raw eggs into his mouth.

He heard a door slam and some voices coming from the house. He scurried back up the ladder and found his place in the corner underneath a pile of hay. At least he had an ample breakfast, as far as amount was concerned; the eggs and milk were enough to satisfy his hunger. What he needed now was a change in attire. He would stick around here today, hoping the farmer's wife would be hanging out a laundry. That might help a little, but he also needed a coat or heavy jacket in this cool weather, heavier than the light jacket he was wearing. Perhaps these farm people were sympathetic to the Allies and would help him. He would listen carefully to everything they said, and he might be able to find out their feelings. He could not make any further move today — he would have to wait until evening. He did not dare be seen anywhere until he knew the safety of the neighborhood.

Lying hidden in the straw, he heard two people, a man and a woman, come into the barn. He listened to their conversation which was in French, and he caught most of what they were saying, but a word here and a word there he did not completely understand; yet he was able to get the gist of what they were saying.

"I know your back bothers you, Jean, so I'll get the hay, you milk the cows," the woman said.

"I don't like being treated like an invalid," the man replied.

"Thank God, you are an invalid, or you would be out there on the battlefield, or in some prison camp."

"I wouldn't be on the battlefield or in prison," he argued. "We've cooperated with the Germans the whole time. They've been very fair to us."

Jay heard these words and knew he must not let himself be found. The woman was now climbing the ladder. She had thrown a pitchfork up into the loft before she started her climb. Jay almost stopped breathing, afraid of being discovered. What if she decided to stick that pitchfork into the highest pile of hay! But she took the easy way, pitching down the hay that was nearest to the stalls of the cows. Then she began her descent.

"Did you climb up here yesterday?" She yelled at her companion.

"No. Why?"

"This looks like a little blood on this ladder. Did you hurt yourself, or hold onto this?"

"I can't see it now, I'm milking."

After a moment of silence, Jean continued, "Oh, that might have come from my hand after I wrung the neck of that chicken a few days ago. I just don't remember wiping my hands off on the ladder though."

"You don't remember a lot of things."

"Don't be so nasty. You forget a lot of things, too."

"Forget it!"

Jay listened for any further conversation, but none came. He heard them leave the barn after the woman had pitched the hay and fed the chickens. He would try to get as much sleep today as possible, so that he could be getting out of here tonight.

But Jay didn't get out of there that night! His leg was bothering him and he needed different clothes. Though most of his clothes were dry by now, his pants were torn from the fall that caused his injury, and his shoes were still wet. He had taken them off when he got in the hay last night, but he found them still damp on the inside this morning. If he could find a place to put them where they could absorb the sun, without being seen by the farmers — there was one small window in the loft, but there was little chance of any sun coming through it, and if it did, it would not reflect on any spot in the loft where he could place the shoes.

He wondered where the people had gone. Were they inside the house eating breakfast now? He peeked down from the hay loft to the ground level and could see no one, nor could he hear anything but the sounds from the cows and the chickens. He ventured all the way down, carrying his shoes. He slipped out on the side of the barn away from the house, the very entrance he had come in the night before. It just happened to be on the east side. He remembered a bush a few feet from the barn. Its leaves had all fallen, but it was thick enough that it should hide the shoes. He put them in the sun, out of sight from the barn or the house. He rushed back into the barn and up the ladder into the loft. Now he would just wait and rest — and hope that no dog or other varmint found his shoes and carried them off — or chewed them up. His last prayer (or hope) was that it would stay sunny, not cloud up and rain.

As Jay lazed away the day in the loft of this unknown farmer, he tended to the wound in his leg. He had unwrapped it, and had been able to cleanse it with water from a faucet which he had not found the night before. He washed out his undershirt that had bandaged his wound, afraid that the blood the woman had noticed on the ladder might have come from his leg. He hung the wet undershirt in a place where it could not be seen from the ground floor of the barn, only from the loft. After washing away the dried blood on his leg as well as the fresh blood, he had nothing with which to bandage his wound until the undershirt dried. He took off his dried shirt and used it for a temporary cover for his hurt thigh. It was cold without his shirt. He kept himself warm by buttoning his jacket tightly around him and hovering in the straw, waiting for his undershirt to dry.

He was thinking that perhaps he should stay here a day or two longer, giving that wound a chance to heal a bit before he strained his leg too much with the running and hiding that would be necessary. He would have enough to eat and drink here, not much variety, of course, but it would keep him alive. He would take just enough in such small portions that the farm people would not notice; yet it would be enough to sustain him. He would be very cautious, not taking any risks. That reminded him of his shoes. Since he had decided to stay a day or two longer, he had better retrieve them and let them dry slowly in the loft, rather than take the chance of them being found by man or animal.

By staying a little longer, he might be lucky enough to find a laundry on the line with clothes that he could filch. That would help him make his way across country undetected until he came upon Allies somewhere. It was aggravating, maddening to stay cooped up here with nothing to do. He wanted to get back to England. He knew he would have a letter, maybe a whole load of letters from Irene. It was all he could do to make himself stay put for a day or two, until his leg got better.

He checked periodically for any movement of the farm people. Late in the afternoon, when it seemed no one was near the barn, he climbed down the ladder and scampered out to pick up his shoes. After he had picked them up, he went back into the barn and scavenged the hens' nests. He only picked up three eggs, though there were many more available, but he had already taken three for his lunch. If he took too many, the loss would have been noticed and a search would begin to find out why. The cows weren't too happy about his milking them in the middle of the day either. He didn't take too much — nor did they give much — for they would have their regular milking sometime around dusk. He couldn't get any milk after those udders had been drained at their regular milking time, so he took just enough for dinner as well as lunch. All he had to worry about now was how long he could go on like this without his presence being discovered.

On the third day after his last forage Jay was lounging in the hay enjoying his food, when both the man and woman came into the barn. Jay listened to hear what they would say, but neither of them said anything much. The man evidently was doing the milking and the woman was gathering the eggs, just as they had each day. It was not yet dusk, and while they were going about their chores, Jay could hear the loud voices of two men who entered the barn and started talking to them. The men spoke German, and it was soon evident to Jay from what he heard that they were German soldiers.

Jay was too far away to distinguish their voices, but he couldn't help but wonder if one of them might be Franz Lubeck. He wanted so much to peek and see those German faces. But he didn't dare! What if one of them had been Franz. Would he have climbed down that ladder to say "hello"? Jay listened and came to the conclusion that the gruffness of the voices he heard could not have belonged to Franz. At least, he hoped not!

"Herr Garin, Frau," Jay heard them address the two farm owners, "we've been tracking an enemy soldier that was shot down several miles from here. Have you seen or heard about anyone in this area? He would be wearing an American or British uniform, I expect."

"Sir," Jean Garin replied, "we have seen no one around the area, but we haven't been off the place in several days."

"But we can hear the shooting in the distance, and it's upset our chickens. They aren't laying as many eggs as they used to," the woman complained.

"And the cows aren't giving as much milk either," Garin chimed in. "When do you think this war will be over, so we and our animals can get back to normal?"

"I think the Allies are prolonging the war. Soon they will have enough sense to surrender. But right now we need to capture that renegade soldier. Will you keep your eyes and ears open for any stranger you might see or hear about?"

"Yes, of course," the Garins answered together.

Jay Fisk lay very quietly in the hay. He had heard every word the Germans had said and his hosts' replies. What bothered him most was the last goodbyes of the soldiers as they left. "We'll be back in a day or two to check again, so be on the watch."

After she knew the soldiers were out of hearing distance, Mrs. Garin spoke, "Damn those Germans!"

"Don't say that," he husband advised. "They are going to win this war, whether we like it or not, so we better be nice to them."

"I said, 'Damn those Germans' and I meant it. Nothing has gone right for us since this war started. Our daughter has run off to join the resistance forces, and we have had to lie to the Germans saying she was working in Paris. We don't know where she is, and we may never see her again."

"It's that girl's fault, that girl she met in Strasbourg — you know, what's her name, Helene something. She got our Joan mixed up in the wrong crowd, off on a suicide track."

When Jay heard that name, he almost bolted upright. These people knew Helene, his old-time acquaintance in Munich. He wanted to drop down from the loft and talk to these people immediately. They knew Helene! But he had to keep hidden! Mr. Garin was not in sympathy with his daughter's convictions. He wondered what the Mrs. thought about it. Oh, he so wanted to talk to her!

Any further conversation between the husband and wife Jay did not hear as they left the barn. That was when Jay laughed a bit on the remarks they had made to the German officers about their chickens not laying as well as they had been and the cows giving less milk! Little did they know! Jay chuckled about it and wondered if he could ever let them know. He had a few English pounds in his pockets. When he disappeared from this barn, he would leave a note, thanking them for the milk and eggs.

Milk and eggs — raw eggs! It had kept him alive and well, but he was getting awfully tired of nothing else to eat for the last two days. He had chewed on some of the grains he found in the bins, a little corn and wheat, but his teeth were not powerful enough to be good grinding stones, and he had given that up. He wished the Garins would go away so he could sneak into the house and get a few slices of bread, and even make a fire and cook the eggs for a change.

Thinking about leaving a note, brought another idea to his mind — why not leave a note saying he was a friend of Helene's and had brought them a message from their daughter? Then perhaps they would talk to him without turning him over to the police. But what would he say? He didn't know their daughter, not even her name or her whereabouts. A bad idea that wouldn't work. He might tell them he would try to find their daughter and have her get in touch with them — if they would help him find his way to the nearest Allied position.

He was still afraid to make himself known to these farmers. He wasn't sure of their political leanings. He didn't know what their reaction would be if he disclosed his presence — whether they would notify the Germans or help him find safety. Caution finally took command and he decided he must leave as soon as everyone in the countryside was in slumber. He would write a "thank you" note, and he would write it in French, so that if perchance the Germans found it first, they would assume that it was from a neighbor or friend. But what about the English pounds? Would that jeopardize the Garins? The more he thought about it, the more he felt that he dared not leave foreign money, but would say that he would get payment to them later. That would sound like a friend who was presently in need, and from the burned-out houses and devastated villages Jay had seen, that could very well describe any family in the area.

All he had to do now was find something to write on, and something to write with. He had neither pen, pencil or paper. He also had to recall his best French words. It hadn't been too long since he had written letters for the importing business thanking French suppliers. Surely he could make the right kind of note to these people whose cows and chickens had contributed to his survival these last two days.

Lying in his hiding place in the loft, Jay conjured up the method he would use to leave a message. He could mix some dirt with water to form a mud, then using a stick for pen he could scrawl on a board what he wished to say. He hadn't seen a loose board anywhere around — he might have to write it on the walls somewhere. The chicken coops were the best place to go unobserved by intruding German soldiers. He couldn't put it on the wall just below where anyone coming into the barn would notice. If he could find a shingle, any small piece of abandoned wood, he could take his time writing it while he was secluded up here in the hay. If he wrote it after dark, he could risk going below, but no light would make the task almost impossible.

Of course! He could use a bucket, the bucket the woman used to feed the chickens. She left it in one of the bins of grain, after she had used it to dip out the mixed grains she spread out in the barn lot where the chickens spent much of their day, pecking at the grains and scratching the soil. Surely she would notice the mud scribbling if he put it on the side of the bucket. But he couldn't do it now, because the animals and chickens were fed twice a day. He would have to wait until around dusk, just after the next feeding. It would still be light enough for him to see what he was doing. He might just as well get some sleep now, because he would spend most of the night slinking through the hills and valleys, avoiding as much contact with habitable places as possible.

Jay slept soundly and was startled when he heard the Garins enter the barn. Mrs. Garin started up the ladder to the loft, evidently to pitch more hay down to the cows. Jay had already buried himself deep in the hay to keep warm, but his face and head were exposed. He buried his head in the closest mound of hay, hoping she would not look into this corner of the loft. He could get the strong scent of the fresh hay as he moved it. He knew the woman would smell it, too. He hoped that she would attribute it to the hay she was handling. He lay as still as he could, taking light breaths. It did not take her long to finish the hay tossing and she was down the ladder.

He wished he knew her first name. He had heard her call the man Jean, and the Germans had called them Herr and Frau Garin. Unless he heard otherwise, he was going to call her Angel, for she had always looked away from him in the loft, unintentionally, he suspected, but it could have been otherwise! He didn't hear any conversation, only the noise of the chores being performed. After a bit, the man called out, "Damn these cows, they aren't giving the milk they should. Do you think they are getting too old. Should we sell them for beef and get some new ones?"

"We can't afford any new cows, and if we tried to sell them, the Germans would just take them off our hands," the woman replied. After a few moments she continued, "It's the war! The chickens aren't laying as many eggs as they should either."

"Then damn the war!" Jean Garin swore.

Up in the loft, Jay Fiske hummed to himself, "Amen!"

The minute the Garins were out of the barns and far

enough away, Jay crawled down the ladder and found the bucket in a grain bin. He set it aside, got a stick from the bushes on the east side of the barn and some soil and water from the cows' watering trough. Back up into the loft, he began his message.

Merci pour le lait et des oeufs, he wrote on the first line, then

Je vais te payer plus tard! J. was his only signature.

When he had finished, he wondered where he would put the bucket. If he put it back in the grain bin, the lettering of dried mud would chip right off. He decided it best to place it on top of one of the hen's nests. He placed it where he was certain it would be seen; then he was ready to leave as soon as light faded enough for him to feel safe.

As darkness fell, Jay climbed down the ladder. He was just out the door on the east side of the barn when he thought he could sneak another egg to take with him. Knowing that they had gathered the eggs just an hour or so before, he remembered one of the old sayings when he was a youngster on a farm. A hen always cackled when she laid an egg, and he had heard a hen cackle just a short time before. If that cackle meant anything, he might find an egg to implement his supper.

He went back into the barn into the chicken coops and felt in the nests. The hens were not on their nests but were perched on the rafters with the roosters for the night. He felt in each nest as he came to it, but no eggs. On one next he found a hen, probably the one that announced she had laid an egg. That old hen didn't cackle, she squawked when he reached under her to pull out an egg. He could feel more than one egg in the nest, and he thought of taking another, but that belligerent hen pecked his hand hard enough to bring blood, and she was making such an fuss that he took the one egg and beat it out of the barn as fast as he could, before she had all in the whole henhouse squawking.

Once outside, he was ready to start the next leg of his journey out of German held territory. Carrying an egg (eggs had such a paper thin shells) was not easy, so he thought he might just as well eat it now. He cracked the end off the shell and started to put it to his mouth to suck out the raw egg, but he immediately caught a strange odor. This wasn't a fresh egg in that shell as he expected, but a half-formed chick. No wonder that old hen had raised such a squall! Jay was laughing at himself and thought all of those animals and fowls in the barn, if they only knew, they would be laughing at him, too.

He wished he knew where he was! He couldn't be near Strasbourg. That was on the eastern border of France, on the Rhine. He remembered it well from years ago, but the countryside he was in now did not look familiar. There were hills and meadows all around this area, but not mountains. The Vosages near Strasbourg would probably be covered with snow. All he could do was head west to get out of trouble. He could cover between fifteen and twenty miles tonight if his leg did not give out on him. He wished he could find a change of clothes; then he could travel in the daytime as well as night and should be able to get by since he could speak both French and German fairly well.

These were Jay's first thoughts as he limped along at a moderate pace. Then he had another devastating thought — what if he should meet the enemy and the German soldier would be his friend Franz? What would they do? Would he shoot Franz? Would Franz shoot him? They had been such good friends, and the last he had heard from this dear friend was that he was serving in the German army under Witzelben on the French border. Tears came to Jay's eyes as he thought about Franz. There was no way, *no way,* he could shoot Franz. Would he just stand there and let Franz kill *him?* He didn't know what the outcome would be should they meet on a battlefield. Each had an obligation to their separate countries. Did they have the obligation to kill a friend who had done no wrong? Jay knew what he would do, surrender! And hope that Franz would do the same, if Jay had the advantage.

The more Jay thought about it, the faster he walked. He had to get to an Allied position, so no such an encounter could happen. He *mustn't* let that happen!

For two nights, keeping up his fast pace in cold night air had generated enough heat to keep him from getting too cold, but he had found little time or place to rest during daylight. Shortly after midnight on the second night, he could see in the distance spikes of buildings that looked like spikes of cathedrals reaching hopefully toward a heavenly sky. He hurried toward the bombed-out town and reached it in the wee hours of the morning. By now his leg was giving him fits. The throbbing had increased and he had a feeling that it might have started to bleed again. He could see no lights in the wreckage of the village he came upon, but he was sure that there would be some of the original inhabitants who had not abandoned their homes. So he moved as soundlessly as possible, hoping to find shelter among the fallen walls, perhaps a rug or blanket that would keep him warm for a few hours' sleep. He needed to find a hiding place that would protect him until morning. He would listen for any conversation that might happen around him — German, French, English or any other signs to warn him on how and when to make his next move.

The first building Jay Fisk came to was a total loss, all the window panes shattered, no sturdy walls left standing, just bricks ready to crumble in a high wind or from a jolt of nearby shelling — and no hiding places. He crept along to the next building, and the next, with no further advantage. As he approached the fourth or fifth building, he had lost track of the number, he could feel a bit of heat emanating from its walls. Someone must be inside to have heat leaking through the cracks. He moved around the building until he found a door. Dare he go in? What if it were occupied by German soldiers? He tried the latch and found the door unlocked. The first slight push he gave produced a loud squeak, like an unoiled hinge. He held his breath and waited a few seconds, then pushed again. The squeaks subsided as he got the door open enough to slip inside. The warmth of the room engulfed him, and though the heat was very limited, it felt like the lap of luxury.

He stood very still to ascertain that there was no one else in the room. As his eyes got accustomed to the dark, he made out that there was a clothesline with garments hanging on it. He felt each one, searching for men's pants, shirts or whatever else he could find. As he felt around, he discovered a man's trousers. Jay could feel they were big enough around, but too short for his own long legs. The shirt was also a bit large, but he decided he would take them both. He put them on, but kept his own jacket and shirt for additional warmth. He could shed them if he anticipated trouble anywhere. It was so nice and warm in here! He found the dying embers of a fire in a fireplace with the cracked chimney. That crack gave out the heat he had felt outside The light from the coals had helped him in exploring the room. He would have liked to curl up in front and sleep, sleep. But he couldn't! He had to make a choice, keep the garments or have a warm night's sleep. The native garments were more essential than the warmth of the room. Knowing the family would miss the clothing the next morning, he knew he must be miles away. But before he left, he found a piece of cloth, a tea towel, or rag, he didn't know which, but he used it to replace the undershirt on his leg wound. Wearing the undershirt gave him one more layer of clothing to fight off the chill in this frosty weather.

Out into the cold again, wearing the large garments over his uniform, he made his way out of the town. He was comfortable with the additional clothes. Besides the pants and shirt, he had also taken a scarf that he found hanging on a hook. He put it over his head and underneath his helmet. It was surprising how much warmer he felt with his head and ears covered.

For two hours he walked. It was still pitch dark, but

he knew that the early light of dawn would be coming soon and he must find another place to hole up. He was getting so tired that he could no longer keep up the fast walk. He was weakening, mile by mile. He felt that he couldn't have covered more than six or seven miles, so he must still push on. He had passed no place that offered him any safety.

Another hour, and still plugging along slower and slower, he didn't know where he was, or whether he was in friendly or enemy territory. He spotted a little church — he had to get there. Weakness was creeping upon him for lack of food for two days, lack of enough sleep, and the festering wound on his leg — he couldn't go any farther! He just had to rest for a little while before he could go on. He could see the church, but it seemed so far away. But he had to get there — he had to get there —

"Monsieur? Sir, are you all right?"

Jordan Fisk awoke with a start! Where was he? He suddenly became tense — had he been captured? There was a young woman and a couple of nuns standing over him. He was lying on a bed in a room that was all white. The last thing he remembered was struggling toward a church. He must have fainted or fallen asleep. He remembered having shed his uniform and hiding it in some rocks before he started his last trek toward the church, not knowing how he might be greeted there.

As he lay there, looking around him, he started to blurt out in English, but caught himself in time to ask in French, "Where am I?

"You are in the Laon Cathedral."

Jay wasn't going to say anything further until he found out about the people around him. He knew nothing about the town of Laon or its cathedral. He knew France had many scattered cathedrals that were famous, and he had visited some of them when he was in school in Munich, but Laon wasn't one of them, so he thought it safe to say, "I need something to eat." And that was very true.

One of the nuns left the room and soon returned with a bowl of broth and some crackers. Jay was famished and disposed of the repast quickly. He thanked them, then tried to get up, saying he must be on his way.

"Where do you want to go? You aren't able to go anyplace just yet."

Again, Jay was cautious about letting them know where he wanted to go. He should be safe in first asking a few questions himself. "What happened? Why am I here?"

"I found you sound asleep on the ground, just a few hundred feet from the Cathedral," the young woman said. "I got the nuns to help carry you inside. You must have been exhausted."

"Yes," was all that Jay answered.

One of the nuns, in a laughing tone, said, "Those pants don't fit you too well, nor the shirt, but you have on good shoes. Are you running away from something?"

"I don't know yet," Jay answered in French; then in German he asked, "How far am I from Strasbourg?"

That last sentence was the right move. Immediately Jay saw the faces around him tighten up, and very formally the older nun said, "We'll get you back to your people."

"You knew I spoke French with an accent, didn't you?" he asked.

Before anyone could stop her, the young woman said coolly, "But I thought it was American!"

Jay noted the same behavior of all of them, not the gentleness he had first noticed. He had to take another chance. "I need to get to Paris," he said in English.

"You *are* an American!" one cried out.

"Or British," chimed in another.

The smiles returning to their faces convinced Jay that he was in friendly hands, and he told them of being shot down and all he wanted was to get back to England and get his leg tended.

They assured him they would see that he got there.

Jay rested and fell asleep thinking of nothing but getting back to his base, and having a letter or maybe many letters from his beloved Irene.

CHAPTER FIFTEEN

CHAPTER FIFTEEN

THE GOODBYE wave to Jordan Fisk left Amy Carter feeling completely debilitated. There was so much more she would have liked to tell him, but she couldn't. She hated to lie to him, but she had no choice — it could present danger to Jay as well as to herself if she did otherwise.

But any thoughts of danger to herself or Jay were soon forgotten as she found herself worrying about the handsome Lieutenant Conway. She remembered the first time she had seen him in the hospital. Her first startled brainwave was one of concern, a mixture of fear and hate … maybe not hate, but more like scorn. But he was a sick soldier, and she *had* to take care of him. With her vital nurses' training and love for her country, she could do no less! After all, he, too, was in our country's service and needed to be cared for so that he could fight again. As he improved in health, she couldn't get over what a handsome man he had become. Day after day, she watched him improve and began to feel flattered that he was paying her so much attention. But there was no way she would let herself get close to that man!

She told her roommate, Erica, about him. Erica showed an especial interest in the handsome Lieutenant that Amy had described, and she wanted to meet him. In fact, Erica made such a nuisance of herself insisting that she meet Billy Conway, that finally Amy told her to come about five o'clock to the big hall of the hospital. She told her that Billy Conway would be there, as he was every day he was off duty.

Billy Conway was not the only soldier that Erica seemed to fancy. Amy thought that Erica seemed to throw herself at all the good-looking boys. She even spent more time trying to entice the officers, whether they were good-looking or not, or whatever branch of service that came into their territory — Army, Navy, Air Force, it didn't seem to matter. Amy herself was quite reserved and had gotten the reputation of being a "cold fish."

Billy had told her once that the other guys in his outfit had told him he was wasting his time trying to get a date with her, that she was a frigid old maid. She had told Billy that she was cautious of all the attention these service boys were giving the nurses, or any other girls they met. She knew they were lonely and she would talk with them, but no way was she going to get involved with anyone.

As the train rolled along toward London, Amy thought again about Erica's meeting with the Lieutenant. Erica was entranced, saying that he was the handsomest man she had ever seen. She didn't lose a minute in applying all the tricks she knew to get his attention. Amy laughed to herself when she remembered Billy's polite "How are you," then how he turned abruptly from her back to Amy saying, "Amy, please give me a chance! I love you."

Amy had never thought of herself as being jealous

of the beautiful Erica, even from all the attention she seemed to attract from the servicemen, but Amy nevertheless got a deep pleasure when Billy Conway practically ignored Erica, as he begged for Amy's total attention instead.

Amy had been lodged with all the other nurses when she first arrived in London. She and Erica had since that time arranged to rent an apartment. When Amy had suggested they make such an arrangement, Erica was delighted, so for the past few months just the two of them shared an apartment.

Tonight, sitting on the fast moving train, Amy thought that once she got back to the base hospital her work would never be the same. The Lieutenant was gone, and she wouldn't see him, probably never again. She knew that tonight she wouldn't have Erica to talk to either, and that once she had made her report, she would never see Erica again. But most of all, she would miss Billy Conway appearing out of nowhere, day after day, telling her he loved her. She had felt an emptiness these last two or three months that she couldn't explain, ever since he had been gone.

As she got off the train and made her way to her quarters, tonight she felt that loneliness more than ever. Lieutenant Conway had been sent across the channel to fight, and she wondered if he was still alive. Amy finally admitted to herself that she loved that man, in spite of herself. Much as she had fought it for the last eight months, she knew her feelings for him were more than she had let him know — and now he might never come back! Why hadn't she told him she loved him. She was crying as she unlocked the door to her room. She was glad that Erica wouldn't be there, so she wouldn't even try to hide here tears. She knew Erica would not be there, and that was her *other* problem.

Amy walked the several blocks from the train station to her abode near the hospital, hoping to organize her thoughts for the report she had to make — and trying to forget the Lieutenant. Once in her room, she turned on the lights, plopped down on the bed and let her tears flow. So many things were askance, and she didn't know what to do about it. After getting control of her tears, she took off her coat, sat down at the small desk in the room and prepared to write the report that was expected from her. She couldn't write it! Erica would be coming in later tonight. There was no way she could risk Erica seeing it!

The next morning Amy awoke before Erica did and dressed quickly.

"Where are you going in such a hurry?" Erica turned over in bed and asked in a sleepy voice.

"To work!" Amy answered hurriedly.

"This early? Hold on a minute, and I'll come with you."

"No, Erica, I'm not going straight to the hospital."

"Where …"

"Erica, I am going to see the Major."

"Wow! Must be important. Now I know I want to come with you."

Amy wanted to shout, 'NO, NO', but that might defeat her purpose, and she calmly said, "Okay, I just wanted to find out if Lieutenant Conway was okay. You might just as well go back to sleep for another hour."

"You are in love with him, aren't you?"

"Could be. Anyway, I'll see you at the hospital," and Amy was out the door and on her way.

When Amy appeared before the Major, he motioned for her to sit down; then he listened to what she had to tell him.

"You were careful not to write any notes down, I notice," the Major remarked.

"I had to be," she replied.

After asking several more questions and some small talk, Amy asked if the Major had any news of Lieutenant Conway, and if he was all right.

The Major said, "Thanks for your help. You've done a good job. Would you like to be an 'angel of mercy'?"

"Angel of Mercy? What is that?"

"We are sending many nurses over to the continent to care for our injured boys. Nurses are badly needed there, but it is dangerous. We don't like to send women into the combat area, but —"

"We are already in the combat area, Major! Every bomb that falls on us here can be just as fatal as the ones on the continent. I want to go!" Amy Carter jumped up from her chair. "How soon can I leave?"

The Major was surprised at the sudden reaction to his suggestion. He also got up from his desk and reached across to take Amy's hand. He knew there had to be someone across the channel that she very much wanted to see. With a grin on his face, he said, "If that's how you feel, you can go tomorrow."

Amy got her orders and joined the other nurses waiting to be shipped across the channel. She no longer wanted to be in the London hospital. There was a chance, just a chance, that she might see Lieutenant Conway. After he had been in the D-Day invasion, she had thought she might never, ever see him again. Even now, she was not sure whether he was dead or alive, but over there in France, she might have an opportunity, no matter how small, of seeing him just once more.

What Amy had not anticipated was the great change in her nursing work and its surroundings on the continent. She was unloaded with the other nurses on a strip of beach, where men, officers as well as the enlisted men, helped set up tents for their quarters. No electricity, no running water, nothing to take the chill off the air. Nothing to stop rain water from running through their tents. All they could say was that they were protected from the wind, and that helped a little in making the tents bearable. They were stuck in the tents for three or four days before being transferred to an old building, which might have been an old schoolhouse, business building or clubhouse, whatever, but it had been vacated and now was being used for a field hospital.

Wounded men from the front poured in by the thousands. These temporary hospital bases were often called the e-vac hospitals, where nurses did what they could to prepare the wounded for evacuation to hospitals in England, Paris or other liberated hospitals on the continent. Many times the injured did not get to the field hospitals until four or five days after they had been hurt.

For several weeks, Amy was working at the e-vac, then she was transferred to the hospital in Epernay, a town about forty miles south of Reims where many injured men from battlefields were sent. It seemed there were hospitals in many of the French towns just south of the Belgium border and they all had a constant need for more nurses.

Amy learned from some of the injured Allied soldiers that there were as many French people sympathetic to the Germans as there were those supporting the Allies, maybe more. She also heard from some of the other nurses who had served on the continent longer than she that was also true in parts of Belgium. It made Amy wonder what would happen if Lieutenant Conway, though not captured by the Germans, would still be in danger from the local people, the people he was fighting to protect. Amy had become friendly with one nurse named Pauline who had the same queasy feeling about the populace around them.

When Amy got her orders to move to a hospital at Mourmelon, she felt sorry to leave some of the nurses she had been with for weeks, but at the same time there was the possibility that any move she made might put her closer to wherever Billy Conway might be — whatever battle he would be fighting.

Amy Carter found that her work in Mourmelon was the same sad situation she found at the other hospitals — young boys unable to overcome their insurmountable injuries, and yet she knew the rewarding experience when she could help pull them through. In Mourmelon she found many young soldiers that she helped bring back to health, and she began to appreciate the atmosphere around her. She was working with more French nurses than she had in her previous location. There was one in particular who made her feel worthy. Her name was Helene.

Amy remembered the day she had first seen Helene. She was a little older than most of the young nurses and was talking excitedly to several of them — in French. Amy was new is this hospital, and she would have liked to get to know the other nurses she would be working with. But Amy was, by nature, a rather reticent person, and she stood quietly by and just watched.

The older woman turned and saw her standing alone and with a bright smile on her face walked up to her and said in perfect English, "I am Helene."

Amy said "Hello, I am Amy." Then in an apologetic voice said, "No parlais vous Francois."

"You are an American, aren't you?"

"Yes, and I am new here."

Helene laughed, looked closely at Amy and remarked, "You look like you've already had experience in this field of nursing, and no offense, but I think you are probably as old as I am."

Amy looked quizzically at the woman, who had a few gray hairs beginning to appear in her dark auburn hair. She could see the good humor in gold/brown eyes that matched the color of her hair. Amy said, "I am thirty-two years old, and I guess anyone that age *has* been around a lot."

Helene laughed again. "I was right about you. I, too, am thirty-two and feel twice that old since the war started."

Helene turned back to the younger girls who were still standing around and told them they were dismissed, then said to Amy, "I am not always here — I am in and out, but I would like to know you better. Shall we have a cup of coffee?"

Helene's appearance at the hospital was irregular, but it became more frequent as time passed. As the days passed, she always took time to chat with Amy. It was through these short visits that Amy and Helene developed a special rapport for each other, yet they had not divulged much of their private lives to each other.

One day, after hours of being on her feet, Amy took off her shoes to relax and ordered a cup of coffee. Leaning back, stretching out her legs, she closed her eyes for a moment of solitude from a frantic day of caring for the injured. Suddenly she was brought out of her reverie by the appearance of Helene. And as Amy had found out from other days when Helene would appear, an otherwise hard day became one of pleasure.

Through these first few weeks of communication, they still knew little of the other's life. On this particular day Helene remarked, "Amy, I notice that every time they bring in these wounded boys, you make a quick inspection of each of them before you start to work. Like you're always looking for someone."

Amy did not say anything for a moment; then she looked closely at Helene and replied, "Yes, there is someone very special to me, and I am always looking for him, for I don't know where he is, or if he is even still alive." Amy looked away from Helene, but the tears forming in her eyes were obvious.

"I didn't mean to interfere in your affairs. But I am your friend. You can tell me about it, if you want."

"Helene, I haven't told you much about me, nor have you told me much of anything about yourself. I know you are a good nurse and take good care of the wounded, but I still don't know anything about your political leaning. I learned quickly that not all French people are against the Germans."

"Amy, did you ever wonder why I disappeared from the hospital for days at a time?"

Amy was careful not to reveal all the thoughts she might have had, and said nonchalantly, "No, I just supposed that you visited your family somewhere."

Helene's voice became almost a whisper, "Amy, I have been separated from my family for years, because I work with the Resistance. My father said we had to cooperate with the Germans because they would win this war, and our whole future depended upon our being friendly with them I left home and have spent much of the last few years recruiting others to help in the Resistance and setting up safe houses. I took up nursing so I could work through the hospitals. I am not a registered nurse like you. That's why I was gone so much of the time when you first came here. Very few of the other nurses know about my clandestine activities." With her voice still low, she continued, "I, too, do not know for sure how all of them feel about the Germans. Since you are an American, I know I can trust you."

Amy listened to every word that Helene said, and it made her think of another nurse she knew in England, another nurse who often made clandestine trips when she had some time off. But she liked Helene a lot. She felt that she could tell her a little of her own affairs that would in no way be traitorous to her cause.

"I have told you about a boy from my home town that I hadn't seen in fifteen or more years until I saw him in a hospital in London. He doesn't know that I care about him."

"Is he married? Do you know how he feels?"

"He says he loves me, and he is not married."

"Are you sure? That's what I was telling those young nurses — to beware of amorous soldiers, they could all say they are not married."

"I know he is not married."

"Then what's your problem?"

"I did not want to get involved. But I wish I had."

The two young women finished their coffee and were sitting quietly at the table, saying little, when injured troops were hauled in. The women hurriedly jumped up to see what help they could administer to the incoming patients.

Amy, as was her custom, started an inspection of each one before she began any duties. She had seen but one or two before one of the drivers, following one of the injured into the hospital, said to her, "This is my friend, he's hurt bad. I want you to take particular care of him. He's our Lieutenant."

Amy looked at the bandaged head and face. She jerked up, looked at the accompanying boy and said, "Is this Lieutenant Conway?"

"Yes, do you know him?"

"Yes, and he's a dear friend of mine, too!" Amy cried out for a doctor, "This man needs immediate attention!"

Lieutenant R. William Conway had considered himself one of the lucky ones who had made it safely to the shore of France on that fateful day, June 06. He had lost many of his men in their push through Cherbourg, and their breakthrough at St. Lo. Their breakthrough was used first by Patton who turned west to Brittany and then back east towards Paris. This movement relieved the pressure on English General Montgomery who was fighting at Caen. Patton and Montgomery had not gotten along from their first encounter, and now Patton felt that Montgomery had fouled up the works again. The Allied Forces were short on supplies, and Montgomery convinced Eisenhower that first priority should go to the British. Because of this, the United States Army got only bare essentials, which literally grounded the American Forces, since the only gasoline they had was in their vehicles. Since Montgomery's plan didn't work out very well, it was the Americans who had to continue the fighting, pushing the German across France toward Paris. It was the Americans who circled the city, captured a trainload of German officers with the loot they were trying to sneak out of Paris; yet, because Churchill had promised the French that they could make the victorious entry into Paris, it turned out to be American trucks with American supplies, that the French drivers had to take when they entered the city.

The movement thus far into France and part of Belgium had been fairly rapid. The native French seemed glad to see the Americans, and though seldom seen during battle, they occasionally made the conquering forces more comfortable by letting them throw their bedrolls in buildings instead of out on the ground.

German soldiers were surrendering around the whole area. Sometimes when one or two would first come out with a white flag, they would be followed by a hundred more. As the ninth Army moved on toward Belgium, Lieutenant Conroy advised his men to be careful, for though the people were friendly in one village, they might not be in the next. The Germans had retreated to the German border near Aachen, but snipers could be hiding in the Schnee Eifel hills.

The Allied forces were spread out, and the Germans wanted to keep it that way, slowing any progress into German territory. The Germans made the Ardennes their main thrust. One of Conroy's men said he saw a German or two slip across a clearing in front of them, and a few shots were fired. Winter had come upon the land with a frightful force, leaving heavy snow, still falling, and with temperatures dropping rapidly. It caused a bitter chill in the spirits as well as to the bodies of the fighting soldiers, affecting both the very young and the more experienced men.

Major Huff, of the American Army, was stopped and told to report to Division Headquarters. When he arrived there, he was advised that German paratroopers had been dropped in the woods around them, wearing American uniforms, and other Germans in American uniforms were driving American Jeeps in the town of Eupen. The American Commanders now knew why some of their Jeep patrols had disappeared and were not returning. The troops were all alerted!

The Major got back to his unit and had just informed his men to be wary of Germans dressed as Americans, when one Jeep returned and came to an abrupt stop. An officer lay hurt and unconscious across the front seat, and the driver shouted, "Lieutenant Conway is hurt." The Major told them to be very careful, repeating the same message Conway had given his men — that the enemy Germans had retreated to the German border, but that snipers could be still hiding in the hills. That's how the Lieutenant got shot — by a sniper.

Nurse Amy Carter did not neglect any of her duties, she was too good a nurse for that, but she did spend every spare moment that she had at the bedside of the injured Lieutenant Conway. Before he had been brought into the hospital, Amy had spent a few minutes extra with all the patients, giving all of them a little extra cheer and what good war news she could bring.

Lieutenant Robert William Conway was special! That's what all the other injured boys around him were thinking. One day when Amy had checked his pulse, taken his temperature and finished with the regular regime, she leaned down and kissed the semi-conscious Conway on the forehead before she left to go to another patient.

A patient in the next bed, now practically recovered from any injury he might have suffered, teased, "Nurse, you never kissed me like that?"

Amy laughed at him and said, "You were never unconscious. I didn't dare!"

After the arrival of Lieutenant Conway, Amy spent as much time as she could the first day or two finding out the extent of his injuries. He had a bad wound in his right chest and had lost quite a lot of blood. Another shot had injured the femur of his left leg. His head injury came from hitting his head hard on a sharp corner of the jeep as he fell when the shell hit his chest. A loss of blood, as well as the blow to his head, added to his extreme weakness and unconsciousness. Amy knew that he was in and out of awareness, but was thankful that with the proper care he should be all right again. She hoped that his chest and leg injury would earn him a discharge, so that he would not have to return to the battlefield.

As he got better, Amy spent more time with other patients and even took time to talk with Helene. When she came in one day, Amy, for the first time in days, took time to talk with Helene. She told her about Lieutenant Conway's precarious condition. Helene, trying to cheer her up, joked about another Lieutenant at another hospital who had given her a few laughs.

"What's the matter with him?" Amy asked.

"He has a broken leg and is going to be laid up for two or three weeks. That gives us two Lieutenants with broken legs." Helene laughed again.

"And you think that's laughable?" her serious friend asked.

"Amy, to understand, you would have to meet this guy. He's a riot!"

"You sound very fond of him, Helene. Are you falling for him?"

"Lord, no! He's only —"

The girls were interrupted by the arrival of newly injured soldiers.

"Talk with you later!" they each called to the other.

In another part of the hospital, Lieutenant R. William Conway had a young American nurse approach him. "You've got a note, Lieutenant." Billy Conroy had just opened his eyes and saw a pretty little brown-eyed nurse sitting by his bedside with a letter. Billy looked all around him, at the many beds, all filled with injured soldiers. He moved his head to find out more of his surroundings.

"Oh, my head hurts!" he flinched.

"You got quite a bump on your head, Lieutenant, but it will be better in a few days. But I think your leg is broken and that will take longer to heal," the nurse smiled.

Conroy had not even noticed until that moment that his leg was in a cast. "How long have I been here?"

"Oh, just a while. You'll be taken back to London, I expect before too long."

Billy had just a fleeting thought that the letter might be from Amy Carter, but she wouldn't even know he was here; yet he had the felling that Amy was near him.

"Do you want me to read it to you or can you do it yourself?"

Billy's head was hurting and he wondered if he could even focus his eyes, but he didn't want any one else to read his mail. "Give it to me, please."

It was from Major Huff. Billy was surprised to hear from the Major. It was so satisfying to know the Major was concerned about him. He read it an re-read parts of it again.

Hitler deliberately picked bad weather for his attack to neutralize American air superiority. By concentrating his forces at this one point, he planned to break through and drive all the way to Antwerp, using captured sup-

plies on the way. Again he underestimated the ability and sinew of the Americans pockets of resistance that refused to give up and became thorns in Hitler's side. Patton's Third Army, which faced east, turned left to attack north towards Bastogne. The defending units had become surrounded, but Patton said "Nuts" to the German's order to surrender. Driving on a lonely road, I held my pistol in my hand. Headquarters was on alert, ready to move out on a moment's notice. Our units held their ground and became the north hinge of the bulge.

The 9th Division's plan to attack east was abandoned, and we attacked south toward Malmedy, near which the Germans had lined up unarmed prisoners in a clearing and mowed them down with a machine gun mounted in a truck. This was referred to as the Malmedy Massacre. The Allied plan, once Hitler's intent became clear, was to pinch the bulge of at its base. The situation was tense for several days. We had only one supply road behind us. Some of our artillery placed its howitzers and fired right from an ammunition dump. Finally, the weather cleared and with the return of air support, the Battle of the Bulge was over.

Lieutenant Robert William Conway, for the first time since his injuries, felt a feeling of contentment. So they had won that battle. How long would it be now before this war was over. The nurse who had brought him the letter had left after he took it from her. It made him feel better to know that his unit had been able to continue the fight. He wondered about how they had all been able to get through the horrors. He could still hear those bullets whizzing past and the loud explosions all about him. Would he continue to have nightmares about that battle. He couldn't remember what had happened to him. He remembered being in the dark, was it a foxhole or a space under his jeep? The next thing was waking up here in a hospital, with a terrific headache. He wished the nurse had stayed a little longer so he could ask her some questions. Was he shot in the head? Or did he fall. He would like to know what happened. Reading the letter had made him glad that the battle had been won, but he felt tired, and just dropped the letter on the bed at his side and closed his eyes. The injured officer felt like the young boy Billy Conway who had just received the best Christmas present ever. And it must be near Christmas! Or had Christmas come and gone? He wished he could talk to Amy about it. His thoughts and dreams of Amy faded in and out as consciousness deserted him again, as it was wont to do since his injury.

Since the two nurses, Helene in and out of the hospital, and Amy who was constantly caring for the many healing or dying young servicemen, had little time for jocular chatter between themselves, they had made a game of it, exchanging a word or two about *their* lieutenants with the broken legs.

Dashing down a corridor of the hospital one day, Amy met Helene. "Hi!" she said, "How's you love life coming along with your Lieutenant?"

"Amy, I told you he is not my love interest, he's just a kid, much younger than I. It's the American nurses all around him with the love bug. I just listen to their talk. When I speak to him, I talk like a mother."

"You're kidding!"

"No, I'm not. He likes to tell me about a cute French girl he met in one town. He says nothing serious, but he said she was fun."

"Well, well. What *about* your love life?"

"It's a long story."

"Tell me about it."

"Maybe I will some day."

No more was ever said about Helene's love life, and Helene continued, "I told you Ed was a fun-loving kid and I liked to talk with him, but that's all. How's your own loving Lieutenant?"

"I am so relieved that he is getting better. He still has moments of unconsciousness, but not too often. I get in to see him as often as I can."

"Have you told him you love him?"

"Not yet."

"Let me know when you do."

And the nurses touched each other on the shoulder and went their separate ways.

The Lieutenant, the one Helene called the fun-loving kid, was not always in a hilarious mood. Sometimes he got tired of the ribald discussions of other servicemen around him. Helene was approaching his area in the hospital when she heard him lecturing the others. "I know we have to take this war with a bit of humor or we couldn't survive, but don't you forget we've a long way yet to go. And all of us will not make it. Think about the thousands upon thousands of men and women, combat and non-combat, who didn't make it at Anzio, in Sicily, in Africa."

Someone muttered, "Those damn Germans and Italians?"

"But Ed's right," another said, "We can't forget our men, but I feel bad for those very young German boys that looked like they should have gotten their mother's permission before they went out to fight."

The conversation had turned suddenly from the smuttiness to heartbreaking memories. Tears came to the eyes of several when they remembered the Italian priest, Don Bosco, who had become an important figure to the allied cause by helping refugees escape the murderous hands of the Gestapo by furnishing food, beds and medicines to the refugees.

Helene listened to them, then she turned quietly away, knowing she had a new awareness of this young Lieutenant, coming from what he called the American Heartland.

Amy stood over the bed where Lieutenant Robert William Conway lay and looked down on the sleeping man, not knowing if he were unconscious or just asleep. She leaned down over him and whispered very softly in his ear, "I love you, Billy."

Suddenly two arms shot up and closed all the way around her. It took her off her feet, and she was lying across the wounded man on the bed. Startled, she jerked back, but was unable to free herself. She looked down into the bright, laughing blue eyes of the Lieutenant.

"I knew It!" he exclaimed, "Will you marry me?" He unleashed her, but still held onto one of her wrists as she picked herself up from her prone position.

"I've been telling you he's a four-flusher!" joked the patient in the bed on Billy's right. "He's been fooling you all along, just playing like he was unconscious. I tried it, but I couldn't fool you."

Amy was not smiling as she shook her head, and looked from the other patient back to Billy. Before she could say anything, Billy, still holding her wrist, asked, "Does your love mean 'yes,' that you will marry me?"

Holding back a sob, Amy said, "I can't. There's something about me you don't know. I am not the person you think I am. If you knew something of my past, you wouldn't want to marry me."

Billy reached out and grasped Amy's shoulders, with his eyes looking straight into her own and said, "*I* am your past, Anna Mae Cowan!"

Amy could hold back her tears no longer. She sobbed, "You knew."

"Will you forgive me, Amy, Anna Mae, whatever name you want to be called? I love you and want you to marry me."

Amy put her hands, one on each side of Billy's face, leaned down and kissed him on the mouth. His arms went around her again, and when she freed herself, she said, "Now you know."

Amy had to get back to her duties. With a light sprint in her steps she waltzed away. She could hardly wait to tell Helene! When would they meet again? When they did, Helene did not have to be told. She saw the beaming countenance and light step and the broad smile on Amy's face, and she knew what Amy had to say.

Helene, though, did not have an easy way to tell

Amy about the serious mood she had discovered in *her* Lieutenant. After congratulating Amy, she said, "I think it would be nice if we could get our Lieutenants together. They are in different Army divisions and probably would never meet, but they might like each other."

"Helene, come over when you can and see Billy. I won't be far away. We'll see what we can work out."

It was a day or two later when Helene came into the hospital section where Lieutenant Conway was located. Amy was not there, but Conway was awake. Helene introduced herself and told him that there was an American Lieutenant in another hospital that she thought he might enjoy knowing each other — if they ever had a chance to meet.

"Well, maybe we don't have much in common. Where is his home in the United States?" Billy asked.

"He says he from the American Heartland. I don't know where that is," Helen replied.

The Lieutenant laughed, "That could be anywhere in the Midwest, but Kansas City, Missouri often claims that title." Billy was quiet a second, then said, "If he is from Kansas City, he might know Roxanne Fisk. She's married and I don't remember her married name, but Jay told me she lives in Kansas City."

"Who did you say?" Helene was studying Conway. She was thinking back ten or more years. That name Fisk had caught her attention.

"Roxanne? Was that who you were asking about?"

"No, I thought you said Fisk."

"I did. I ran into Jay Fisk in England and he told me his sister, Roxanne, was married and lived in Kansas city."

"Is Jay Fisk a tall, slender, blond-haired, blue-eyed boy? Did he study music in Germany ten or more years ago?"

The Lieutenant was nonplussed. "You knew him?"

"We were good friends. And his friend Sam helped us get out of Germany in time."

"I don't know what you are talking about," Billy said. "I just know Jay was very musical, and left our town when he graduated from high school. I never saw him again until we ran into each other at a pub in England. He's still tall and slender, his blond hair is a little thinner, but aside from that, I knew him the minute I saw him."

"I want to see him," Helene said. "Where is he now?"

"I don't know. He's with the Air Force, and I have no idea where he is stationed."

Amy Carter came in while Helene and the Lieutenant were talking. Helene ran to Amy and said, "I know now why we were destined to become friends. I knew Jay Fisk when we were students at Munich University over ten years ago. I hear you are his friend."

Amy and Billy promised to tell Jay about their friendship with Helene if they ever saw him again.

"Oh, the encounters of war!" they thought.

Little did the three of them know that three weeks before, Jay Fisk had been close by, making his way through enemy territory to safety.

CHAPTER SIXTEEN

CHAPTER SIXTEEN

THE NUNS THEMSELVES, in the Laon Cathedral, could do nothing about getting Jay Fisk through the enemy lines, because they were watched closely. However, they did all they could to protect anyone who came to them for help. When Fisk was brought in by a native woman, the nuns were quick to find clothes of French design and the right size to fit him. When the woman left the hospital a few hours later, she was accompanied by a man, who to all observers looked like an old, stooped Frenchman helping a woman carry a load of wood from the Cathedral to her own home. All around were signs of massive destruction. The people, with the help of the churches, tried to apportion what supplies they could muster to the many who had lost all their belongings.

Jay Fisk helped the French woman distribute the wood to several homes before she said she could get him to a safe place. They heard the newscasts of the war's progress. When territory was not in their definite control, the Allies moved their field hospitals from place to place until the area was captured. One day an e-vac hospital came close to where Jay was in hiding. His hostess took Jay to it. There was a small landing strip where the C-47s came in, picked up the wounded and took them to England.

Though Jay Fisk's leg was getting much better, he was one of those listed for evacuation.

"At last!" Jay thought, "now I can get back to base and collect my mail." He expected he would have many letters from Irene by now. He knew she would have wondered why she hadn't heard from him for such a long time. So, this time he had a big story to tell her!

When Jay Fisk reported back to his unit, he was informed that he had been promoted. He was given a purple heart, which surprised him, for he thought his was such a minor injury. He was now a Sergeant, and his job would be instructing the new men who were arriving. He would no longer be flying missions to the continent. He was relatively safe — another thing he could tell Irene. No longer would she be worried about his being killed in action! He hurried as soon as he could to get his mail, thinking that soon his joy would be complete!

His mail! There were only two pieces, and neither one of them from Irene. He opened the first one. It was from a lawyer enclosing the papers of a completed divorce proceedings that Irene had filed, a letter that stated that Jay's consent was not required, because the reason for the divorce was that he had agreed to accept her religion when they got married, and he had refused to do so. The shock left Jay stunned! The letter couldn't be right! He and Irene had never, ever once discussed religion!

Something was wrong here! But before he would read it again, he opened the second letter. It was from his bank. His last deposit was questioned — did he want to re-open his old account that had been closed out, or did he want to start a new one?

Jay sat there in a stupor, looking at the two letters lying in his lap. Irene had divorced him, cleaned out his bank account, and had not even advised him of her actions. He was in a war, alone, broke — the only money he had was the meager sum of his last pay check.

He looked at a group of soldiers clustered around a table, but he didn't see them — he saw a brown-haired, bright-eyed girl sitting around with him and a bunch of their friends at The Village. He looked out the door at a row of Quonset huts, but he didn't see huts — he saw that upscale house in Stamford or Tappan that he and his love had anticipated buying.

Jay wanted to cry, but he couldn't. He was in too much shock to feel anything. Moving as if in a trance, he felt around in his locker. The only musical instrument that was still in his possession was a harmonica. He picked it up, sat back down on his bunk, and let the melancholy tunes pour forth. He played and played!

For the first few days after Jay Fisk got the devastating news, he was an automaton and went about his duties like a mechanical toy soldier. His superior officer called him into his office one day and remarked, "Fisk, these new boys coming in need a friend. You are in a position to pep them up, give them a feeling that their job is worth the effort. I know you like music. Maybe some of these new boys like music, too. Find out about that — take them into the city for a shopping tour for instruments they could play while in service. Make them part of your life."

"I thought I was doing my job — teaching them communications," Jay answered in a flat tone of voice.

"Fisk, you are not the only soldier in this war that has received a 'Dear John' letter —"

The officer was interrupted by Fisk, "I have been trying to keep my troubles to myself, not to inflict them on other people."

"That is your trouble, Sergeant — keeping too much to yourself. Open up to those around you. You will be better off, and so will they."

Jay Fisk took those words of advice to heart and tried hard to find an outlet for the extra spare time he had, now that he was no longer making the regular C-47 fights to France. He had not heard the results of his own last flight, whether his companions had escaped the fiery annihilation of their plane, whether they had been captured or killed. All his enquiries had resulted in no information whatever. All that was known was that the plane was lost and he, Jay Fisk, the only known survivor. Being in a new unit, now that he was no longer flying, Jay had not made an effort to acquire new friends.

After the short conference with the officer, Jay decided he would see if he could find his long time acquaintance, Lieutenant William Conway. He thought the best way was to contact him was through the nurse, Amy Carter. He went to the hospital where she had been stationed, only to find out that she had been sent to France. He remembered his last conversation with her — at the train station in Ely.

That memory gave him another idea. He had wondered for months about the true identity of the beautiful suave nurse who called herself Amy Carter. He had felt so sure that she was none other than a girl he had known in his childhood days, a girl named Anna Mae Cowan. True, the teen-age girl he had known had been a shy, scared young girl. Could she have developed into this debonair, perfectly groomed, educated young woman called Amy Carter? She was certainly the right age. Jay took it upon himself to find out about her. He remembered the story she had told him at the Ely station. Only Anna Mae Cowan would have known that story. But he also felt that Amy Carter was lying to him at Ely, lying about something, but what?

Sergeant Jordan Fisk had found a project to take his mind off his personal troubles — his investigation of the nurse, Amy Carter. His first foray was to talk with the other nurses she worked with at the hospital before she was sent to France. He remembered very well the gorgeous Erica. That would be his first call.

When he arrived at the hospital where the two of them had been stationed, he asked for Erica Brown. No one could tell him anything at all about her. All he could learn was that she was no longer at the hospital. Had she been sent to France? No one knew. Was she working at another hospital in England? No one knew. The more he talked, the more answers came back negative. They all said that one day she just did not show up for work, and no one knew why. He talked with these same nurses about Amy Carter. Did they know about her? Oh, yes, she was an"Angel of Mercy."

The more he visited with the nurses still working at the hospital, the more he arrived at the same conclusion that they had all reached, that the very sexy and dazzling Erica had run off and gotten married to some rich man. They all agreed that she had set her aims high and that she had probably found one that met her requirements. But they didn't know that for a fact, it's just what they all guessed. But not Amy? Wasn't she just as pretty? Well, in a different way. She was not that social — someone even called her haughty.

Seeking the information about Amy Carter had brought Jay's mind a bit away from his loss at home. So many of the evenings of the last two and a half years he had spent writing letters to Irene. She was no longer there for him. One evening after coming from the hospital with the little news he had about Amy Carter, Jay decided he would write to his sister, Roxanne. He would write to her regularly, just as he had earlier written to Irene. He knew Rox would always be there for him! Jay wrote her about Irene's getting the divorce without even telling him she was getting it, about her cleaning out his bank account and leaving him broke. As he wrote, he began for the first time to feel an anger, and it took away some of the hurt.

He found another solace, music! His harmonica was his only source at first, but he followed the advice from his officer friend, who had told him to mingle with the new recruits coming in who were lonely and might also had an interest in music. One night when one young soldier named Joe told him he liked to hear him play his harmonica, Jay said, "How would you like to go shopping with me?"

"Shopping?" the boy asked, puzzled by the question.

"It'll be fun," Jay told him. The next night they went into the city, and Jay with what money he could dig up bought a used guitar and an old accordion and told the boy that now the guys in the barracks could hear a variety, not the same instrument every evening.

"Will you let me play your instruments sometime?" the boy asked timidly.

"Of course, if you can really play them. The guys around get upset when I produce a screech now and then."

The different instruments made a big difference to the rest of the soldiers in the barracks, too. They began to enjoy Jay's nightly concert, not complaining when it didn't interrupt their card games or other activities.

Jay had suppressed his personal heartache as much as he could, going with the rest of the boys to the pubs occasionally. One night they went into a pub where a piano sat over in a corner. One of their accompanying airmen, really expecting to bait Jay, called out loudly, "Sergeant Fisk, I suppose you can play that old piano, too."

Jay shrugged his shoulders, muttered, "Ummm, I guess so," and sauntered over to the piano, sat down and hit a few chords, then began to sing. He started with a song he had learned as a boy, *A Thousand Miles Away from Home.* He followed that with *When It's Springtime in the Rockies.* His voice was as good as his playing, and soon not only were all the airmen from his own unit surrounding him, but others from the pub were listening and crowding around, too. Soon they were asking him to play and sing that first song again. Because the mileage in England and in all of Europe was not as great as in the United States, he changed the words a little so that it reached all the homesick boys who were listening, as he sang, "***So many*** *miles away from home, just waiting for a train.*"

After seeing tears come to the eyes of some of the boys, Jay Fisk knew that he was not the only one to whom this war had brought the pangs of grief and loneliness.

Jay did not give up on his investigation of Amy Carter. When he had time enough, he decided that he would go to the town of Ely where he had last seen Amy Carter. He would check out her story about visiting relatives there. He thought also about going to the base near Ely where he was stationed when he flew his last mission to France with Quentin, Ray and Shelby. Perhaps he might be able to find out something of their plight. It would take him two hours to get there on the train. Jay didn't think that was a very good speed for the one hundred fourteen kilometers (less than seventy miles), but he thought it was still the best way to go.

Though winter had set in — the day was sunny and cold. Jay did not expect to be caught up in one of those smoggy black-out nights as he had months ago. Bombs still fell, but not as often as they did back in September when Germany had first dropped their V-2 rockets on London. As the train passed through Cambridge, Jay wished he had time to explore the University there, but he could do that on another day. Now that he didn't have any flight missions, he had time to see more of

England and perhaps Scotland. He didn't want to think about Irene at all, he wanted to concentrate on Amy Carter. Who was she? What was she doing that time so far from London weeks, no, months ago? Was she really calling on relatives?

From the train station in Ely, Jay tried to cover the steps he had taken when he met Amy. He tried to remember the location she gave as the address of her relatives — she said just a few blocks from the train station. Jay found a telephone book and looked for addresses. There was no one named Carter listed, and Amy did say her mother's relative was a Carter. After finding no telephone listed under that name, Jay walked rapidly, covering an area of blocks, in and around the station, seeing if he could find the name of Carter anywhere. About four blocks from the direction Amy had come that night, Jay found an empty house. It was boarded up.

He called at the house next door. An old woman answered his knock on the door. Two little children clung to her skirts. "Ma'am," Jay said, "I am looking for a family named Carter. Could you tell me where they might live?"

"I know of no one named Carter in this town, and I've lived here most of my life. Of course, there were some people who rented the house next door, but their name wasn't Carter." The woman did not invite Jay to come in.

Standing at the door, Jay asked, "When did they live there?"

The woman looked at Jay suspiciously, "Why do you want to know?'

"Ma'am, we're checking the disappearance of some

important people. We heard that they were here in Ely." Jay couldn't think of any other explanation.

"Spies, huh?"

"We don't know. The people who rented that house — when did they live here?"Jay asked again.

"They came about two years ago, a very nice couple, but they left suddenly about two or three months ago." The children, tagging at the woman's dress, were crying and asking for attention. The woman picked up the smaller of the two, told the other one that she would get her a cookie in a moment, then she explained to her caller. "These are my grandchildren. I take care of them while their mother works."

Jay nodded, but was not deterred from his line of thought. "What was the name of the people who rented that house?" Jay asked.

"Joan and William Davis. They kept pretty much to themselves, but Mrs. Davis offered to care for the little tots if I wanted a day off now and then. I thought that was nice, but I never did take her up on it."

"Do you ever see anyone else around here that you do not know?"

"Oh, the Davis' had company now and then — sometimes men, sometimes women, but they never stayed long."

"Well, thank you for your help." Jay gave a slight bow to the woman as he left. Sergeant Fisk thought he had some very important information that needed to be put into the right hands. He caught the train back to London, eager to get back to his base and thinking he should get in touch with his CO.

Jay's attention was quickly diverted from his Ely journey upon his return to base. He had a letter from Roxanne! He was surprised and delighted that she had answered his letter so soon. The first part of the letter was commiserating with him on Irene's betrayal and inquiring about the condition of his leg injury. He was reading another part of the letter about a First Lieutenant from Kansas City that Roxanne knew. It amused him, and his laughing about it caught the notice of one of his bunk mates, one who wanted to share in his mirth. Jay read that portion of the letter again, this time out loud:

There is a First Lieutenant from Kansas City here that everybody seems to know. He's not a kid, almost as old as I am. His heroic activities have been told to his family and friends. I was wondering if you knew him. His name is Edward J. Reardon. He is with the Third Division. The funny thing was that he fell out of his jeep and got a broken leg. He was in a hospital in France for three weeks. I thought you might have run into him while you were hurt in France.

Jay told his companion that he was laughing about the fellow getting a broken leg by falling out of a jeep. He had no idea how it happened, and Roxanne had given no further details. He would have to write Roxanne that there was little chance that he would ever run into First Lieutenant Reardon — for one reason, the Lieutenant was in the Army and Jay was in the Air Force, and they did not often mix. And the second, unless he was a personal friend, Sergeant Fisk would not likely be in close relationship with the higher ranking officers. It had been different with Lieutenant R. William Conway. Conway had contacted him because they had been acquainted since childhood days. Conway would be the one who might know Reardon, since he, too, was in the Army and a Lieutenant.

Jay enjoyed the rest of Roxanne's letter, about the preparations for Christmas she was making for her two little girls. She told him his Christmas package was on the way.

It was the following day before Fisk had an opportunity to talk with anyone about his findings in Ely. He didn't want to tell just anybody. He wasn't sure that it was worth reporting at all, and he certainly did not want to cause undue trouble if it was not warranted.

When he had a few minutes the morning after his excursion, he went into the large lobby where the commanding officer sat at his desk. It was a large space on the ground floor of the administration building, and soldiers of all ranks passed through it, in and out at all times of the day. Jay went up to Commander Burke and said, "If you have a few minutes, I want to tell you about a strange incident I found on a trip I took yesterday to my old stomping ground near Ely."

Commander Burke smiled, leaned back in his chair, looked up at Sergeant Fisk who still standing in front of his desk. He did not invite the sergeant to sit down, but said, "Okay, fire away."

"Well, it's about a nurse, Amy Carter." The minute Jay uttered her name, a frown came over the face of the

Commander and he leaned forward.

Jay Fisk continued, "I do not think her name is Amy Carter. I am sure that she is a girl I knew many years ago —"

The Commander was on his feet and a round the desk. He looked at the numerous people who were coming and going through the building. He took Jay by the arm and said very quietly, "I think this better be a private conversation. I hope you haven't spoken to anyone else about this."

"No, no," Jay mumbled as he was being led from the spacious room through a door into a small private cubicle.

When they were inside and the door was closed, the Commander asked Jay to take a seat, then he said, "Now tell me your story."

Jay told him about suspecting Amy Carter was really a girl named Anna Mae Cowan, a girl he had known in his home town, years ago. Because he wondered about the name change, and because she acted as if she had never seen him before, he began to wonder what she was up to. Then Jay told about running into her that foggy night in Ely, and about her telling him she was visiting relatives named Carter. Yet when he checked it out, just a day or so ago, there was no family named Carter in Ely, and from what a woman had told him, there never was a family named Carter that lived in that town. Jay told him about the empty rental property and a couple who had lived there for a short time only.

"I appreciate your concern, Sergeant Fisk, and the loyalty you feel toward your country. Now let me tell you a story. Because our plans were foreseen by the

Germans, we knew there was a mole, a leak, somewhere in our forces here, in the Army and in the Air Force. How did they know to be ready to meet our thrusts at just the right time in just the right places. We figured that it might have come from a woman, or maybe women, because it was being felt in both the Army and the Air Force. We sent an agent, a registered nurse, to supervise the nurses in the London hospital, agents to mingle with the soldiers in every outfit, trying to find that leak.

"One day the nurse at the hospital said she had heard Amy Carter talking with some of the other nurses. The girls were remarking on the beauty of a girl, a brunette with a satiny olive skin and gorgeous brown eyes. Amy Carter told the other nurses that when she had made those remarks to her roommate, Erica Brown, Erica had seemed almost angry. She flared up and said how could anyone say she was good-looking — all those dark-skinned people just looked dirty to her. The agent nurse stepped in and asked Amy how she had replied. Amy told the nurse that she just shrugged her shoulders and said to Erica, 'So you and I are fair-skinned, blue-eyed and blond, so what?'

"The agent nurse reported this nurses' conversation to us, saying she thought Erica sounded just like Hitler, she might be the one we were looking for, so we checked out Amy Carter, thinking she was the one who had the opportunity to watch Erica Brown. We found that after Amy had been raped in her teen years, she was ostracized by her community. She finished high school, went to Chicago —"

Jay finished the sentence the Commander had started,

"Changed her name to Amy Carter, became a top ranked nurse and —"

Now the Commander interrupted, "So you already know that. Then what's your problem?"

"Why did she lie to me in Ely?"

"Sergeant Fisk, Amy Carter was on a mission. She couldn't tell you what she was doing. We recruited Amy Carter to spy, yes, spy on Erica. She might find her innocent, or maybe guilty of the leak to our enemies. We did not know. We asked her to check on any travel outside the hospital that Erica might take. Amy followed her to Ely two or three times, found the address where she went and reported it back to us. That was when we arrested a couple who called themselves Davis, Joan and William, just as you stated. They were German agents and had a powerful radio in that house. As you probably know, Erica Brown was one helluva good-looking gal. It wasn't too surprising that with enough drink, she could wheedle information out of some of the lonely service men. Amy told us that Erica made a habit of directing her advances toward the officers whenever she could.

"We told Amy she had been a great help in finding the source of our leak. We caught the Davis couple, but Erica has disappeared. If you want to keep your eyes open for Erica, we would appreciate it. Oh! If and when you see Amy Carter again, congratulate her on her patriotism."

"I would like to have a chance to do just that," Jay Fisk said, as he rose to leave. "I feel like a fool, doubting her as I did. I heard she is in France now. Will she get in touch with you if she ever comes back to England?"

"I expect she will, but I don't know."

"Please let her know that I would like to see her, will you?"

The Commander assured Jay that if he should ever again be in touch with Amy Carter, he would give her Jay's message.

The news Jay heard from the front in the middle of December was bad. Because of bad weather, the Air Force was stymied in its need to relieve the Americans who were surrounded by the Germans near Bastogne, France. The days pressed on and the English people, in spite of the war news, did not want to forget the coming of the Christ Child. Already most families and the churches were preparing for the Christmas celebration.

Christmas day came, and in spite of the good intentions of the English people doing all they possibly could to make Christmas a time of joy for the nonnative soldiers, they could not dispel the depth of loneliness for home and family that lingered in the hearts of these foreign boys and men.

Many of them, like Jay, received the most welcome gifts from their loved ones at home, food! But welcome as it was, it did not lift the despair among them, nor the despair that they might lose this war, even after sacrificing the lives of so many young men. That was the feeling Jay and most of his companions had on Christmas Eve and Christmas Day.

Then came December 26, the day after Christmas. The sun broke out from the days of dreary gloom, and the air Force went into action! Fair weather, they could fly!. Sergeant Jordan Fisk was sorry that he would not be on one of the C-47s that were flown in droves to relieve the American boys struggling to stay alive against the German Ardennes Offensive. It was one of the turning points of the war.

In January, the Soviets captured Warsaw from the Germans. In February, President Roosevelt, Winston Churchill and Stalin met at Malta to discuss plans for the complete surrender of the Germans. Step by step, day by day, through the early months of spring, more German strongholds fell to the Allied Forces and more German soldiers surrendered to the Allies.

One day Sergeant Jordan Fisk was asked to report to his commanding officer. Jay had not spoken with Commander Burke for some time, and he wondered why the Commander wanted to see him.

Burke was smiling when Jay appeared before his desk. He put out his hand to Jay and said, "There is someone here who wants to see you."

Jay thought immediately of Amy Carter, but it was Lieutenant William Conway who came out to see him. The two young men shook hands, expressed their pleasure in seeing each other. Then Lieutenant Conway said, "Jay, I have a favor I want to ask of you."

"Okay, what is it?"

"I want you to be Best Man at my wedding."

"I would be glad to if the place and date are agreeable. I assume you are talking about marrying Amy Carter. Am I right?"

"Of course." Conway called out to Amy, and she walked out the same door that Billy had a few moments before. In her regal manner she approached Jay and said, "I have a surprise for you. You'll never guess who I have asked to stand up with me." She led Jay over to the door, opened it, and Helene said, "Hello, Jay! Do you remember me?"

No one had said her name, yet Jay realized the young woman before him looked familiar. Jay paused a moment before he said, "Can you be Helene Dolmet, a girl I knew over ten years ago?"

After the mutual greetings of the four, Jay turned to Commander Burke, "Did you help them plan this dramatic entrance, one at a time, until they had shocked me out of my senses?"

The Commander laughed and told the four to get going on making plans for the wedding. What the Commander did not know was that plans for the wedding had been made many weeks before. It was the subsequent events and conditions that made implementing those plans a troublesome chore.

While Lieutenant Robert William Conway was still bedridden, he had been assured of the reciprocal love of his adored nurse, Amy Carter. At once they began contriving the kind of wedding they would have. The first obstacle was presented by the Lieutenant himself. He wanted to first get himself in good health, so that he could be a good top class husband — not a dilapidated, incapacitated invalid hanging onto her skirt tails.

Amy agreed to postpone the wedding until he was well on the road to recovery. Her desire was to have the wedding in London, the place where they had met as Amy Carter and Lieutenant William Conway. The Lieutenant would have to get permission to be allowed to return to London while still in the service, and so would she, as a nurse.

Other plans they discussed would also take a bit of doing. After they had decided upon London as the place for their wedding, Bill Conway said he would like to have Jay Fisk to be his best man. He did not know where Jordan Fisk was stationed at the time, so they would have to locate him as soon as they could and see if he would serve in that capacity. All they knew was that he was in the Air Force and was in communications on the C-47s that flew supplies to the Allied Forces in France.

Amy had a plan also, that would take some International planning. She wanted to have her French friend, Helene Dolmet, be the Maid of Honor. Helene agreed at once that she would be glad to have that honored position, but she had no money and, at the present, no way she could get permission to leave the country.

While they were working through these impediments, things were happening in the war and around the world. The Soviet Army had captured Warsaw in Poland, Finland had declared war on Germany, the United States First Army had crossed the Rhine River at Remagen — then the city of Cologne, Germany fell to the Allies. A blow that shocked the world, especially all the Allied nations was the sudden death of The American President, Franklin Delano Roosevelt, on April 12, just a couple of months after he had met with Churchill and Stalin in Malta to make plans on their occupation of Germany.

With so many signs now pointing toward the end of the war, the Allies expecting Germany to surrender soon, plans for the wedding fell easily into place by the end of April.

Lieutenant Robert William Conway and Nurse Amy Carter exchanged their marriage vows attended by Jordan Fisk and Helene Dolmet and many other casual service friends.

But the marriage vows were not the only vows exchanged. The bride requested that the bride's only name would be Amy Carter Conway, no time would she ever be referred to as Anna Mae Cowan. The groom also had his own request — never would he be called Billy. He would go by his proper name William, or he could be called Will, the short name used by most of his business friends at home.

The war was over! The newlywed couple were ready to depart for home in May, looking forward to living happily ever after. Their two close war-time friends, Helene Dolmet and Jay Fiske, told them of their own plans before they bid them farewell, promising to keep in touch in the days to come.

Helene told the other three the story of her own lost love, the story she had promised to tell Amy months ago. When the Germans occupied Strasbourg, France, Helene's father had chosen to collaborate with the Germans, saying that the Germans would win the war, and that they had no other choice if they wanted a future in their own homeland. When Helene argued that she would join the Resistance, her father forbad it. What made the matter even harder for Helene was the attitude her beloved Pierre had taken when he agreed with her father.

When Helene left her music schooling in Munich,

Germany, she had returned to Strasbourg where she and Pierre Caen had fallen in love. She and Pierre had known each other from the time they were children, since they both came from two of the most influential families in Strasbourg. They had paid little if any attention to each other until they were in their early twenties. They fell in love and made plans to marry when they were both through the University and had their careers settled. Then came the war. Helene quarreled with Pierre when he sided with her father. She ran away from Strasbourg, to the west of France where she joined up with the Resistance Force fighting the occupation of the Germans. It had been years since she had gotten in touch with her family or Pierre. It had not been safe for her to contact them through these war years. She had given up her study of music and had taken up nursing to help with the war wounded. She told Amy, Bill and Jay that she had several offers of marriage from boys she liked a lot, but no one had taken the place of Pierre.

"Oh, yes," Amy said, "there was a Lieutenant from America in a hospital with a broken leg, the same as Bill. She liked him a lot. His name was Eddie"

"Amy! I told you he was too young for me. He was just fun to talk to," Helene protested.

"That's the same soldier Roxanne wrote me about," Jay joined in the repartee. "She hears about him from her friend and asks if I have ever met him."

"Listen, you guys," Helene laughed a moment, then became very serious. "I have to go back to Strasbourg. My family will probably need me more than ever now. Many of the people wouldn't state whether they were for or against the Germans, and now in Strasbourg, just as I've seen in the rest of France, many will say they've always been for the Allies. At least my father took a stand! But he will probably be ostracized by the rest of the community. That's why I need to go back. I also want to find out what happened to Pierre. Maybe he's married and has a family. I don't know, but I have to find out."

Jordan Fisk told them of his heartbreak, getting the "Dear John" letter. He did not tell them that Irene had cleaned him out of all his possessions, left him flat broke.

"I have nothing to go back to," he said. "They need me to stay here, probably six or more months after the war, to go to all the concentration camps. Since I speak several of the European languages, they want me to go to many places, find out where these poor people live and help them get back to their native countries. As you know, I have already gone to Dachau." Jay shuddered as he spoke the name. "There is much more work in that place yet to be done."

The happily married couple said goodbye to their two friends, one of them seeking the uncertain reunion of a divided family in Strasbourg, the other to face the horrors of the death camps.

PART THREE

The Aftermath

CHAPTER SEVENTEEN

CHAPTER SEVENTEEN

FLYING LOW OVER PARIS! That was the only way to get a close view of a lovely city, unharmed by the wide-spread devastation elsewhere. It brought a wave of joy and rapture to Sergeant Jordan Fisk, Jr., replacing momentarily the underlaying melancholy that had engulfed him for months.

Though other officers and enlisted men were still moving about in the European war theater even after the conflict was over, most of Jay's acquaintances and friends, with whom he had fought alongside these last few years, had returned to the bliss of home and family. But not all of them. He had learned that his pilot friends, Quentin Peterson and Ray Goins, had both gone down with the flaming plane from which he himself had escaped. And he couldn't keep a choking lump from coming into his throat whenever he thought of them — or of the wife whom he had loved so much, the wife who had divorced him, cleaned out his bank account and married another man. From those bits of heartbreaking events, he had found a bit of warmth in the coincidental meeting of childhood friends of long ago — but they, too, were no longer around. He was glad, of course, that a happy Billy Conway and Anna Mae Cowan (Amy Carter) had returned to the United States, having reaped a love and marriage from the ravages of this war.

Jay looked down again on Paris, his plane flying at a lower altitude than any commercial plane would do, and felt the enchantment of the place, letting it crowd out the bitterness of his personal loss, even making him forget memories of pictures of Dachau that he had seen only a few days before, and in the news pictures taken by those who had observed the freeing of 33,000 prisoners from that death camp. The euphoria of viewing the charm of a Paris, intact from battle wounds, did not last long. Jordan Fisk knew his stay in Paris would be short-lived, that he soon would be going back to Dachau, the first of many other concentration camps where prisoners were being held.

Munich was the city that Jordan Fisk, Jr. had grown to love in the years he had lived there as a student. He would be going back again soon after these years of war, and he wondered what the city be like now? And the University where he had enjoyed his study in music — would it still be there? And what had become of the close friends he had made? How many of them would he find now? Munich had been the center, the heartbeat of the Nazi uprising. Would the Nazis still be in control there? The Dachau Death Camp was established while Jay was in school in Munich in 1933, and he was completely unaware that this, the first of the German concentration camps, only a few miles away, was imprisoning political opponents, clergymen, and any undesirables opposed to the Nazi regime. It was operated by the organized SS and Gestapo elements, which became known for their terror and brutality. Jay Fisk did not have time before he was sent on to Dachau to investigate the damages of the Munich he remembered from years of long ago.

Jay didn't see it, or even know about it, while he was in school. He saw Dachau for the first time in the aftermath of its prime. Though the prisoners had been freed, the dead were not yet all buried, and there were others dying. Before he went there the first time, he dreaded what he would to find; yet he had little knowledge of the horrors he would face, nor could he foresee, not in his wildest imagination, the full extent of the atrocities.

His first impression when he arrived in Dachau was one of surprise. The place looked like an ordinary military post, nothing noteworthy in the appearance of a brick wall around it. On the back side of the complex, away from the front gate, there was a water-filled moat and guard towers all around. The guard towers had been manned by several hundred SS troops and Gestapo agents, but those remaining on duty had been captured, others had fled before the arrival of the Allied forces. What still remained, however, exemplified what Jay had seen first-hand and in news pictures shown all over the world. What those pictures did not show was the close view of the corpses that still remained unburied, or did they reveal the stench that permeated the whole area.

There were different barracks, some used as infirmaries. They were filled with the dead and dying. What the liberating forces soon found out was that the camp at Dachau could not be cleared out overnight. The original camp was built to imprison a few thousand, but had expanded to hold many more. The exact number of prisoners that were sent here, died or were rescued is not known, but one General estimated the number to be around 300,000.

Jay also saw what was designated as the "experimental station." There was gruesome evidence of biochemical work that had been done on prisoners to find how they would react to certain diseases with which they were forcefully infected. He learned from live prisoners that anyone who tried to escape and was recaptured was sent to the Gestapo agents for torture and death.

A rifle range was outside the prison area. Jay was told that at least six thousand Russian prisoners had been executed there, besides the thousands of unknown others who met a similar fate. It was estimated that between thirty to fifty thousand people were executed here at the rifle range, most all of them political prisoners, not the condemned Jews. Some of them were none other than good German citizens who protested the brutality ordered by Hitler. Jay couldn't help but wonder if any of his good German acquaintances might have been in that number. He especially thought about one of the last letters he had received several years ago from his friend Franz Lubeck, telling of the assassination of the brother of their mutual friend, Grenythe Karstein. Jay thought it very likely that her brother could have been one of those killed here in Dachau, since it was so close to Munich, his home. He wondered if he had been shot on the rifle range, or had he been executed in the gas chamber — and in either case, was his body disposed of in the crematorium? The more he thought a bout it, the more he wanted to find his friend Franz, Grenythe, or any of the other students he had known, students who did not condone the brutality that was becoming evident, even before Jay finished his studies in Munich — before his return to the United States.

The individual barracks at the camp were constructed to hold about 200 prisoners each, yet Jay found as many of 1600 in one of them, jammed in with those already dead, and others dying. Jay had to leave that place for a time to keep from being sick from the foul odor of stale vomit and rotting flesh.

Besides the boxcars of corpses, they found cement structures used as a crematorium for the dead bodies. There was also in the structure a gas chamber, another means of extermination.

One day Jay was talking with one of the troops who had arrived at Dachau earlier than he, an enlisted soldier named Joe Kerry. When he first met him, Jay suddenly felt his own age. This young enlisted man had asked him question after question. Jay felt that the youngster had assumed he would know all the answers, not because of his rank, but because he was an older man. The boy was barely old enough to be in the service, and his light complexion gave no hint that he had shaved or had ever needed to. He had arrived with the evacuation hospital sent here to aid the rescued prisoners who were sick. On one occasion, when Jay was helping with the live victims, the boy Joe spoke to him again, telling him that once while they were unloading the corpses he found one man alive, a man that was so thin that every bone in his body could be counted.

"What did you do with him?" Jay asked.

"It was horrible! At first I didn't know he was alive. When he moved a hand, I thought it was just our movement of the other dead bodies that made the hand move. The smell was so bad that I kept turning my head away. I couldn't look at that pile of emaciated bodies any more. Finally, the sergeant told me to keep moving these bodies out of the car. I turned back—" The young soldier stopped talking and tears came to his eyes.

Jay put his arm around the boy's shoulder and said. "I know it was awful — it still is. You don't need to tell me any more about it, if you don't want to."

"But I need to! It won't leave my mind. When I turned back to move that corpse, he moved again — just a slight move of his body. I hadn't moved any other corpses, so I thought something was different about this one. I put my hand under his shoulders and his hips and lifted him very carefully. Then I called out to the doctors that were outside and told them a live man was in there.

"Several others came into the car and helped me take him out. They got him to the hospital. I insisted that he was alive. The doctor said he could hear a heartbeat, but he didn't think there was a chance the man would live."

"Did he?"

"No!"

"I'm sorry. I know you hoped he would recover. What we must remember, Joe, is that there could be others in like circumstances that we can save. There are a lot of other concentration camps that we have to go to. We mustn't forget to search for others like that poor man. Maybe we can restore a life somewhere."

"I can't forget that man though. He was thrown in with all those other dead people when he was alive. I wonder how many others were treated the same way?"

Jay shuddered as he listened to Joe tell the story. Yes, how many other skeletal bodies had been pitched aside with the dead. How many of them could have been saved? Gruesome though the incident was, it would stay forever in Jay's mind as he was sent from one prison camp on to another. He shook his head and in a soft voice said, "Joe, we are treating those captive SS officers and Gestapo agents a lot better than they treated their prisoners."

"We are, aren't we?" Joe Kerry suddenly changed from his serious mood and started to laugh, then continued, "It's a lot better than how one General treated a Lieutenant Colonel here a day or two ago. You think the only war would be between the Allies and the Germans, wouldn't you, but wait until you hear about this!" And Joe was laughing again.

"Well, tell me about it! I need a laugh," the still glum Jay bid. And Joe told him the story:

"It was on April 29, when the 157th Infantry Regiment, under the command of Lieutenant Colonel Felix Sparks, came to this death camp here near the little town of Dachau, a short distance from the city of Munich. The first thing Sparks and his crew saw was that line of forty railway cars near the camp entrance — all of them loaded with decaying corpses of men and women. Attached to Sparks command was the 191st Tank Division, Battery C of the 158th Field Artillery and engineers from the 120th Engineers Battalion. Though Sparks' task force was first designated to head for an attack on Munich and that task took them through the little town of Dachau, it did not include the concentration camp. Sparks new little or nothing about the death camp at all, not until he received another order telling him to take the camp before going on to Munich. Included in that order was the message to keep a tight guard on the camp and let no one enter or leave.

"The camp was guarded by two or three hundred SS troops and guard dogs, so Sparks' command went over the wall around the camp to start the attack. His forces captured the German troops in all the areas in the camp. When the last of the German guards had been taken, the prisoners seemed as cowed by the liberating forces as they had been under the Germans. It took over an hour after Sparks had entered the camp to convince the prisoners that they were there to free them. They informed them that food and medicine would soon be coming. When the prisoners knew that they were to be freed, they rushed to the fences, trying to push their way out, endangering themselves and those in their way. Sparks ordered soldiers to stand guard to keep them in order, and while he was doing that, three vehicles from the 42nd Division drove up to the gate. Sparks remembered his orders to 'let no one out, let no one leave' and sent one of his men to inform the approaching group that they could not enter.

"It just happened that a Brigadier General was in one of the approaching jeeps, and he had a reporter with him. When the messenger told him he could not enter, the Brigadier General whacked Sparks' messenger over the head with a riding crop that he was carrying. Sparks immediately went to rescue his messenger, and pointed to the orders posted on the gate — that no one was allowed to enter or to leave. Then that woman reporter jumped out of the jeep, dashed up to the gate and tore off the order!

"After having his man struck by the approaching general and his orders torn off by a reporter, Sparks lost his cool and delivered some unkind epitaphs to the General, upon which the General told Sparks that he was removed from his command. Sparks drew his pistol and again asked the General to leave — which he did, but not without telling Sparks that he would see that he was court-martialed."

"What happened to Sparks? Was he court-martialed?" Jay asked.

"That's all I know. Lieutenant Colonel Sparks put Company I in charge of rounding up all of the German guards, and you see what is going on now — we learned from the prisoners that most of the German guards had left the camp and only about two hundred were left to be captured by the Americans, but some of them were killed by mistake."

"Killed by mistake?" Jay asked, "What do you mean?"

"When we first arrived here and were capturing the German troops in all directions, Sparks heard gunshots from where soldiers were guarding the German prisoners, and he rushed over there and kicked the gun out of the hand of one of our boys. Sparks asked him what he thought he was doing, shooting German prisoners. The boy was about 19 years old and scared. He said he was afraid the Germans were trying to escape. Sparks was angry that those twelve German prisoners had been killed. He said it would cause the Americans to get a bad reputation. We would be labeled as bad as the Germans, executing war prisoners."

"Where is Lieutenant Colonel Sparks now?" Jay asked.

"I don't know. I know that part of his command left to take Munich. The Seventh Army came in on April 30th and we arrived a day later."

"Where did you hear that story about Sparks and the General?" Jay asked.

"Oh, everybody was talking about it when we got here!"

After talking with Joe, Jay went about his work, talking with emaciated prisoners, getting them to tell him where they came from. It wasn't easy. Many of them did not want to give their home town or country, fearing reprisal to members of their families who might still be living there. It was a gruesome task, heartwarming when he gained the trust of those poor people, yet heartbreaking when they did not live long enough to return to their homeland.

Jay wanted desperately to find time to seek out his old haunts of years ago — to trace the whereabouts of those two good friends, Franz Lubeck and Grenythe Karstein. His few days with Helene Dolmet had given him no clue to whether either of them were still alive. When he was off duty, he hoped he could slip away for a few hours to Munich. He wanted to explore the area where he and Samuel Bradshaw had lived in a pension, and maybe find the house where he had boarded with the Weis family. He remembered seeing the Weis boy,

Paul, spirited out of the country while he was living there. He knew that the Weis father had disappeared. Whether he had left to find a safe place for his family or whether he was a victim of the Hitler regime, Jay never learned. The Weis family were very secretive on that subject. And Mrs. Weis! What had happened to her? Had she been able to join her son or husband, or had she, too, been sent to the death camps by the SS troops and the Gestapo? Jay would do all he could to find out!

When the first opportunity came, Jay Fisk traveled the short distance into Munich. He did not see the bright lights and gay atmosphere that he remembered from his school days here. The lights were dimmer, the streets, though not deserted, were shy of the hustle and bustle of happy citizens. Not like the former bouncy city with the spirit of a merry maid, Munich now resembled more the image of an old woman without hope. The people on the street looked neither to the left or the right, but with heads down, moved ahead as if they dreaded their destination.

This shocking impression of Munich left Jay feeling heartsick, that what he remembered as a wonderful center for learning and music had become a forlorn remnant of its former self. A soon as he got his bearings, he made his way toward the pension where he had first lived, wondering if the building was still there

What he found was worse than he expected. Even though he had heard from other servicemen that the pension was nothing but a brothel, Jay saw it more than a bawdyhouse — to some of those young girls it was more like a prison. This is the way that Jay described it, when he wrote to his sister, Roxanne.

Roxane, he wrote, *you could never believe what this war has done to the people of Germany. Not from the bombs we have dropped on them, but from what they have done to themselves. In a war, soldiers were getting killed by the dozens, as you would expect, and Hitler played upon the patriotism of young girls, telling them that they must produce more and more children to fight for their country — and the male soldiers went right along with that. My old pension had turned into a house for girls, where the soldiers went whenever they were in town, and these girls, not all of them, felt like they were helping with the war effort by just being whores. I cannot believe so many would fall for such a line of malarkey.*

Jay's hasty visit at the pension increased his despair on finding anything he would really enjoy in Munich, but he was determined to look anyway. The drabness of Munich was likely increased by Jay's own dispirited self, a mood he had never been able to cast completely aside, not from the very day he had received the "Dear John" letter. What was it about Munich that Jay hoped would lift his spirits? The place? The people?

Leaving the pension, he walked along the streets, looking into the faces of everyone he met. Was it possible that he might see some face he would recognize, someone, even something that might bring back the joy he had felt walking along here so many years ago? He walked out toward the University, not knowing whether he would go there first or stop at the Weis home, which was nearby.

Jay just had a few hours to explore, then he must get

back to base at Dachau. He knew he had done about all he could at Dachau, and would soon be sent to another death camp — he did not know where. That was the reason this visit to Munich was so important to him now. He walked fast until he came to the street where he could turn to the Weis home or continue on straight to the University. He hesitated, then turned to the house where he had lived in 1932 and 1933.

A smile came to his face as he looked up from the street. The house looked much as it had so many years ago. He was pleasantly surprised to see that it had been well kept through the last twelve years, the years since he had been here. He skipped up the steps and knocked on the door, having no idea who might answer — if anyone. It was late in the afternoon and working people could possibly be home. He hoped so!

When he did not get an immediate answer, he knocked again, louder this time.

He was about ready to knock once more before leaving when the door opened. The woman who answered was a slight woman, too thin even for her natural medium frame. There were a few white streaks in her otherwise blonde hair. She did not have a smile on her face, yet she was not frowning either. She just opened the door, with a questioning expression on her face. Jay looked at her, then looked again. She looked familiar, yet for a minute he couldn't be sure where he had seen her before. Then, with a query in his voice, he said, "Grenythe?"

The woman's brow furrowed, her attention directed fully at Jay for a moment, just long enough for him to think he might have made a mistake. This woman could be thirty-five or forty years old, thin and her hair a dulled blonde and cropped short, not the long flowing, corn silken hair he remembered on the young girl student, Grenythe Karlstein. He was on the point of offering an apology, saying he had mistaken her for someone else, when she asked, "Are you Jay Fisk?"

When they both recognized the other, Grenythe stepped out the door, and they fell into each other's arms. They hugged each other tightly, then were kissing each other, on the mouth, the cheeks, and hugging again, like two forlorn lovers, at finding each other after a long separation.

Just as suddenly as the hugging and kissing had started, it stopped. They both pulled back from the other, both a bit embarrassed by their sudden vehement greeting. After all, they had only been friends a decade or more ago. Then they had never engaged in the same hugging and kissing that they had just experienced this last moment. Many times while they were in school, Jay had put his arm around Grenythe's shoulder, had given her a pecking kiss on the forehead or cheek, and she had treated him likewise. They had been just good school friends, enjoying each other's company in their mutual studies.

Now they stood staring at each other, then grinning. Jay said, "I am so glad to see you, Grenythe. I came into Munich hoping I would find some of my old friends. Can we have a time to catch up on our lives since we've last seen each other?"

Grenythe put her hand on Jay's arm. "Jay, I do need

to talk with you, for a long, long time, but I have to be back at school very shortly. I am a teacher now at the University and board here. Can you come back Saturday or Sunday for a full day, or perhaps for an hour or two tonight after I am through with my classes?"

"I can't stay tonight, but I can try to get back here Saturday or Sunday. I don't yet know what my schedule will be. I have to go to the prison camps and help get people back to their native homes. I'll come to see you whenever I can get away."

The two gave each other another hug, and Jay Fisk smiled a happy goodbye as they parted.

CHAPTER EIGHTEEN

CHAPTER EIGHTEEN

THOUGH SERGEANT JORDAN FISK was glad to leave Dachau, he was sorry the leaving made it impossible for him to get back to Munich on Saturday. Anyone with no higher rank than a sergeant did not specify where or when duty would send him next. Dachau was just one of many concentration camps scattered around Germany. All of them needed help in the repatriation of the many weak and injured inmates. Jay, though not fluent in all dialects, was kept busy because of his ability as a linguist in several European languages, a need in the many concentration camps.

On leaving Dachau, Jay hoped to erase from his mind what he had seen of the terror system there. It had begun with the establishment of the camp by Heinrich Himmler on March 21, 1933. It was a model for the rest of the death camps, and often called the "murder school" for the SS. Surely the next camp where he was being sent could not be as bad. The four gas chambers that were built at the Dachau camp for cremation were never put to full use, because thousands upon thousands died of starvation, sickness, exhaustion, beatings and torture, long before they would have been sent to the gas chambers for elimination. Surely no other camp could be as bad!

Disappointed that he could not get back to Munich to see Grenythe, Jay was still amazed at the fortunate circumstance that had brought them together. He had been so glad to see her, and she had seemed just as glad to see him — or had she? Jay remembered that she had not invited him into the house — that instead, she had stepped out on the stoop to talk with him. Was there someone or something in the house that she did not want him to see? Maybe she was not as glad to see him as he was to see her — she had dismissed him hurriedly, saying she did not have time to talk now. Then he remembered how fervently she had embraced him, how lovingly she had kissed him, not once, but again and again. He had to see Grenythe again. He knew they had so much to tell each other!

His mind was suddenly brought back to his present mission by the quick stop of the jeep he was riding in. It brought his attention to his present surroundings. On their way from Dachau, they had come upon another concentration camp. It was much smaller than Dachau, and they found out from the American Company K that had already been stationed here for a few days that it was a slave labor camp and contained about eight thousand prisoners. These prisoners had been selected from the most hardy specimens so that they could carry out SS supervised labor.

Jay soon learned that most of the big death camps had sub-camps, such as this one where the more hardy prisoners were forced into making war weapons. The same horrors they had found in the main Dachau camp were repeated here in the sub-camp, but in a far lesser number, though not in degree.

The released prisoners came through the opened gates, barely able to walk as they greeted the American soldiers. Most of them were so emaciated that they were unable to take but a few steps, and those slowly. Jay Fisk noticed that one of the victims was considerably heavier than the others, that he was not nearly as weak, even though he had a limp. As Jay watched him, he noticed the man sometimes did not limp, and when he did, the limp was not consistent. Jay also noticed that other prisoners were shunning him, and some were yelling at him. Jay understood enough of what they were saying to call the officer in charge of the liberation and told him it might be wise to investigate that victim, for in all probability he was one of the SS troops trying to escape capture by appearing as one of the prisoners.

Jay's commanding officer took the man aside and found that he was truly one of the guards at the subcamp who had shed his uniform and dressed in the dirty, worn-out clothes of one of the deceased. He was just *one* of several guards in the SS and Gestapo who were trying to escape the punishment they feared from their captors.

As the American Forces advanced toward the death camps, many of the healthier prisoners in them had been driven out like cattle by the SS and Gestapo troops, hoping to get them to any other camp held by the German forces, and where they could still be used to produce more weapons. Along the way, the Americans found very shallow graves where the driven prisoners had fallen, too weak to go any farther. As the frenetic departure of the SS and Gestapo with their victims increased, in some instances time was not taken to bury those that had fallen. Those that were not already dead were shot in the back of the head and left for scavengers.

The Americans following their path learned from residents who talked with them along the route that they, the residents, were the ones who had picked up some of those fallen bodies and buried them before the conquering army came through.

Jay was glad that his unit went no farther than the sub-camp of Dachau on their first stop. They were closer to Munich than they had been at Dachau, and Jay, along with many other servicemen, were happy that they could spend an evening in Munich.

As soon as Jay arrived in the city, he went at once to the Weis home, hoping to find Grenythe there. He didn't believe he would be in danger by knocking on the door — after all, the war was over and Germany had surrendered completely, but he was still disturbed about Grenythe's attitude the other day, her hurry to have him leave.

The dark shadows of evening were falling, precipitated by a cloudy sky in the west. Jay looked around him before he took the steps up to the door. There was no one in the street. Why he had expected to see little children playing out there at this time of evening, he admonished himself, was ridiculous. They would most probably be inside eating their dinner. That made him think about Grenythe and how thin she was. He knew one of the reasons the Allies were successful was Germany's lack of supplies of all kinds — food, shelter, clothing. All the wealth of the German nation had been spent to produce war weapons, leaving many of their own people, as well as political prisoners, starving.

Jay knocked, and almost immediately a nice-looking young woman opened the door. She was tall, with long light brown hair and blue eyes. She was slender, but not nearly as thin as Grenythe. Jay looked at her a second, and not wanting to put Grenythe in any danger by saying he was a friend, he took a more formal stance and in German said, "I am Sergeant Jordan Fisk of the United States Air Force, and I would like to speak to Grenythe Karlstein."

He noticed the wave of fear that crossed the woman's face. What caused her such alarm? Quickly Jay said, "Are you her friend?"

"We both live here in this house."

"Is she here?"

The woman hesitated, and Jay, in his kindest manner, said, "I would like to talk to her about her University days."

The woman relaxed when he mentioned the University, and not saying anything further, she went to the bottom of the steps and called to Grenythe, saying there was someone here to see her.

Jay was still standing on the stoop, but the door was open and Grenythe saw him by the time she was halfway down the stairs. She turned immediately, ran back to her room, grabbed her purse and was out the door, taking Jay by the arm as she hurried him down the steps to the street.

"Don't look back," Grenythe whispered, as she guided

him down to the street.

Until they were out of sight of the Weis house, neither had said another word. Then Jay asked, "What was that all about?"

"It's a long, long story, Jay. I want to know about you."

"I want to know about you, Grenythe, and I want to know about Franz. Do you know anything about him?"

Tears came into Grenythe's eyes and she said, "He's dead. They murdered him!" Her voice broke and Jay put his arm around her as he, too, fought tears.

"Jay, Franz and I got married. You know we were always good friends. I don't know whether we would have married in normal circumstances or not, but when the SS and Gestapo were almost forcing all the young women, those who weren't married, into having babies by any soldier who came along, I asked Franz to marry me to save me from that type of hell."

"Tell me about Franz?"

"We married about two years after we got out of school. We didn't plan to have any children until after the war was over. I don't know whether we wondered if we would stay married or not. We loved each other, Jay, but just like wonderful friends. That's why I don't know whether we would have stayed married after the war, or if we would have fallen in love and married anyway. I feel like I can say now that I truly loved Franz and I think that he loved me, too."

They had reached the Englischer Garten across from the University. In the last of June, the war had payed no role on the voluptuousness of nature, and the park was filled with blooms of many flowers and bushes, unattended, but still bursting forth in a riot of color.

Jay reached out and put his arm around Grenythe's thin shoulders and led her to a bench where they sat down.

"Tell me about Franz," Jay urged.

"I can't talk now." Grenythe's voice was choked. "You tell me about yourself."

Jay told of his courtship and love of Irene. How they had saved to buy a house in a fine neighborhood near New York, and then came the crushing blow — Irene had divorced him, stolen all his money and left him alone and broke in a foreign country, fighting a war. His voice broke a time or two as he told his story, but he did not cry. Grenythe, however, could hear the heartbreak in his voice. She put both arms around him and pressed her cheek against his cheek.

The two turned to face each other, noticing the tears in the other's eyes, and first one grinned then the other, and soon they were chuckling at themselves.

"Two old warriors, crying over lost battles!" Jay remarked.

They sat quietly for a few moments, holding each other, then Jay pleaded, "Tell me about Franz. He was my best friend while I was here in Munich."

Grenythe began her story with Franz's dislike of Hitler, yet he was forced into the armed service anyway. "He was a good and faithful German soldier, Jay. He loved his country, but he thought Hitler was a fiend. But when he was ordered into the service of his country, he went willingly. He was serving under Field Marshal Erwin von

Witzleben. He liked serving under him and was glad to follow any orders that were given him.

"Franz told me that Witzleben was the paragon of honor and justice in a good soldier's tradition. Witzleben was a Prussian and Hitler hated the Prussians, because so many of them hated what he was doing. Witzleben was ordered to lead the German Army in the invasion of France. That was where he and Franz became such good friends. It was there that Franz joined the group of soldiers and scientists that opposed Hitler. There was more than one organization. Franz told me that one was called the Wednesday Club. It had sixteen top scientists, military surgeons and professors that met under cover of darkness, so as not to get attention. Another was called the 'Red Chapel organization' with members in Germany, France, Belgium and the Netherlands. Their central leadership was in France and they operated by couriers and radio.

"There was one man, high in the German command — he was head of German Counter-Intelligence. His name was Admiral Wilhelm Canaris."

Jay interrupted, "I know about him! He was hanged just a few months ago for giving the Allies information."

Grenythe continued, "He risked his life many times to save people from the Gestapo. He was hanged in April, along with many others."

"Is that what happened to Franz?"

"What happened to Franz happened to many others who tried to get Hitler out of power. They could not abide by Hitler, his SS troops and the Gestapo for their torture and brutal treatment of other people.

"They formed a group to assassinate Hitler. They were good men, most of them soldiers who would not follow Hitler's order to kill and torture anyone who opposed them. Many of them were arrested after their plan to get rid of Hitler failed. They had mock trials — in what they called 'the people's court.' Count von Stauffenberg was the one who volunteered to plant the bomb to kill Hitler, but the bomb wasn't strong enough to blow up everyone in the shanty-like building where the designated meeting was held. It would have worked in a cement building, but in this weak wooden structure it just blew out the walls. The Count had gone. He had left the building before the explosion, but he did not take his suitcase. That's how they knew that he had something to do with the explosion, so he was arrested and tried, along with another Count, Peter Yorck, arrested because he was a Christian who opposed Hitler from the beginning. And there was Helmuth Stieff and, of course, one of their wonderful leaders, Field Marshal Witzleben. He was relieved of his duties when he wouldn't follow orders to torture his captives and he was sent to prison. Because Franz refused to testify against Witzleben, he was also arrested and they were both hanged in August 1944."

"Franz was a great person, a good man!" Jay muttered when Grenythe stopped speaking. The horrors of what he had seen in the camps made him appreciate the supreme courage of Franz to stand up against the authority that ordered such atrocities.

Grenythe was speaking again. "I'll have to tell you what Witzleben said before they hung him — he said, 'You can have us hanged, but in three months' time the people will drag you alive through the gutter.' Another General said, 'You had better hang us in a hurry, otherwise you'll hang before we do.'

"When the Allies began to close in on the German strongholds, Hitler, for no reason at all, demanded the hanging of others who were in prison. They were not all soldiers. One was Dr. Carl Goerdeler, a civilian, Dietrich Bonhoeffer, a theologian — just hanged this last April.

"I'm telling you all of this, Jay, so you'll know that we Germans are not all as bad as Hitler and his henchmen."

"You don't have to convince me, Grenythe. I know you and Franz."

"Now tell me more about you, Jay. I've talked about me and my sad life so much. Now, it's your time to talk."

"Why don't we go get something to eat? Aren't you hungry?"

"I'm always hungry. I can't remember how long it's been since I've had enough to eat."

"No wonder you are so thin. Come along." They both got up and started walking toward the center of town.

They strolled along until Jay asked, "Is that little cafe open — the one where we six used to go for our confabs after school?"

"It's still there and I go by it once in a while and think about those fun days. It seems so long ago!"

They had been walking leisurely until they neared the old kaffehaus neighborhood where they had spent much time years ago. As they neared it, they were hardly conscious of the fact that their steps speeded up until they came to it. It was still open, but not as crowded as it had been in their early years. They had no trouble in finding an empty spot. They took a small table, not looking for the largest in the place as they done in those college years, when they always had six or more in their group.

They ordered a meal and beer. Grenythe seemed ravenous, and when she was finished, Jay asked her if she would like something more to eat. Grenythe nodded, then shook her head. "I never feel like I've had enough to eat, but if I gorge, I can make myself sick. For years, I have eaten barely enough to keep alive. I don't want to overdo it."

"I'm going to order something else — that *deutsches beefsteak* was not enough. I want dumplings and strudel. You can share it with me." Jay, being used to having all he wanted to eat, the hamburger had been sufficient, but he thought his thin companion would gladly accept something more to eat if it were right before her.

They talked of trivial things while they ate, both of them steering away from the subjects that had brought them both such sorrow. At first they refrained from that consciously, so before long they were laughing and talking about anything that came up. They even laughed at some Allied servicemen who came in for beer, and the antics they performed when some German girls came in. That some of the servicemen were enlisted in Jay's outfit made no difference to Jay. He was having such a pleasant evening just being with Grenythe, and she, too, seemed to be having a wonderful time.

They naturally got back to talking about their music. Jay told Grenythe about the hard times he had in finding a new instrument of any kind in the new locations, for during his last two or three years in the war he was moving from one base to another, and he wasn't allowed to take the instruments with him. "I didn't go out scouting for girls, like many of my buddies — I was very true to my wife. I opted for music instead of chasing girls."

As Jay told Grenythe about that, his words astonished him. For the first time he didn't cringe inside when he thought of Irene. He realized that he would and could get over that blow that had hurt him so much. He continued to speak of music, "Do you remember when we were all here after the opera? We had seen Tristan and Isolde, and we were telling about that last scene when Isolde died —"Jay stopped speaking. His words were broken off in laughing.

"Oh!" Grenythe was laughing, too, remembering the scene in the opera where Tristan had in some way touched the prone Isolde and the dead character had jumped, causing the whole audience to erupt in laughter. "I'll never forget it!"

The two of them were giggling like school kids, and Grenythe said, "Jay, tonight I feel like I've been tickled just like Isolde was that time, and that *I've* been brought back to life."

The two were having so much fun that they were unaware that a couple of enlisted American soldiers who had come in for beer were watching them. The soldiers sauntered over, not stopping, but walking very slowly in front of their table where Grenythe and Jay sat. They acted as if they were talking to one another, but spoke loud enough that Jay could hear them. And one soldier said to the other, "Is this really that sad ol' sourpuss sergeant that hangs around our base?"

The other one answered, "I don't think so. I thought for a minute he looked like Sergeant Fisk, but the Sergeant never goes out with girls, or never has any fun. It must be someone else."

Jay caught their insinuations and looked up. "Okay, you guys," he said as he waved them away, "shove off!"

The enlisted men left, but kept looking back at their sergeant, as if puzzled by finding him with a female companion and having such a good time. Grenythe and Jay watched them leave, then looked at each other. They both let out a quiet little chuckle, then became more serious. They realized that by their being together, they had both broken through a depressive wrap that had held them captive for months. They moved closer together, a little more sedate than when they had been in the lighthearted mood, but still aware of their happy togetherness.

"I don't want to spoil our fun, Grenythe, but I would like you to tell me more about you and Franz."

"It's a long story. When I saw him the last night, we made love, and I kissed him goodbye when he left for France with Witzleben. I didn't know if I would ever see him again. I told you that we got married to keep me from having to join what we called the 'pack of soldier comfort stations.' We had always liked each other, but after a very few years into our marriage we really loved each other." The tears were once again coming into Grenythe's eyes.

Jay put his arm around her shoulders and pulled her close, "You know, I loved him, too." He patted Grenythe's shoulder, then in a cheery voice said, "Go ahead and get it all out. I want to know all about you, and when you have finished, I have a surprise story to tell you."

Jay tightened his grip on Grenythe's shoulder and wondered how on earth he might be able to help her through the trauma.

"Franz had been gone just a few months and I had not heard from him. It was weeks and weeks since I had heard from him. I knew he was fighting the French, and we were losing men every day. When I didn't hear for so long, I was afraid that he had been killed. Sometimes I thought that he just wanted to abandon me. You can't imagine the torment I went through, not hearing from him for such a long time.

"I finally got a letter. I was almost afraid to open it, but when I did, I gave a triumphant yell. I was living in the same room that I live in now, but the people who were in the house then were my friends. When they heard me shout, they came to the stairs to see what was the matter. I told them that I had just heard from my husband and he was well. But then the more frightening news. He said he knew that bombs were falling all over our country, and Hitler was getting meaner and meaner, arresting everyone who raised a voice for any atrocity he ordered.

"This was when Witzleben and his cohorts decided that Hitler had to be stopped. In 1943 Witzleben took time off from his military position, saying he had to have an operation for appendicitis. He was relieved of his command shortly afterward. Franz was arrested along with him, both of them accused of treason and imprisoned. The SS and Gestapo came to arrest me, too, because I was the wife of a traitor. But for some reason they decided that I was needed to continue at the University." Grenythe was crying now, but still speaking through her sobs.

Jay thought it was time for him to do what he could to take Grenythe's thoughts from her sorrow. Grenythe and Jay had been sitting at their table over an hour and had let the time slip by. Jay said, "It's time for some fun talk. Do you remember Helene Dolmet?"

"Why, of course! She was one of my good friends."

"Do you ever hear from her?"

"No. You know she was against the rise of Hitler over ten years ago, and told us there would be trouble. What do know about her?"

Jay spent the next thirty minutes telling Grenythe about his encounter with childhood friends and the American nurse, while serving in France, and how she had become acquainted with a nurse named Helene Dolmet. He told Grenythe about the wedding of the two Americans and about his being best man and Helene being the maid of honor.

"Where is Helene now? I would love to see her."

"She has gone back to Strasbourg. Do you remember when we were all there as guests at her home?" Soon Jay and Grenythe were reminiscing about their student days and were once again engrossed in chit-chat, just glad to be together.

The happy hours could not last much longer. Jay had to get back to base, so he reluctantly bid Grenythe goodbye.

"I'll get back to see you whenever any opportunity comes," he told her.

"And I'll be waiting!" she answered.

Jay wondered where his next military stop would be. Weeks had passed since the end of the war, and not nearly all the concentration camps had been taken over by the Allies, nor all the prisoners released. Many of those who had been released were wandering around the streets in the area where they had been freed, not knowing where they were. There was always work for the linguists to help relocate these poor souls. Discussions were held among the officers before they selected the next destination. Jay heard the mention of Regensburg, a principal city of East Bavaria.

Jay couldn't wait to tell his companions about Regensburg. "I will really enjoy going there again. I heard them say that the old city there had not been damaged by the war."

"Why is that so important?" one of his buddies asked.

"You have to see it to appreciate that old town. A bunch of us came here when we were at school in Munich. It was originally an old Celtic town, but was taken over by the Romans two thousand years ago ..."

He was interrupted, "Fisk, are you trying to give us a history lesson on some old town?"

"Well, if we get to go there, I just wanted to tell what there is to see. But I'll shut up if you don't want to hear it."

Two or three others asked how long they expected to be there. No one knew the answer to that, then one young man said, "If we have just a few free hours, maybe

Jay could tell us what we should see."

Jay hurriedly told them about a Roman fortress located on a narrow street named Unter den Schwibbogen (Under the Arches) and about an impressive Roman tower. He told them there was a Palace of the Princes of Thurn and Taxis in the southern part of the city, but they probably wouldn't have time to see that if they took time to see the magnificent cathedral that claimed it couldn't be surpassed in German Gothic architecture by any other cathedral, except possibly the ones in Cologne and Strasbourg. The city became a center of commercial importance in the Middle Ages. Jay hoped he would see it again.

When they got the word that there was a camp they needed to liberate just south of Nurnburg, any call at Regensburg was canceled. Jay was very disappointed, as he remembered how he and his friends had had so much fun there. He also took a lot of ribbing from his companions. "Don't bother to give us any more travelogues on any place — we probably won't be going there," they said.

The reason to skip Regensburg was a good one. En route to Nurnburg by way of Augsburg instead of Regensburg was important because Patton was stationed at Augsburg, and they might learn from him the places where they were most needed.

After they reached Augsburg, the officers arranged to meet with Patton, and while they were thus engaged, the lesser men in the military had the time to see the city.

"Have you been here before?" several friends asked Jay Fisk.

"Yes, several times," Jay answered.

"Then will you be our guide?" they asked.

"Now, wait a minute! I thought you didn't want any more of my travel talk."

With much persuasion, Sergeant Jay Fisk reluctantly told them he would guide those who wanted to go with him. Several of his companions went with him to the city, hoping that much of the things worth seeing had not been destroyed by the war. He told them that there were so many things to see that they could not possibly see them all. He asked if they wanted to see cathedrals or fountains or business buildings. He told them a little of the history of Johan Fugger and his weaving trade that made some of the finest fabrics in all of Europe. He told them about the compromise between the Catholics and Lutherans, giving both the right to build their churches and each to be free to worship as they chose. Then he told them about the fountains, fountains almost as beautiful as those you found in Rome.

His companions chose to see the fountains. They had only time to see five of them — the three outstanding ones were the Herkulesbrunnen (Hercules on a pedestal killing the hydra) and the Merkurbrunnen (Mercury with a cherub playing at his feet) were on Maximilianstrasse, and the third they saw, the Augustbrunnen, close to the Rathaus, was made by the Dutch master Hubert Gerhard. The main figure standing on a column in the center of the fountain is of the Roman Emperor Augustus, founder of the city.

While they were sightseeing, they ran into some other Americans also viewing the illustrious fountains. Jay saw one face among them that looked familiar, one he thought he had seen just a few weeks before. He called out, "Joe!" He would have called the last name, but he couldn't remember what it was. He thought the face he saw belonged to the same boy he had seen in the medical corps at Dachau, the one who had found the live body among the corpses.

One soldier turned immediately, looked at Jay and said, "Is that you, Sergeant —?" He didn't remember Jay's name either.

"I'm Jay Fisk. I met you in Dachau. You told me about finding a live body among the dead."

"Oh, I remember now. Oh, I've something else to tell you! You remember I told you about the dispute among the big shots, that there was a General who wanted to have a Colonel court-martialed?"

The companions of both men busied themselves viewing the figures perched all around the large basin of the Augustbrunen and its many spouts of water crisscrossing in an elaborate pattern of streams while Jay and Joe exchanged greetings.

"What happened to the Colonel — what was his name?" Jay asked.

"His name was Colonel Sparks and when he was arrested, brought back for court martial, his case was brought right here to Augsburg and placed in front of General Patton. You know what Patton did? He just read over the file, tore up the papers, patted Sparks on the back and complimented him on being such a good soldier. No court martial!"

"What happened to the General that tried to have

him court-martialed?"

"I don't know. I think he tried hard — through the press — to take full credit for the release of the Dachau prisoners, even though Sparks had already done it before the General ever got there. I have no idea how it will be listed in the record."

After their short conversation, Joe Kerry and Jay Fisk moved on about their sightseeing, each with his own group, not likely to ever to see each other again.

Jay's unit passed by the camp near Nurnburg, then into Nurnburg before heading north into East Germany. In one camp they came upon they found that most of the prisoners had been released, but there was one woman whom no on could understand. She was an older woman and she spoke German. The soldiers had tried to learn from other prisoners who spoke German what she was trying to say. When Jay's unit came into the camp, the situation was explained to his superior officer, who immediately called upon Jay.

"They say this woman keeps talking in German, yet no one understands. When they bring in other Germans, she refuses to say a word. They don't know why she clams up as soon as other Germans appear."

From the time Jordan Fisk, Jr. had been a little boy in his small town of Bluewater, he had been called the "peacemaker." He had a friendly personality, always calming and pacifying those around him. When he met the woman, he did not even ask her to tell her name. He talked with her at first in schoolbook, or high German, but she would not talk with him until they were alone. When he told the other Americans to leave, he spoke to her in high German, but she paid little attention. Then he dropped into the low German vernacular, saying he had many German friends who hated Hitler, and he told of the brother of Grenythe who had been imprisoned because he opposed the brutality of the Hitler regime. He urged her to talk with him.

"Many Germans still support Hitler!" she told him.

"Even these other prisoners?" he asked.

"Perhaps some of them," she answered laconically.

"Is that why you wouldn't tell about your home to them?"

"Yes."

"Will you talk to me, tell me your home. I want to help you."

The woman looked at Jay, then around the bare room, with just a small desk and a few chairs. When she had made the survey, she looked again at Jay and spoke, "I was sent to this labor camp because I helped my little granddaughter get out of Germany, ten or more years ago. She was only six years old. We lived in the northern part of Germany, and our family is Jewish."

Jay gasped, "Then you are lucky to be alive!"

"I am only one-half Jew. Hitler's Germans didn't know that or I would have been annihilated years ago."

"Now that Hitler is dead and Germany has surrendered, why are you afraid to speak out?"

"I know there are many of the young that are still inebriated with hatred for the Jews. I want to be sure my little Hanna is safe before I go back to our town.

"When did you last see her?"

"It was in 1933. She was six years old and had just

gone to her first day of school. When she got home, her mother asked her what she had learned that day. Little Hanna made a salute and said, 'We learned to say, *Heil Hitler!* ' My daughter sent her to my house to keep her safe."

"What happened to your daughter?"

"She and her husband were collected by the Gestapo and sent to one of the death camps, I feel sure."

"Where is Hanna now?"

"I don't know! I used the only way we knew to get her out of Germany, but I don't know if she got away or where she went. That's why I must know she is safe before I can go to my former home."

Jay stood up and put his hand out to the woman. "She's a grown woman now, if she has survived. We need to take care of you and get you back to health. While we are doing that, we'll do what we can to find Hanna for you."

Jay told his commanding officer about the woman and her granddaughter Hanna, and asked if the army could do anything to help find her. Perhaps getting the woman back to her own town would be the first step.

When Jay's unit left that small concentration camp, Jay didn't know where their next stop would be. The job of finding the girl Hanna was no longer his, but he hoped he might keep in touch and know if the grandmother ever found her granddaughter. His thoughts roamed back to Grenythe. When could he get back to Munich to see her again?

CHAPTER NINETEEN

CHAPTER NINETEEN

AUGSBURG was a pleasant surprise from the many other stops in Germany in what the American servicemen called the "mop-up" operation. In Augsburg, Jordan Fisk and his group found that the American army, under the command of General George S. Patton, was in complete control. Jay and his friends had enough free time to enjoy the historic landmarks that abound there.

Jay had found another release from the tensions that had held him for months. Until just recently, every time he walked on any street, every dark-eyed, brown-haired girl he saw reminded him of Irene and he felt an empty hole inside himself. Jay was always slender, but the loss of appetite that came the day he got the "Dear John" letter had made him lose more weight than was good for his health. After the total German surrender, he had accepted the assignment for these extra months in Europe because he thought he had nothing to go home to, nothing socially worth his time, and even his old job at the importing company did not appeal to him.

When the war against Germany was over, he and most of his unit would ordinarily be returned to the United States, then to be reassigned to service in the Pacific, if hostilities had not ended there. Jay was dismissed from that routine when his linguist qualification made him a desirable asset in helping correct the abuse that had taken place in Europe under the command of the Gestapo and SS forces.

Jay's depressed state of mind from Irene's action was not leavened in any way by the atrocities he came upon in Dachau, seeing the horror chambers where real live people resembling moving corpses just added to his despair. He wrote a letter to Roxanne expressing his feeling:

> *After VE day, May 1945, we left England for France.*
>
> *Some of us were taken to the liberated concentration camps. That was a horrible sight. Men were lying on bunks so starved, their thighs were the size of my forearm.*
>
> *We saw many rows of lined-up corpses. These camps were in Germany and Austria. The sides and roofs of the buildings where they were held were often made from the uneven edges of boards from the side of the trees with no attempt to make them air or water-tight. At one abandoned camp we saw little tin containers where prisoners had attempted to cook acorns and cones for something to eat. It was a nightmare which has haunted me for days.*

When Sergeant Jordan Fisk, Jr. had taken on this "after-war" assignment, he was hoping to find somewhere a mite of brightness to assuage his despair. He had gone to Munich and there he found Grenythe!

Jay no longer felt like a soldier, plodding along doing

his duty. He felt as if years had fallen away, and he was more like the same happy youth he had been so long ago. How could that one girl make such a difference in his whole being? For the first time in months he felt alive, really alive. He took his job seriously, glad he could make a difference in the plight of some of the displaced prisoners. With each success, the buoyancy he felt was enhanced by the luxury of seeing Grenythe again.

It was in that lighthearted mood that he left Augsburg, with the next stop Nurnburg. He looked forward to visiting the beautiful old landmarks there, landmarks that he and Grenythe and their mutual friends had enjoyed together when they were young.

The buoyancy in Jay's spirit took an abrupt plunge when they entered the city. Wartime raids had almost totally wiped out all of medieval Nurnburg! Jay had viewed most of the results of the war with satisfaction where his own Air Force had dropped bombs on enemy targets. Why had the ruins in Nurnburg seemed different? Why had the drab and darkened Munich depressed him so? Nurnburg, Augsburg, Regensburg — all had been part of a happy youth at the time when he had enjoyed living in Munich a decade before. It seemed hard to accept those dear posts as enemy territory. The momentary shock Jay sensed when he first saw the ruins of Nurnburg, though, disappeared rapidly as he remembered the destruction that had fallen all around him in England.

But now this was no longer enemy territory! Someday under American direction, he mused, the happy days would come again. He thought of his dear friend Franz, who had given his life trying to stop the utter destruction that the mad Hitler had brought upon his own people. Here in Nurnburg, gone were the Imperial Castle (Kaiserburg), Knight's Hall, Burgrave's Castle (Burggrafenburg), and the Imperial Stable (Saiderstallung). Jay remembered that below the western part of the fortress there had been a picturesque small square with the Tiergartner Gate and the Albrecht-Durer-Haus, and the St. Sebaldus Church, built in the 13th century with its mixture of Romanesque and Gothic style architecture. Gone with the ravages of war!

Jay wondered if Grenythe knew of the destruction in Nurnburg. He would talk with her about it when he saw her next. He knew she would remember well that Tannhauser lived in Nurnburg for awhile, and that Nurnburg was the birthplace of Durer, probably Germany's greatest painter. These were Jay's thoughts as the American forces took note of the ruins, but moved on to where there was much more vital work to be done, death camps with prisoners not yet repatriated.

The American palliating units had moved from the western and middle of Germany through the forests to eastern Germany, stopping at a concentration camp near Kassel, before coming to Buchenwald. Buchenwald! It was no longer in operation when Jay's unit arrived, but the size of the place was astounding, the largest of any they had yet seen. They had an opportunity to hear what the liberating force had found here just months before.

Buchenwald had been set up in July of 1937 with 238,980 prisoners passing through it before March 1945. Of that number, over 43,000 of these were killed, dying from the brutal surroundings here or unable to survive forced marches to other camps.

Again, the size of the place and the comfortable habitations for the SS and Gestapo troops amazed the liberating forces, as well as other relieving forces that came later. They found a good paved road that led through the green forest to the center of the compound. The large barracks for the guards, eighteen individual quarters in yellow buildings with red roofs, were on a curved road around the drill ground with a spacious dining hall for the guards. Headquarters of the political department (Gestapo and SS troops) was in the center of "The Karakho Path" or the "caracho-weg." It was a section of the road where dogs were set upon prisoners to make them run, while the Gestapo and SS watched from their comfortable quarters and called it an entertaining sport.

Prisoners were separated into categories and kept in separate blocks, Block 22-Jews, Block 38-political prisoners, Block 8-Children and young people, Block 47-Gypsies, etc. The well educated people in Block 22, teachers, physicians, scientists and lawyers, were called the "Singing Horse Jews" and were required to clean the latrines.

When Jay's outfit arrived here, they met two survivors of that camp, a Frenchman named Jean Mialet who made a much quoted statement about the place, "This is what hell must be like!" Another survivor was a young boy from Austria, arrested because he was a gypsy. He was first sent to Auschwitz, then to Buchenwald. He was just fifteen years old. He told them that what they had seen was not the total prison of Buchenwald. His last imprisonment had been in Mittelbau Dora, the underground prison where inmates were forced to produce the supersonic V2 rockets. An estimated twenty thousand prisoners died while making these rockets. The boy named Franz Rosenbach said he didn't know how he had been able to survive.

There were ten ovens in the crematorium to dispose of the victims of torture and abuse. The young Rosenbach told of the naked number of corpses that had been shoved into these ovens. The American boys who heard the description of the abuses that went on here reacted in numerous ways. Some showed intense anger, others became sick and vomited, even though they were not seeing the actual gut-heaving acts, as they had in Dachau. The liberating officers in charge, along with the soldier boys, wondered how much more of this they could endure.

Jay Fisk was relieved that all of them would have a little time off before they were scheduled to move into Poland. Jay, of course, got back to Munich as soon as he could. He wanted to see Grenythe. Would she be waiting for him as she promised? Thinking of her was the light that erased the abhorrent memories of Buchenwald and other unbelievable revulsions.

Getting to Munich by train was not as easy a task as Jay Fisk expected. He could speak German without an accent; he had traveled a great deal on the trains in Europe, and making the necessary changes in different stations had never given him any problems. But things were not the same as they were years ago. The speedy routing he wanted to take to get to Munich was not available.

Important bridges had been blown up by the Allies, and they had not been rebuilt. It was a roundabout way to get from the little town of Weimer to Munich, and it took some of the precious time that Jay wanted to spend with Grenythe.

He felt disheveled and dirty when he finally arrived in Munich, but his time here was so short that he wasted no time in hurrying from the train station to the Weis house. Oh, he hoped Grenythe would be there. He wanted so much to see her!

He jumped from the street level to the top step of the stoop and banged on the door. His heart was in his mouth as he waited for an answer. He heard footsteps before the door was opened and prayed it would be Grenythe, not the jailer he had met earlier.

It was Grenythe who opened the door, but even she presented a surprise to the waiting Jay. The drab blond hair, poorly arranged when he last seen her, was now very becomingly cut and set, and there was a brightness to the dull blond hair that he had seen years before. The hair was not the only change Jay noted in the pretty young woman before him. She was wearing a sleeveless summer dress, a yellow print that emphasized the yellow blond of her hair. Her manner was upbeat, almost bubbly as she opened the door, reached out and said, "Come in, Jay. I'm so glad to see you!"

Jay stepped inside and looked furtively around the room and said in a low voice, "Where's the ghoul?"

"She's no longer here. I am the only one here now."

"You look beautiful, Grenythe. I was feeling so sorry for you the first day I saw you, but you look wonderful and here am I, dirty and tired from a tedious journey. I need to clean up before I take out such a gorgeous gal."

Grenythe patted him on the shoulder, hesitated a moment, then said, "Would like to go up to your old room and clean up?"

"I would love to, and I would like to see my old room anyway. I suppose it has changed. And what about the rest of the house?"

"Very much the same, but your room is the one I've been living in for years, so it may not look like a boy's room any more, but you are welcome to use it."

They had moved just a few steps into the living room as they carried on this conversation. When Grenythe made the last statement, Jay, knowing the house well, hurried across the room, took two steps at a time up the stairs and disappeared on the upper landing.

Grenythe waited downstairs, trying to read, but she couldn't concentrate on the book in her hand. When she heard the shower turn on, she dropped the book and ran up the stairs. She suspected Jay would have left his clothes in the room, and if he had, she would pick up his wrinkled shirt and slacks and press them for him while he was in the shower. The door to her room was open when she got there. She noted his bag was on the bed, open, with his shirt and pants lying across it. She assumed that he had gone to the shower in the same underwear he had been wearing, perhaps taking clean ones with him. When he got back she would offer to launder them for him. That was something else she could do besides pressing his shirt and pants. It would let him know how much she valued his company.

The press job took longer than Grenythe expected, and when she got back upstairs, the door to her room was closed. He would wonder what had happened to his clothes! She knocked on the door and called out, "Jay, I have your slacks and shirt. I pressed them for you."

Jay opened the door and Grenythe saw that he was fully dressed in another shirt and pants. Jay was grinning as he pulled Grenythe into the room with one hand and took his clothes with the other. "Thanks a lot." Then teasingly he said, "When I saw they were missing, I thought you just wanted to be with me *without* clothes."

Jay no longer had hold of her arm, and Grenythe, turning a beet red, started for the door. Jay caught her again and apologized, "I was just teasing. Grenythe." He turned her around to face him, held her close and kissed her. He quickly let her go and said, "Where shall we go this evening?"

Jay laid his hand on Grenythe's arm and steered her for the door. He hoped he hadn't ruined this wonderful friendship by his suggestive remark.

It was August, and the evenings were getting cooler. Neither Jay nor Grenythe was wearing a jacket. They had gotten as far as the park with no decision on their destination. Their conversation had been limited up to this point, and they sat down on a park bench, both determined to end the slight tension that had arisen after Jay's remark in the bedroom. They had not sat long before the chill of the air made them move closer together. Jay hesitated a second, then put his arm across Grenythe's shoulders, hoping she would not move away. Instead, she cuddled even closer to him. Jay was aware of the freshness of Grenythe's scent — not of perfume — she probably could not afford perfume — more like a soap flagrance. He looked down at the top of her head and said, "Grenythe, I like you an awful lot."

She cuddled even closer, and murmured, "And I like you, too."

"Let's find a warmer place to stop," Jay suggested. They decided to go back again to their favorite place, the old kaffeehaus where they had always had such a good time. They remembered the first evening that they had spent there in renewing their acquaintance, and they still had so much to tell each other.

When they got inside and ordered a beer, Jay asked, "Have you heard the latest news?"

"What news?"

"Just the other morning while we were eating breakfast, a soldier came in and announced that an atomic bomb had been dropped on Japan, and the war in Asia was over."

"Yes, the whole world heard that news, Jay."

"Well, overnight my plans were changed. I will not be re-assigned and sent to the Pacific when I finish my stint here in Europe. My last assignment is Poland. When I have finished there, I will be heading back to the United States. I have so little time here before I am mustered out. I want to spend as much of it as I can with you," Jay told Grenythe.

"I wish you didn't have to leave, Jay. I feel like I've come to life again."

"We'll have to work something out. I told you what I

have yet to do; what happened to you while I was away? What happened to that woman who lived with you in the Weis house?"

"Her husband was arrested and she moved out, but I don't know whether she will face any kind of punishment because her husband was an SS man. I heard that the house will be returned to the Weis family — if they can find them."

"What happened to Mrs. Weis?"

"I was living there, just as I am now, when the Gestapo came and got her. I have no idea where they took her, or if she is still alive."

"You probably know about Helene helping Paul get away while I was still here in school."

"Yes, Franz and I both knew about it, but we did not divulge it to the rest of our companions, mainly because we were afraid Tony and Georg would have reported it to the Gestapo."

"I have often wondered what happened to either of them. Do you know?"

"Tony went back to Italy, and Georg, the last I saw of him, he was always saying 'Heil, Hitler.' He quit school and joined the army."

"Franz wrote me about your brother. He never did give me any of the details. It was in a code that something had happened to him. You can never guess what he wrote. I kept the letter for a long time, and would probably still have it —" Jay stopped talking a moment, then continued, "Irene may have thrown all my things out. I won't know until I get home."

"How could he have written you about it without

getting into trouble?"

"He asked if I remembered a blond-headed girl that he was always telling to take better care of her health. He said her brother had died of the same disease, and that she was now taking better care of herself."

"How did you figure that out?"

"You were the only one that Franz was always telling to keep your criticisms to yourself. I took it that something had happened to your brother because he was too outspoken."

"It wasn't because of what he said, it was because he tried to help some of our family friends who were Jews."

"What happened to him?"

"We never did find out. The Gestapo picked him up one day at work and we have never heard from him since. I don't know if he is in some prison camp somewhere, or even if he is still alive."

"What happened to the Jewish people?"

"That's what is so tragic. It wasn't all tragic, just part of it. The family name is Kahn, and they were friends of our family. We lived in the same block. It was seven years ago, more like eight, when my brother Robert came to dinner one night saying that his friend's sister had left the country, and Fried was grieving about it. Robert must have been grieving, too. He sat at the table and just picked at his food. He sat there awhile, then asked my father if he couldn't do something to stop what the SS troops and Gestapo were doing to the Jews. My father told him that there wasn't anything he could do, and that he thought matters would get worse before they got better.

"Father told Robert he had better tell his friend that

he should follow his sister and get out of Germany. It was about six month later when Robert told us that Fried had disappeared. Robert had always been a good friend with Fried, they were both exactly the same age, eighteen years old. They had always been together in school until the Jews were no longer allowed to attend. Then Herman Kahn, Fried's father, lost his job. Robbie missed Fried, so he went to see the Kahns to ask about him; the Kahns wouldn't talk with him. I think they were afraid. I don't know whether they didn't trust Robert, or thought he might be forced to tell what he had learned. Later he found out from some of his other Jewish friends that Fried and his sister had gone to Israel, and these other friends were trying to get out, too, just as soon as they got enough money to pay their fare out.

"Robert said he supposed that the Kahns had enough money to send their two children to safety in Israel. The sister was older than Fried and she went first. I don't know how they managed it. Maybe they got out before the Gestapo clamped down on anyone leaving. They especially wanted to collect the Jews and dispose of them; they didn't want them to find safety anywhere.

"My brother wasn't the only one who knew about it — the whole block did, when the Gestapo came and took Mr. and Mrs. Kahn out of their house. They were taken to Dachau! Everyone knew that was the same as a death sentence. But Mr. Herman Kahn had gotten a visa to go to England, and he was allowed to leave. He told his wife, Paula, that he would send for her just as soon as he could get another visa. He would have to work in England and get the money to pay for it. Everything he had in Germany was lost to him.

"Robbie was a soldier. He asked for work at Dachau. That was probably the stupidest thing he ever did, but I believe he would do it again. He thought by being there he could help get Mrs. Kahn out of Dachau with a visa for England, just like Mr. Kahn had been able to do.

"The prisoners were dying by the dozens at Dachau, many from starvation, some from overwork and exhaustion, and others from torture. Robert told us that he slipped food into Mrs. Kahn whenever he could. He also wrote to England trying to get a visa for her, but he got no answer. I doubt if his letters were ever sent. Robert was not careful enough. Some other guards at Dachau, some of the ones Robert called the goons, must have known what he was doing, and when I or my mother and father tried to contact Robert, we got no answer.

"Father was afraid for the rest of us, now, because of Robert being in our family. We tried to be very careful in everything we said or did. I guess that's what Franz meant when he told you that I was taking care of myself. We asked Franz, who was an officer in the army, to try to find out for us what had happened to Robert and what happened to Mrs. Kahn.

"He did find out that Mrs. Kahn was killed at Dachau. That's all he could tell us. About Robert — he said there was no trace of him at all. Whatever had happened to him was erased from the records. As far as the army records show, he never existed. My mother and father felt certain that he was shot and buried right there at Dachau. The Gestapo and SS made lists of all the Jews they annihilated, bragging about their savagery, but they never listed Robert. My dear brother was just one of *many* good Germans who disappeared without a trace. I've already told you about Franz and his superior officer, Witzleben. The Gestapo liked to publicize the execution of any of the great men who opposed them, thinking, I guess, that it would make them seem more powerful. I don't know what they thought."

Jay listened to Grenythe tell her story, and then he told what the Allied command had found out. There was a conspiracy, called the "White Rose" society, made up of students at Munich University, claiming to be the only true ones who fought against Hitler.

"I know all about them," Grenythe said. "That is the group that Robert joined — secretly, of course. He told us that 573 of them had been buried in a mass grave."

"The Allies also heard about all those others who tried to assassinate Hitler, but the Allies didn't dare take them seriously when they were saying they were trying to stop Hitler. They suspected it could just be competition for another Hitler-like authority to arise from their midst," Jay said.

"How do you judge people? How do you know how they will act? There will always be some Germans here who will aggrandize Hitler and continue his hate for the Jews. I wonder if any other country will have such a split personality," Grenythe mused.

Jay chuckled lightly. "Grenythe, no matter where you go, there will always be people who disagree, some on a friendly basis, others with hate. That happens in our country, too. Slavery came to an end nearly one hundred years ago, but there are some people in the south who still disparage the Negro." Jay was laughing now. "Let me tell you what happened in Africa. We had a stop in Liberia on our way across the desert. Natives were hired to take care of us, seeing that we were properly under the mosquito netting at night, etc. They spoke pretty good English. Early one morning, they were told to go around to each bed and shake the soldiers awake. They were told to go around the second time, and if a soldier wasn't up, to lift him up by the armpits and stand him out of bed. Some of our men were Southerners and didn't want any Negro putting his hands on them. One of them swore at the native, 'Don't touch me, you dirty so and so.' The Negro (he was big and strong), he just laughed, paid no attention at all to the Southerner's words and lifted the soldier out of bed with no hesitation. The soldier knew if he laid a hand on this fellow or fought back, it would be the guardhouse and he would not be able to continue his journey. I enjoyed this scene and purposely stayed in my bed, just to let that Negro lift me out of bed."

Jay was grinning when he finished the story and Grenythe was laughing, too. Jay put his arm around Grenythe and kissed her on the cheek.

Since Jay and Grenythe had entered the small coffee house, many others had arrived. Most of them were servicemen from the different countries of the Allied forces, French, English, Americans, etc., and along with them there was smoke of an untold number of cigarettes that nearly filled the place.

"Let's get out of here!" Grenythe urged, and started to slip away from the table where they had been sitting for nearly two hours.

Jay followed her out and teasingly whispered as they were leaving, "I remember an incident many years ago, at this very same place you wanted to leave. That time you said it was because of the smoke, but when we got outside you told me you didn't want to hear any more about Hitler. Is it the smoke this time, or is it all those servicemen that were giving you the eye?"

"Oh, Jay! It's the smoke! It bothers me more than ever. I remember that you gave up smoking when we went mountain climbing. Did you ever start again?"

"No. I quit then, and I'm glad I did. I had no idea when I first smoked that it was so habit forming or so expensive."

When they stepped outside, they collided with the chill night air. A strong wind had arisen since they had gone into the coffee house. Grenythe shivered as she hovered close to Jay. "Let's go home. I need a wrap." It was not a long walk — a walk Jay had made many times while he was here in school. This evening, because of the chill, they decided to take the train. Though he had no jacket, the long sleeves of Jay's uniform offered him protection, but Grenythe's summer dress was sleeveless and her bare arms were covered with goose pimples from the cold. Jay pulled Grenythe right in front of him, and standing very close behind, he folded his arms around her, as they stood there waiting for the train.

Jay needed to pick up his bag, so when they got to the Weis house, he went inside with Grenythe. It seemed so natural for him to go on up the stairs to his old room. But tonight it seemed special, because Grenythe was going up to the room with him!

After he had packed his bag, he turned to Grenythe, put his arms around her, and said, “I don’t want to say ‘goodnight,’ Grenythe.”

“I don’t want to say ‘goodnight’ either!”

CHAPTER TWENTY

CHAPTER TWENTY

THE HAPPY THOUGHTS of Munich that Sergeant Jordan Fisk, Jr. took with him as he began his journey through one after another of concentration camps across the eastern portion of Germany and into Czechoslovakia did not prepare him for the utter destruction and ruin the Germans had inflicted upon the city of Warsaw, Poland. Nowhere had he seen any city so completely wiped out, even those hit hardest with Allied bombs. The Germans had threatened that they would wipe Warsaw off the map, and they almost did, leaving that city just a pile of rubble. It was not all caused in war bombing — it was a purposeful action to totally destroy every landmark, every building and everything of importance to the inhabitants of Warsaw. But they couldn't wipe out the spirit of the Polish people!

What Jay saw when he arrived at the ruined city was a forlorn people wandering around, scrounging through the rubble, searching for something they might find that belonged to their past. A sad sight to behold!

It was October and Mother Nature, right on schedule, was buffeting the area with cold winds, denying the impression of warmth flaunted by the red and yellow leaves still left hanging on the trees. The chill in the air promised instead the harshness of the winter yet to come. But nature was not the only snag that Jay Fiske found along the way. He knew before he left Munich that the Russians did not want any of the other Allied forces coming into Poland, Czechoslovakia or any portion where the Russians had defeated the Germans. The only reason Jay could make this journey at all was because he came with a party of international investigators, and there was no way the Russians could interfere with the Allied Investigation of war crimes committed in any part of the transgressions.

Most of the people working in the rubble of Warsaw were underclothed for autumn temperatures. Some of them were almost in rags, while others were better dressed, but none of them looked warm enough or in any way prosperous. There were a few unimportant buildings and a few tents lining the edge of the devastation. Jay wondered how these scant shelters were going to keep the people warm when winter arrived in full force. He saw that one man wandering around was more warmly dressed than the rest. He caught Jay's attention, because he seemed to be distressed. He was a small man, very slight of stature, and he looked as if he had been undernourished for months, maybe longer. Jay watched him picking his way over the rubble. He moved slowly, looking keenly at the people who were digging through the debris and ashes, inspecting one person after another.

Jay figured the man was looking for some person or persons, rather than for any object. Jay left the companions with whom he had been viewing the Warsaw ruins and approached the man. Jay did not speak Polish and wondered in what language he might question the man. Jay was afraid that if he spoke German, the man might refuse to talk with him, so he asked, "Do you speak English?

The man raised his head, looked at Jay and quietly said, "Yes, of course!'

Jay was taken aback by the quick and decisive answer. He thought, this is an educated person, and though he has an accent it is not pronounced. Jay introduced himself and said, "I noticed that you seemed to be looking for someone. Can I help you?"

"I don't know if you can help. I am looking for my family."

"How long have you been looking for them?"

"I just got here. I was a prisoner in Russia."

Jay noticed how thin the man was, and questioned, "A prisoner in Russia? Were you in one of the concentration camps?"

"No. I was in prison with other captured German soldiers."

By now, several other Americans had joined Jay and were listening as the little man spoke. A soldier gasped, "Then you are a German soldier?"

"I am not German, I am Polish, and I am also a Jew."

The journalists thought that they had come upon a good story, and before the man could answer, one journalist asked, "How the hell did you end up here in Warsaw now?" Another asked. "Then why were you detained with German soldiers?" Questions were coming from the Americans, several at a time.

Jay, who been the first one to contact the man, said,

"Let's go get something to eat." He turned to the little man, "Why don't you join us? Perhaps we can help you locate your family." Jay saw how thin the man was and thought he would welcome some food.

As they turned and walked toward the American camp, Jay said, "Do you mind telling us your name?"

The Jewish refugee was Wilhelm Vlastok. His hunger for a full dinner was apparent when he sat down to eat with the Americans. His hosts let him eat in peace before they started once again to bombard him with questions.

"Why were you imprisoned with the Germans?" was the first questions asked the second time.

"Because I was a German soldier. The Germans made me a part of their army," Vlastok answered.

The numerous questions continued, "How long did you serve with them?" "Did you want to be part of their army?" "Where is your family?" "Did they know you fought with the Germans?" "How did you learn to speak such good English?" and on and on. Wilhelm Vlastok had little time to answer one question before another was asked. Finally Jay rose up from the table where they were sitting around, some of them still eating, and in a firm voice said, "Mr. Vlastok is having trouble in answering all your questions. Why don't we let him finish his meal, then he can tell us his story. If we still have any questions, we can ask them later. Okay?"

Everyone around the table agreed. When Wilhelm Vlastok had finished eating, Jay turned to their guest and said, "Mr. Vlastok, why don't you tell us why you were out there searching in that rubble, who you were looking for, and tell us all that has happened to you and your family since the Germans invaded Warsaw."

Jay had addressed the Pole with respect, even though he suspected Vlastok was younger than he. He knew from the way he spoke English that the Jew was well schooled. Jay, reached down to this little man sitting beside him and pulled him up to a standing position. "We want to know about you, Vlastok. Then perhaps we can help search for your family."

Wilhelm Vlastok looked around at the ten or twelve men who were facing him, some journalists, and some commissioned and non-commissioned officers in the American military service. His thin face with its sunken cheeks could not hide the shyness he felt on standing before these strangers, nor did his quivering mouth completely suppress his emotion.

"My family and I lived here in Warsaw — we had lived here all our lives, my mother and father and my three sisters. My father was a teacher in the University. Two of my sisters were older than I and one younger. We were not rich, but we lived comfortably. We had a good many friends. There were over a million people living in Warsaw before the war, at least half of them were Jews. There was no friction among us, or none that I was conscious of. I was only seventeen years old when the Germans invaded Poland in 1939.

"First the bombs fell on us, and then by the end of September the German troops arrived. They came in Polish military uniforms. They plundered our city of all its treasures. They stole all our great art works and tore down all our important monuments. You should have seen our beautiful Warsaw, our old city ..." Vlastok paused. His voice choked as he pointed out to the right of the rubble from which he had come, and said, "That was the Castle Square with the monument to King Sigismund III, and there was a bridge there that crossed the river into the old city. The Royal Palace, St. John's Cathedral — all gone! The old market square where we had such good times! And all our people …"

Wilhelm's voice portrayed his grief as he continued, "I can't find anyone I know. Our family had many, many friends, and I can't find any of them. They must be gone, just like the city — all gone!"

One of the journalists said, "We hear there are some other Jews that have come back to Warsaw."

"Where are they? I was looking for someone, anyone. I want to see them!" the little man cried, as he reached out toward the American.

Jay interrupted, "Mr. Vlastok, these men need to hear your story. We want to help you find your family and friends. Go ahead and tell us what happened to you."

Wilhelm Vlastok sat down, "It is too long a story for me to stand up and tell you all of it. As I told you, the Germans took all our treasures, paintings, sculptures, and then they turned on the people. After a few months, in 1940 they started gathering up all the Jewish people. They forced us out of our house, just like they did all of our friends. They herded us into small quarters over on the other side of town. They not only put the half million Jews of Warsaw in that small walled ghetto, they collected Jews around the country and crowded them in with all of us into that twenty-six-square-mile space.

"For three years they kept us there, without enough

space to live, nor enough food to eat. Then the Jews rebelled. The German troops killed many of us. Later they crammed many men, women and children into box cars to ship them off to concentration camps. My mother, father and sisters were shoved into one of those cars. They were not allowed to take anything with them. I waved goodbye to them. That was the last I ever saw of them.

"I did not know what the Germans were going to do with me. I thought I would probably be shot, but instead they gathered a whole group of us boys, from age fifteen to about twenty-five, and forced us into the German army. We were made to do all the dirty work of the camp until they finally sent us to Russia.

"We Jewish boys were put on the front line. I think the Germans thought this was an easy way to kill us and protect themselves at the same time." Vlastok stopped talking for a second and a grin came over his face. It was the first time since they had been talking with him that any semblance of a smile had appeared on his face. "A few of us got ourselves captured by the Russians instead of getting killed.

"I wasn't released until recently. The Russians still thought I was a German soldier, and that's the way I was treated when I was a prisoner of war. When the war was over, I finally convinced them that I was Polish and a Jew and had been forced into the German army, and they let me go. I told them I wanted other clothes instead of the German soldier uniform. They furnished me these peasant clothes. It was enough for me to get by the Russian and Polish soldiers and find my way back here to Warsaw. The Russians and Polish troops got here in Warsaw last January. They didn't let me come back with them, just kept me a prisoner, for the war wasn't over then. That's why I didn't get here until just a day or two ago. I am looking for my parents and sisters. I guess you already know that it was just a little over a year ago when the Russian and Polish troops were approaching Warsaw, that the Germans began systematically destroying our beautiful city. We have so much to be proud of. Poland is the birthplace of two very important world-known men — Chopin, the great musician, was born right here in Warsaw, and Pulaski was born in Cracow. He is the one who helped you Americans in your revolution against the British."

Jordan Fisk's stay in Warsaw with his companions was short and, as usual, when night fell he pulled out his harmonica to play a bit before he turned out the light. On this night after spending several hours with the Jewish refugee, he felt he should record how much he had learned. He didn't want to carry a notebook around with him — that would be a nuisance. He would write Roxanne a letter and tell her to keep it. He could copy it when he got home, or ask her to let him have it back.

He was also going to write to Grenythe. He felt happy that he could now send her mail and know that it wouldn't be intercepted by the "jailer" who had guarded her for months. Since Grenythe already knew enough about the horrors of the war, he wouldn't write her about the death camps he had seen, but tell her of the little reconstruction the Russians had already started in Warsaw. Grenythe most probably knew the history of Warsaw, so he needn't tell her that either. He would just tell her how much he missed being around her, and that he and his group were not going to be gone much longer. He told her that he expected that they had already seen the worst of the death camps — Dachau and Buchenwald, so he should be coming back to Munich to see her soon. He sure hoped she would be waiting.

In his letter to Roxanne, Jay wrote much of what he had learned from Vlastok, and even more from the information he and his companions had gotten from the Russians here in Warsaw. He wrote her that ninety percent of the city had been wiped out, 670,000 residents of Warsaw killed, 375,000 of them Jews. He wrote that he and his companions had asked Vlastok what had happened to the rest of the million residents of Warsaw, the ones who had not been killed. Sadly, he told them that many non-Jews had sided with the Nazis in persecution of the Jews, while others had fled the city to join Polish forces, fighting with the Allies. Vlastok said many of the Jews were sent to Auschwitz, where they were killed. It was a concentration camp near the city of Cracow. Jay read over what he had written to Roxanne. So much of it was tragedy, he wanted to end his letter on a more cheerful note, so he finished it with a less gruesome note.

I want to tell you how this city got its name. It seems that a mermaid in the fourteenth century came up out of the river Wisla (Vistula) and predicted that a city would arise on the river's banks and be named for two children, Wars and Sawa.

Our last stop before I come home is Auschwitz,

a the large concentration camp here in Poland. The Jewish refugee, Wilhelm Vlastok, is going with us to Auschwitz. We have learned that his family were sent in boxcars to that camp. He is anxious to find out if any of them are still living.

I'll write you about Auschwitz, or tell you about it when I get home. Did I tell you in my last letter about Grenythe? She's a girl I knew when I was in school here, and I ran into her in Munich. I'll tell you about that, too, when I get home.

Love, Jay

After Jay had finished his letters, he reached for his harmonica again. It was his way of getting his mind off the lamentable situation here in Warsaw, all the trepidations he had seen and heard today. There was no way he could imagine what lay ahead in Auschwitz. As he later said, "It would have blown his mind!"

Jay Fisk and his companions, accompanied by the Warsaw refugee, arrived in the lovely little city of Cracow. The town with its Wawel Castle, its Market Square, its Wawel Cathedral and the University showed few signs of any war damage. They looked over these sights before receiving directions on how to get to Auschwitz, the death camp about forty miles away

They had never imagined the immense size of the Auschwitz complex. It consisted of two camps, Auschwitz I and Auschwitz II (Birkenau). They even saw the nearby sub-camp Buna, called Auschwitz III, where many prisoners were worked to death. The total area of the

Auschwitz compound covered about twenty-four square miles, the largest of all the concentration camps in the Nazi network.

The first sight that came to the attention of Jay Fiske and his party was the administration building and its wrought iron gate with the sign above it, "Arbeit Macht Frei" (Work Brings Freedom). Jay and his friends were taken through the Auschwitz I complex by the Russians stationed there. Locations of the different inhumanities were slightly pointed out, but no detail given. They saw two different signs that had been posted, one read "Jews are a race that must be totally exterminated" and the other, "We must free the German nation of Poles, Russians, Jews and Gypsies."

Jordan Fisk, Jr., being a sensitive person, was affected by these sights and signs, much as he had been by those he had seen in Dachau. He did not feel the full clout of what went on at Auschwitz until later. As they were moving out of Auschwitz I, past Birkenau and into the little town of Budy, Jay caught sight of a youngster walking on the street. The minute the child caught sight of the men, some in uniforms, he started running. Jay would have paid little attention if the boy had just kept running, thinking he was in a hurry to get to his destination, but the boy came to a niche in the wall of a building and he hid himself in it, watching the soldiers and journalists. Jay was not close enough to see the boy's face, but his actions expressed fear, fear of anyone in uniform. Jay turned to one of the Russians soldiers who was accompanying them and asked, "Did you see that little boy? What's he afraid of?"

The Russian said, "Oh, he's an orphan. We've tried to get him to talk with us, but he refuses."

"Is he a Jew?"

"No, he's a Pole, but some of them are just as stubborn as Jews."

Jay didn't like the tone of that answer. It reflected the prejudice of that Russian soldier. Jay wondered if it was the attitude of all the Russian military force here in Cracow. Jay didn't ask him any more questions, for deep in his mind he knew why that little boy refused to talk. He was as afraid of the Russian soldiers as he was of the Germans, even though it was the Russians who first stopped the imprisonment and slaughter at Auschwitz. Jay wanted to talk to that young boy. Perhaps he had more to tell them about Auschwitz than they had yet heard. Jay knew he would have to approach the boy without the Russians, but how? If he left now he would have no way of finding that boy again. And if he spoke German, that would frighten the boy even more.

Wilhelm Vlastok made it a point to stay with the American investigating group, rather than the Russians. Vlastok had a feeling that his family had been in a boxcar headed for Auschwitz, and since the Russians were already stationed here, he asked them if they could find out if his family had been imprisoned at Auschwitz. They found no trace of them at Auschwitz. What they did find out was that each person after arriving was called by name, then tattooed with a number — no longer identified by any name. Since none of the *surviving* inmates here belonged to the Vlastok family, the Russian authorities had told Vlastok that he might as well go back to

Warsaw. Wilhelm said he did not want to go to Warsaw. The Russians advised him that they would see that he was transported to Switzerland, but from there he would be on his own to go wherever he wanted.

If Jay were to get any help in the Polish language from Wilhelm Vlastok, he would have to do it right now, because tomorrow Vlastok would be gone. Jay walked over to Vlastok and spoke quietly to him, saying he needed to know a few words in Polish, enough that he could contact that boy hiding in the wall.

"What do you want to say to him?" Vlastok asked.

"Tell him I am an American and need his help."

Speaking in Polish in a pleading voice, Wilhelm Vlastok called out, just loud enough for the boy to hear, "This is my friend, an American, and he is helping me to look for my family. He wants to talk with you. He says he needs your help. Will you please talk with him?"

The boy didn't move, then Jay asked the rest of the party to move on, leaving just the two of them. Fisk and Vlastok informed the rest of their party that they would see them all later, that they were going back to Auschwitz I.

When the two stood alone, Vlastok repeated the same message to the boy. The boy took a step or two toward them, hesitated, then moved a bit farther out of his hiding place. Out of the shadows, Jay could see the boy's face. First he could see an expression of fear, replaced bit by bit with hope and trust, first to the Polish Jew and then a smile at the American as he approached him. That wasn't too surprising, because Jay was one of those people who had a certain kind of glow in his being, a personality that appeals to others, so that he could gain their confidence and trust.

Jay asked him how old he was.

The boy told him that he was twelve years old. Jay noticed how small he was for that age, and attributed it to lack of enough nutritious food for a growing boy. Very softly Jay asked him if he could tell him about what happened at Auschwitz. They boy said that he was only eight years old when the Nazis took his mother and his father. Vlastok asked if he could take them through the compound. He looked at Vlastok and said he would have to ask his grandmother. She would be the one to take them through the compound at Auschwitz and show them exactly what happened to him and his family. Then he looked at Jay and slowly in an accent said, "I speak a little English."

"Will you help us?"

"Let me get my Grandmother."

The twelve-year-old boy's name was Robert Bertold. He told Jay and Wilhelm to follow him. He walked so fast that the two men hurried to keep up with him. They came to a ramshackle house, and the boy went inside and motioned for the men to come in with him.

His grandmother was Maria Kunas. She jumped up from her chair when two complete strangers came barging into her house. Wilhelm Vlastok spoke up immediately, "I am a Pole, a surviving Jew. Your grandson said you could take us through the Auschwitz compound and tell us what happened."

After they had gained her trust, she took the hand of the boy and led them back the way they had come. The boy Robert was the one who started their story. "I was just eight years old and was living with my mother and father in our own house. My father was an attorney, and my mother stayed home with me. My mother and father both spoke English and German. I speak a little of both. The Germans came and called at our house and wanted my father to become a part of their army. They asked him to give them the names of all the Jews he knew in our town. My father refused to do it at that time. They told him they would be back the next day to get that list, and he should have it ready for them.

"As soon as they left, Mother packed up all of my things and took me to my grandmother's house. She told me not to tell anyone where I was living, that she would come see me there. The next day the Germans came again, and my father said he did not know any of the Jews. They took him away. My mother came to live with my grandmother, too, but the Germans came and they made her work many hours every day, sewing. I hardly ever got to see her. She was so tired when she got home. We did not have much to eat, any of us. The Germans took most of our food for themselves and we got only what was left. My mother died last year."

"She was starved to death," the grandmother said. "She gave most of her food, as did I, to Robert. Before she died, she was too tired to stand up. She was worked to death as well as starved." The bitterness in the grandmother's voice was not hidden.

As the grandmother spoke, tears came to Robert's eyes, but he did not cry.

He and his grandmother took Jay and Wilhelm to the entrance gate, but they did not stop there. They led them through the long wired corridor to the part of the camp with brick buildings. These buildings were numbered block by block, usually just one building to a block. Their hosts took them to one isolated building, called block Number 11. "This Block #11 is where they had trials for all the non-Jews, Poles, Czechs, Russians, etc., but the outcome was always the same, and the inmates called it the 'Block of Death.' My father was tried here, and like everyone else, found guilty, and they killed him. All the inmates were not always killed the same way. Just to this side of Block #11 is the shooting wall, called the 'wall of death.' "

That wall connected Block #11 with Block #10. The wall was as wide as the block buildings. Robert pointed to the pock-marked wall, evidence of the bullets that had taken the life of thousands. "This is where they shot my father!" he said.

Grandmother Kunas and Robert next pointed in the opposite direction from the "wall of death" to a gallows, where selected prisoners chosen by the executioners were hung instead of being shot. Why some were hung and others shot was a mystery.

Then they came to building #10! This was where SS doctors conducted experiments on prisoners much as Jay had seen in Dachau, except here the experiments were mostly on women. A Dr. Carl Clauberg had chosen as his victims women on which he could find the quickest method of biological extermination of the Slavs. His idea was to train surgeons to sterilize thousands of persons per day.

Next they were taken to a low building. Inside Jay

and Wilhelm saw the cells where the prisoners had to live. They saw blocks filled to capacity of low berths (Robert said they looked like chicken houses), damp and cold. The aisles between the berths were covered with a slimy mire. The straw used for mattresses in the berths had been pulled off the adjacent farmhouses and had become rotten and stinking.

Blocks 4, 5, and 6 proved to be the most gruesome of them all. One room held shoes and boots taken from the corpses, the floor of another room was knee deep with spectacles, another held various clothing. There was one with bags of human hair, and mixed with them the grotesque scalps from which the hair had not yet been removed. Next to the room with the scalps was a room holding the material made from human hair.

While they stood before those scalps, Grandmother Kunas told of one young woman forced to work in the factory making the material from human hair. One day a scalp was put in front of her and she screamed. She recognized the scalp as that of her mother. She screamed and screamed and refused to work. Other inmates said she had really lost her mind. She was beaten and told to work on that scalp. She was beaten and beaten again, but still refused to work on her mother's scalp. She was taken to the hanging stake, tortured to death, then cremated. Other prisoners thought that particular scalp was purposely put in front of the daughter, just another example of the cruelty of the Nazis and their treatment of prisoners.

Outer wire fences were electrified so anyone trying to escape would be electrocuted. Some victims chose that course, rather than live in the adverse conditions of starvation, brutality and heartbreak.

Robert and his grandmother took Jay and Wilhelm down the fenced corridor where thousands each day went either to the gas chambers or to forced labor. The prisoners never knew which destination they faced. At the end of the wired corridor there was a raised block or mound. It was small, about a six-by-six square, and not more than two feet high. On it was a hanging stake, the very stake where the girl who refused to work on her mother's scalp was tortured. A prisoner was punished here by tying him or her by their arms to the stake and lifting the body so the toes could not reach the ground. The prisoner would be beaten as well as tortured otherwise, to the amusement of the tormentors. He or she usually died on the stake, and the corpse was then thrown into the furnace. This stake was at the end of the fenced corridor near the main entrance gate, and right next to it was a walk leading to an underground building. It looked very much like the driveway to an underground garage of a modern home.

It was at this point that Robert got teary-eyed. He was the one who led them down the driveway, opened the door and went inside.

"The prisoners were told they were going in here to the showers," Grandmother said. "You can see the shower-like mechanisms scattered over the ceiling. Sometimes as many as two thousand people, men, women and children were crowded into this space — it would comfortably hold only two hundred. Instead of water coming from those devices in the ceiling, a poison gas was released, and in fifteen or twenty minutes the shower-takers were corpses. But they were not immediately sent to the crematorium. Before the corpses were put on these little train cars, they were stripped of all their clothes, gold teeth were pried out, and scalps were removed, then they were loaded into the cars that took them to the furnaces, next door here."

Jay Fisk and Wilhelm Vlastok stood speechless as they saw how the corpses were loaded into the rail cars, rolled into the furnace room and dumped into the furnace.

Once back outside, Robert pointed to the sign that read, "Work Brings Freedom," and his grandmother said, "They brought car load after car load of people in here from all countries, France, Holland, Hungary, Greece, and after they closed these gates, they told the prisoners that they were now in a concentration camp and that there was no escape except through the smoke in the chimneys."

Robert said, "That's where they burned my father!"

Standing just behind him, Wilhelm Vlastok murmured, "And my mother, father and sisters."

The grandmother nodded to the sign close by, "Arbeit Macht Frei in this place means 'Work Brings Death, not freedom.' Four million people were murdered here."

Jay worried about the young boy and wondered how was he reacting to all this horror that they were hearing and seeing. But then, Jordan Fisk, being the perceptive person that he was, realized that this twelve-year-old boy had already experienced more terror and heartbreak than they, the observers of the aftermath, could ever fathom.

That little boy in years to come would be telling these same stories over and over again to the rest of the world, so that they would never, ever be forgotten!

CHAPTER TWENTY-ONE

Munich

CHAPTER TWENTY-ONE

THE DAYS WERE COOL, as would be expected in late October, and the nights colder still, yet Jay Fisk could not blame the weather on the chills he felt running through his whole body when he got back to his base in Krakow that night. After spending the whole day in Auschwitz, he wondered if he would ever feel warm again.

He lay on his bunk, fully dressed, yet covered with a blanket, hoping to ward off the chill he felt within. The walking skeletons Jay had seen and spoken with, the harsh surroundings of their captivity, portrayed without a doubt the fiendish character of the madman Hitler. But Hitler could not have implemented such widespread ruthless acts by himself. He needed the aid of hundreds, no thousands of other Germans, men and women, who took sadistic delight in the monstrous hurt and torture they inflicted upon innocent human beings.

He wanted to write to Grenythe, but his mood was so gloomy that he couldn't think what he would write that wouldn't make her unhappy, too. The only thing he could say was that he was leaving tomorrow, glad to be on his way back to Munich. He shuddered. Just getting there as soon as possible seemed urgent, getting away from this earthly hell!

There was no way he could ever forget the torture chambers he had seen in the larger death camps, but neither could he forget the released prisoners he had seen in the small camps where the prisoners were left to starve — the one camp, a little camp in Austria where prisoners were mad with hunger, he found one living skeleton chewing on the arm of a dead man next to him. That was probably the most frenetic scene he had come upon. Jay desperately wanted to be with Grenythe, thinking that she might make him feel better — fleeting thought — how could she, she was German, wasn't she? How could he have liked Germany so much in his school years, and now knowing that so much evil could spring from the same source a few years later? Grenythe was German, but Jay couldn't forget that she was also intelligent and lovely. How could she explain what had happened to those he had thought were such wonderful people? His emotions were mixed — despising German actions, yet feeling a closeness with Grenythe. Thoughts of Grenythe hadn't really changed his overall depressed mood. He wondered what direction his conversation would take when he met with her soon. His wondering was interrupted as one of the other servicemen came into the room, waving a piece of paper in the air.

"Fisk, don't you ever call for your mail any more?"

Jay sat up at once. Jay did not anticipate mail call — not since that day of Irene's digression. He no longer expected any mail. He had been thinking about Grenythe — maybe he had a letter from her. "Is that a letter for me?"

"Yeah! How much will you pay me for it?"

"I'm not in a very good mood, guy — give me my letter."

After a bit of horsing around, his friend finally handed him the letter. It wasn't from Grenythe, it was from Roxanne. He was disappointed that the letter was not from Grenythe, but Roxanne always had something interesting in her letters, so he opened it impassively. Half through the letter, a frown came over Jay's face. Why was Roxanne writing him about the front page news in the Kansas City paper concerning one soldier's return from the war and praising some of his experiences?

He read on, and a smile replaced the frown. Of course! She wasn't writing not just about her acquaintance in Kansas City, but about the person he had first heard about when he was in England. Roxanne wrote about the soldier, an American Lieutenant that had been in the 81st General Hospital in a little French town of Suippes. He was in the hospital because when he was driving a jeep, he stopped to get out, stepped into a sewer and broke his leg, a very serious break that kept him hospitalized for three weeks. He had described it to the journalists of the Kansas City paper, a stupid thing to do.

Jay read the letter the second and third times, enjoying the description that Roxanne had said she read in the paper. She liked the story about his bringing back three German helmets and German pistols, even a German Swastika flag for his three little brothers. Jay found that he was enjoying the news from Roxanne, news of an American soldier that he had never met. Jay had first called Roxanne's attention to him from one of his own European friends, the French girl, Helene. But all he had heard from Helene was about the broken leg and the hospital stay. He had heard nothing about the coming home scene. And Helene would know nothing about that either. Now he had some exiting news he could share with Grenythe. He read the letter two or three times. There was so much in it that he thought Grenythe would like. He would see her in just a day or two, and she should enjoy hearing the news about Helene's Lieutenant. Jay had already told Grenythe about his meeting their mutual French friend, Helene Dolmet, and her knowing a lieutenant from Roxanne's city. Now this letter from Roxanne had given Jay a whole new prospect for his time with Grenythe. He could hardly wait to see her as soon as he got back in Munich.

He read the letter again — there was news about what that soldier thought was the greatest thrill he felt while he was in the European war scene. The soldier said probably the greatest thrill was just getting out of Italy after a year and two invasions at Salerno and Anzio. It was an additional thrill to see the ships gathering for the biggest invasion of the war in southern France, with Winston Churchill in a launch weaving in and out between navy battle ships, cruisers and all other types of carriers, with a "V" for victory sign. He said everyone in his and the other vessels cheered and blew their horns, the 15th day of the invasion.

This was all new information and maybe it wouldn't mean much to Grenythe, but she already knew about this soldier's contact with Helene. Jay's imagination came into full play. Why couldn't he and Grenythe take the train from Munich to Strasbourg and have a day's visit with Helene? If the trains were working as they did years ago, it would take only five hours for them to get from Munich to Strasbourg. If they got there by noon, they could visit the rest of the day and take the night train back to Munich. Wouldn't Helene be delighted to hear all that news about her Lieutenant? Jay was sitting up in his bunk, the letter in his hand, grinning.

"That must be the best news you could possibly have, Fisk," the companion who had brought the mail commented.

Jay looked up and was conscious of where they were. His face turned serious again. "Yes, it is a letter from my sister telling me news of a man we both know about. He was a hero in the war, and his hometown paper gave him quite a homecoming welcome. It's news like that can make one forget, for a moment anyway, what we've just seen here."

Jay was eager to start back to Munich. He had so little time left. Once he left his service in the Armed Forces, he would no longer be getting any pay. He was broke financially, and he had to get mustered out of the service before he could be on his own. His time in Munich would be short. He needed to see Grenythe as soon as possible. He wondered if there was a night train out of Krakow to Munich and, if so, how long it would take him to get there.

He was up and out the barracks, with others of his party asking where he was going in such a hurry, but he paid little heed. Out into the cold, he didn't take time to turn back for his jacket, but rushed to the station to learn what would be the first available train leaving for Munich.

The time had come for sergeant Jordan Fisk, Jr. to complete his service in the armed forces. He had already served over six extra months past the end of the war, days where his linguist knowledge had helped repatriate prisoners from the concentration camps to their rightful homes. He thought of the numerous extermination camps he had seen. It seemed there was no end to them — Treblinka, Belzec, Chelmo, Solibor, Dachau, Flossenburg, Sachenhausen, and the largest and most horrible of them — Auschwitz! Jay had not seen them all, but had come in contact with displaced and tortured people from all over Europe, Jews and non-Jews. He was glad he had been able to help, but he had done all he could — it was time to go home!

There was one task yet to be done! It was in Munich, and he smiled when he thought it. He had visions of the blond, blue-eyed young woman, matured beyond her years, yet a loving, delightful companion to have around. The pleasant thoughts of Grenythe were soothing, yet Jay reminded himself that he must not get too comfortable, fall asleep and miss his train connection, ending up in Berlin instead of Vienna. He knew his time in Munich was limited. He did not have enough money to stay over and pay his own way back to the States. He would have to go at the hour and on the day when the designated Air Force plane left. He wished this train to Munich did not have to have so many stops, making the hours on the train pass slowly. When Jay had signed up for these extra months of service, he had been told that he would be home by Christmas. He was glad when he heard that he would be going home before Thanksgiving, glad that the distressing calls in those scenes of slaughter were over — but he was sorry that there was not more time to spend with Grenythe before he had to leave.

Jay Fisk's steps were hurried, as he almost raced from the train to the door of the Weis house. The hour was in the late afternoon, and Jay had already figured that the hour of his train arrival was perfect. Grenythe would be through with her classes at the University and should be home before he came knocking at her door, and he expected her to be alone, since that Gestapo woman guard was no longer living in the house.

He knocked on the door three times, waited a second or two and impatiently knocked again. When the door opened, Jay was ready to step into the house, enfold Grenythe into his arms and kiss her. But the figure who opened the door was not Grenythe, it was a man. He was a tall, slender man who wore glasses, not quite as tall as Jay, possibly a few years younger. Had Grenythe acquired a new friend in the several weeks that he had been gone? The shock must have shown on Jay's face, for the man almost laughed as he said, "You're Mr. Fisk, aren't you?"

The moment Jay had laid eyes on the man, he had a flash of something familiar about him, but it was lost in the shock of seeing a man here in the house with Grenythe. When the man called him Mr. Fisk, recognition came at once. No one had called him Mr. Fisk for years. Jay's face broke into a grin as he followed the man's motion to come into the house, grabbed the man by the arm and said, "You are Paul — all grown up!" The two men, hands clasped, were bidding each other a fond welcome when Grenythe came down the stairs.

"I told Paul that we might expect you any day," she said. Jay crossed the room to meet her, put his arm around her waist as he spoke to Paul.

"Then you didn't recognize me when you saw me — " Jay began before being interrupted.

"Yes, I knew you at once. You haven't changed that much, Mr. Fisk."

"Paul, you remember years ago when I was helping you with your English, I told you to call me Jay, not Mr. Fisk."

"You didn't know *me*, did you?"

"You looked familiar, but you were just a little squirt when I saw the last. You are a grown man now. I want to hear about you and all that's happened to you in these last dozen years." Jay had lost no time in letting Paul know how he felt about Grenythe. He had kept one arm around her waist as he talked with Paul, but Grenythe had pulled away and suggested that they all sit down while they continued their visit.

Paul Weis told of his escape in 1933, an escape engineered by his uncle. He told of the secrecy and help he received from other German Jews and the French resistance movement. He said Helene was the key person in getting him into France, then later into England.

Jay broke into his story and asked, "Have you kept in touch with Helene?"

"No, after I was whisked into England, I never saw or heard from her again," Paul answered.

Jay told him about his contact with Helene in England, how she was the Maid of Honor at a friend's wedding. Jay told about Helene's boy friend and their separation during the war, and how she was going back to Strasbourg to see if she could rekindle their lost love.

"I could stop in Strasbourg on my way back to England and try to look her up, but I have no idea where to start!" Paul said.

Grenythe and Jay both started talking at once, telling Paul the address of the home of the Dolmet family in a suburb of Strasbourg. "I wish we could all go to look for her," Grenythe said wistfully.

"If you go to Strasbourg, there is something you can tell her." Jay pulled Roxanne's letter out of his pocket. "There is a lot of information in here about her American Lieutenant. I'll let you read it before you go if you decide to stop in Strasbourg." Jay put the letter back inside his pocket. He had carried the letter with him, planning to tell Grenythe about it. He would wait and see whether or not it would be of interest to her.

Jay laughed, "Maybe we better let Paul get back to his story. How were things in England? And why are you back here?"

"Why am I back here? Jay, this is my home, or was for fifteen years of my life. I had to come back, hoping to trace the whereabouts of my parents. Grenythe said they took my mother away a few years after I left. I never heard from her after the first two or three years. This house should belong to me. The Nazis took it from my mother, but when the war was over, they were out of power. I have come back to see it I can establish ownership. It may not be possible, but I want to find out. Grenythe says she will help."

Paul was speaking English most of the time. After living over twelve years in England, English had become his customary language. Once in a while he would revert to German. It made little difference to Grenythe and Jay for they could converse in either language. As Paul continued his discourse on living in London those first years with Jewish relatives, Jay remarked, "You sound very English, Paul."

"I do? In London many tell me I sound like an American. I tell them it was because I had an American instructor in Germany." Paul laughed.

"I don't know which years were the worst for me," Paul continued. "In the early years I was treated like a child, then in September 1940, when the first blitz occurred, I was twenty-two years old, no longer a child, and I had volunteered to fight in the British army, but I was a German. The authorities were not sure whether they could trust me or not, but being a Jew convinced them I was against Hitler, German or not. That blitz lasted into November. But others followed. Over forty thousand people were killed, including my Jewish relatives. I would have died, too, had I not been away, training for the service.

"It was always a matter of luck, whether a building stood or was blasted away. Right in London, the St. Paul's Cathedral was left intact except for the blackening from the intense smoke. Yet through that same reign of terror, just northwest of London, the Coventry Cathedral had a devastating hit. You were in London through much of that, weren't you, Jay? The blitzes went on well into 1942."

"No, Paul, I did not get to London until 1943, but I saw the ruins left by the blitzes, and I, like you, many times had to take shelter in the subways, along with rows of others, looking for a place to sleep in safety. I was glad most of the children were sent to the country."

Paul reminisced, "Then you remember how the noise of the trains rushing by hardly disturbed us at all. We rolled up in our blankets and slept through it all. It is amazing what you get used to in times of war. The noise of the trains, the shells bursting all around, yet we slept!"

While Paul was speaking about the noise of trains whizzing by, Jay's attention reverted back to the apartment in New York where he and Irene had lived and loved. A moment of hurt and pain was quickly dispersed by the present company.

Paul continued, "I was glad that I was finally allowed to wear a British uniform and serve as a soldier. It was the least I could do. Now I am here, with a great decision to make. Grenythe, there is something I haven't yet mentioned to you. I am going to get married. I met a sweet Jewish girl in London, also an escaped German. She comes from the north, near Hamburg. We both can work in England, where she already has a good job, or we can come back to Germany. That's another reason why I am here, to see if I own a house, and the other important reason to see if somewhere I might find my parents. What should Risa and I do? Stay in England or come back home? We really have *four* choices — stay in England, come back here, go to Israel or go to America.

"I've talked enough about me," Paul stopped a moment. "I think you two would like to have some time to yourselves."

"Why don't we go out for something to eat?" Jay suggested. "I'll clean up a bit — I've been on the train a long time."

"I should have taken you up to your room as soon as you got here ..." Paul started.

"My room? Great, you mean I can share it with Grenythe?" Jay clapped his hands together as he chuckled.

"Now, wait a minute —" Grenythe put in her few words.

"I apologize! I meant that you would stay in my old room, you know where it is. I have been staying in my parents' room downstairs since I have been here. Okay?"

Jay let them know that he knew very well what Paul meant, he was just teasing as he ran up the stairs with his kit. While Jay was gone, Paul discussed their plans with Grenythe. He said he knew she and Jay would like to have some time alone, and that just the two of them should go out together, that he would make other plans. Grenythe told him there was no way that they would go off without him. When Jay returned, Paul made the same observation to him that he had made to Grenythe, that the two of them should go without him.

"Why would you think we would go off without you, Paul. Grenythe and I have all day tomorrow together. I do not have to leave until Sunday. I look forward to having some more time with you." The three decided they could have the most fun at the old Hofbrauhaus down in the center of town. It was where both young and old go to forget their troubles and while the night away.

A November evening in Munich can be especially cold if the winds come down from the mountains. The three friends bundled up in warm wraps, stepped out into the bone-chilling night air and started walking toward Ludwigstrasse. It was less than one mile to the Hofbrauhaus, but as soon as they had walked a short distance, they decided to take the underground rather than face the blustering winter wind.

The Hofbrauhaus was not filled, yet there was a good crowd assembled, many of them members of the Allied Forces who were stationed near by. There were also Germans of different classes, not social classes, but more political. It was true that there were still many who had not yet given up their faith in the Hitler movement, and those who had opposed it from the start.

Foreigners, that is, tourists or visitors for the first time at the Hofbrauhaus, look for an unoccupied table. Munich dwellers or most other Germans, will fill up a table not yet fully occupied. When Jay, Grenythe and Paul came in, they looked for a table that had three spaces available. They sat down at a table occupied by other Germans, totally unaware of the political affinity of those already seated, nor did they care. The three were graciously welcomed and they soon ordered their meal — along. of course, with a draft of beer. Music in the background gave a sense of gaiety to the whole atmosphere, and these three friends, a German woman, a Jewish German/Briton and an American soldier, though all of different life stories, could not have found themselves enjoying the evening more. Nor was their festivity in any way hampered by their table companions — that is, not for the first hour or two.

At the table where Jay Fisk sat with his friends, conversations between a few of the men and women with some of those at the table next to them became more argumentative as the evening wore on. By the second hour, after a good consumption of beer, several persons at both tables were in a very ugly mood.

"Hitler was right — the Communists are a big threat to our country!" claimed a high-pitched voice from the three friends' table.

"We are the PDS, Party for Democratic Socialism, and we will save this country! We are the only antidote to Hitler's brutality!" came the answer from across the aisle.

When the discussion between the two groups of Germans on their political viewpoints became more and more vociferous, Jay remarked, "Why don't we move to another table? I don't want to get involved in their differences."

Grenythe got up immediately and moved toward another table where no one else sat. "This is closer to the music, too," she said. They sat back down at the other table and each ordered another beer, but their joviality had waned and they had become more serious.

Paul had become the most serious of the three. "I think that little episode has made up my mind about one thing — I do not want to come back to live in Germany. Mark my word — this country will be split before it ever recovers completely from the war."

"Why do you think that, Paul? What will split it?"

"Jay, you've been too buried in the war effort to learn what is going on around the world. The Communist party is agitating with great skill, attacking all existing systems of government. In England they have made headway in the labor groups around Liverpool. They are especially effective — the Communists, around the unskilled and unemployed. Even many skilled people have gone along with them without joining the party," Paul exclaimed.

"Paul, you are a pessimist," Jay said.

Grenythe had said little during the brouhaha at the other table, and now she said, "Many people think our society has to be reformed. Perhaps they think the Communist system will do it."

"That is wishful thinking, Grenythe!" Paul spoke forcefully. "That is the very propaganda they spout. But Russia is now taking the place of Germany in trying to get control of all of Europe, and Russia is doing it through the Communist party, while Hitler tried to do it by way of the Nazis. Just watch what will happen to Finland, Czechoslovakia, Bulgaria, Rumania, Poland. They all fell to the Nazis, and now Russia is in control. Do you think Stalin will let them be free nations again? I don't think so!"

"Thank goodness, the United States is not in such a precarious position!" Jay said.

"Don't be too sure. I am sorry about your President Roosevelt dying, but he must have been sick to let Stalin get the better of the bargain when they signed that agreement in Malta," Paul advised. "Some of the English papers mentioned that."

Grenythe spoke to Paul, "What do you think of socialism in government?"

"Totalitarian remnants of power still exist here in Germany. Socialism has a strong appeal against capitalists among the youth, the unemployed and the poor. I am poor, but so far I do not feel that I have to have a government supporting me. What about you, Jay?"

"I want to stay out of all arguments. That doesn't mean I am a 'fellow traveler' with the Communists. It means I want to have a good time tonight and forget politics. I don't know when I will have a chance to be with you two again, so let's not carry that table's argument over here. Okay?"

"I think you are right about tonight, Jay. I am more interested than either of you, because I am in the process of choosing a country, and its politics will help me decide."

Jay did not say anything to that, but he leaned over against Grenythe, put his arm around her shoulders and pulled her up close. That gesture brought another speech from Paul. "I think I will be heading back to the house and let you two spend as much time out as you wish." Paul got up with a smile on his face and said, "See you in the morning!"

"Don't be in a hurry to leave, Paul," Jay said. "We've got all day tomorrow, and besides, I'm going to take Grenythe home with me."

Paul did not sit back down, but waved them goodbye and was out the door.

Jay and Grenythe did not stay very much longer at the Hofbrauhaus after Paul left. They got back to the Weis house, and Jay followed Grenythe into her room.

Jay pulled her down beside him sitting on the bed.

"I need to talk with you, Grenythe. I meant that when I told Paul that I wanted to take you home with me."

"I can't, Jay, I can't!"

"Tell me why! I don't want to leave without you," Jay pleaded.

"I can't! Jay, much as I would like to, you know I can't leave Germany.

"You haven't told me why."

"I'm not the same girl you knew a long time ago, Jay."

"I know! Your hair isn't the same corn silk yellow. Well, mine isn't the same either. There's a lot less of it!"

"That's not what I'm talking about. I just can't leave, and I don't want to talk about it any more tonight."

"We'll talk about it tomorrow then." Jay pulled Grenythe close to him and they fell back, side by side on the bed.

On Saturday morning when Jay and Grenythe came into the kitchen, Paul was already there making coffee. Grenythe took over the task of getting breakfast for all three of them. While they sat at the table eating, Paul said, "I have decided to go by Strasbourg on my way home. I hope I can see Helene again. I owe her so much."

Jay jumped up from the table and ran upstairs. In a few minutes he came back holding a letter, which he handed to Paul. "See if you can read America script, Paul. It is the letter from Roxanne, and her handwriting is very legible."

Everyone was quiet until Paul finished reading the

letter. "Wow!" he said. "He was quite a soldier to get all that publicity, wasn't he?"

"Give it to me! I want to read it, too," Grenythe commanded in an enticing voice, as she reached out to take the paper from Paul's hand.

"I am glad you both find it interesting," Jay laughed. "Just don't tear it up, or there won't be anything left for Helene."

Both Grenythe and Jay were prodding him for his decision in which country he would make his permanent home. They wanted to keep in touch with him. He was undecided. "I do not think it will be Germany. Any other place will depend upon where Risa and I both agree."

Jay took Paul's hand and said, "I don't know where in the United States I'll be. You understand why I don't want to stay in New York. I think I'll stop by and pick up anything I may have left, then head for Missouri to see my father and sisters. Where I'll go from there, I don't know, but I would like to keep in touch with you."

Paul Weis left shortly after they had finished breakfast.

Grenythe and Jay spent the whole day visiting their favorite haunts of years gone by. They laughed, talked and ate, the day of delight passing all too soon for both of them. Every time Jordan Fisk would bring up the subject of Grenythe going to America, she would change the subject, saying we'll talk about that later.

Some of the little bars and coffee houses where they went were nearly empty when they stopped in, usually after the lunch hour and before the evening crowds came in. In one almost empty place in mid-afternoon, they saw a piano sitting unused across the room. Grenythe and Jay sauntered over to it. Jay was the first one to touch the keys. He sat down and played a little, then started to sing. Soon Grenythe joined him. They played and sang some of their favorite opera numbers

As they played and sang, people began gathering around them. Jay started some wartime songs, those most familiar to anyone who might be listening, like the old songs from the first World War, *Pack Up Your Troubles in Your Old Kit Bag*, and *It's a Long was to Tipperary, and* then a few of the newer songs. He played and sang, *Don't Sit Under the Apple Tree with Anyone Else But Me.* Grenythe did not know that song and asked him to play it again, she wanted to learn it. Then she played and sang a beautiful war song, *Lili Marlene*. Jay was fascinated by the beauty of that song and wondered why it was not better known.

How quickly the afternoon passed as Grenythe and Jay enjoyed their music — much as they had shared their love of it in those school days in years gone by.

When evening came, Jay and Grenythe were sitting at the kitchen table in the Weis house enjoying a late cup of coffee and some cookies. Jay leaned over the table and said, "You promised to talk with me later. It is later, much later. Give me a good reason why you won't come to America."

"You aren't going to let me get by with 'no' answer, are you? Remember when I said that I was not the girl you used to know?"

Before she could continue, Jay interrupted, "I like this one better!"

"Jay, listen to me. Remember when I told you about Hitler's plan to make all the girls whores to raise as many new soldiers as possible, that was the reason I married Franz?

"Yes." Jay was ready to hear Grenythe's story.

"Before I married Franz, I was one of those girls made available to the soldier boys. I didn't want it to happen, it just did. I could call it rape. Anyway, I became pregnant almost immediately. Several months later, I gave birth to a baby girl. I named her Darlene."

"Do you know her father?"

"I have no idea who he was — is! I got help caring for her, because I had to keep on teaching. I had friends, a couple, living in this house with me. The woman cared for children of all ages during the day. The man had to work. The war was getting bad. Bombs were falling all over the country and Hitler was getting meaner and meaner. That was when I pleaded with Franz to marry me. I did not want another child, or to be a pleasure station for any soldier.

"When my little girl was three years old, she was taken from me. They said she was not being raised in the right atmosphere. I didn't know why they took her. Franz had been gone for several months. I wrote to him. I was frantic! I thought he would be in France with Witzleben. I knew that in France we were losing men every day. When I didn't hear from him, I was afraid that he had been killed. Other times I thought that he might want to abandon me. You can't imagine the torment I went through, not hearing from him for such a long time. I thought maybe that since I didn't have my daughter any more, he didn't feel he needed to stay married to me.

"I finally got a letter. I was almost afraid to open it, but when I did, I gave a triumphant yell. I was living in the same room that I live in now, but the people who were in the house at that time were my friends, Hulda and Ernst Peebles. When they heard me shout, they came to the stairs to see what was the matter. I told them that I had just heard from my husband, and he was well and that he said when this war was over he would help get my little girl back. My friends celebrated with me that night.

"Shortly after that, with the war going badly for Germany, Hitler started arresting everyone who raised a voice for any atrocity he ordered. This was when Witzleben and his cohorts decided that Hitler had to be stopped. In 1943 Witzleben took time off from his military position, saying he had to have an operation for appendicitis. He was relieved of his command a little later and was arrested, and Franz along with him, both accused of treason and imprisoned. The SS and Gestapo came to arrest me, too, because I was the wife of a traitor. But for some reason, they decided that I was needed to continue at the University, but I had to be supervised."

Grenythe was crying now, but still speaking through her sobs, "I believe my little girl is still alive somewhere. She has been gone over two years, and I don't know where they took her, if they still call her by her name or if they have brainwashed her until she thinks she is someone else entirely."

"Don't any of your friends know anything about her at all?" Jay asked. "How long did you say she has been gone?"

"Ever since they arrested Franz. That's over two years ago. They hanged him in August 1944 — just a little over a year ago. Much as I want my child as a mother, I feel I also need to find her and save her from all the brain-washing she has been exposed to in these formative years. What they have done to her in these many, many months, I can only guess — and as you must know, my guesses have been nightmares.

While Grenythe talked, she had her hands crossed on the table, first squeezing one hand with the other, then reversing the process. Jay noticing her nervousness, reached across the table and covered her hands with one of his own. Leaving his hand on top of hers seemed to relieve her tenseness.

"My friends, the Peebles, who lived here, were taken away, and that woman you met moved in. She was put here to spy on me and report every move I made. Since the war ended, I have not seen my jailor or her husband. He is probably a prisoner of the Allies, and I have not seen her since the day she left. I'm still afraid of her though, for if she was not arrested, she could cause me trouble when I start asking what they did with my child."

"How old would Darlene be now?"

"She would be nearly six years old. I don't know what they call her, wherever she is. I am going to change her name to Francine, in memory of Franz, if I ever get her back."

Jay got up from the table and moved around to Grenythe. He put his arm around her and helped her out of the chair. As she got up she said, "Now, Jay, you understand why I can't leave Germany, don't you?" Grenythe turned her tear-stained cheeks toward him.

"Yes, my love!" Jay held Grenythe close before he said any more. Then very softly Jay said, "I was feeling so sorry for myself, so bitter, thinking this war had robbed me of my love, my life, everything that I valued, and then I found you, who have suffered so much more. I will do what I can to get our servicemen stationed here to do what they can to help you find your daughter. Our battlefield encounter has shown us both that we can love and be loved again."

"Yes!" Grenythe hummed, as they left the kitchen, leaving behind the unwashed coffee cups. Together they climbed the stairs with arms around each other.

Sunday morning came. It was time for Sergeant Jordan Fisk to say goodbye. He stepped out the door with Grenythe, held her tight and kissed her goodbye.

Grenythe watched the back of the tall, straight soldier as he gradually vanished in the distance. As she stood peering down the empty street, the echo of his words "a battlefield encounter" resounded again and again, pervading the atmosphere. In time those echoes would fade, but they would never die, because that battlefield encounter had left an aura of hope and joy in the hearts of two war-wounded souls!

ACKNOWLEDGMENTS

Many thanks to the following friends
who have helped so much in collecting
the details and facts needed for this novel:

G. Russell Huff, Colonel, USAR-Retired

Lieutenant Edward J. Reardon-retired

Mr. Fried Kahn; Mrs. Hanna Kahn

John Gentry Frost